The
Anatomy
of
Hallucinations

Fred H. Johnson

The
Anatomy
of
Hallucinations

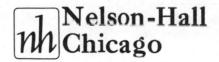

Nelson-Hall
Chicago

LIBRARY OF CONGRESS CATALOGING IN PUBLICATION DATA

Johnson, Fred H.
    The anatomy of hallucinations

    Bibliography: p. 187
    Includes indexes.
        1.   Hallucinations and illusions.   I.   Title.
[DNLM: 1.   Hallucinations.   WM200 J66a]
RC553.H3J63   616.8'9   77–22711
ISBN 0–88229–155–6

Manufactured in the United States of America

10   9   8   7   6   5   4   3   2   1

To My Professors

Contents

Preface

There are still many undiscovered areas in medical science, and one of the most mysterious is the brain. Circuit diagrams of neurons are essential to the understanding of the design and function of the central nervous system, but today many regions are still marked unknown. Often what is observed has no clear meaning as a part of a larger system of connections in regard to comprehension and correlation of knowledge from fields like physiology and psychology. My field, neuroanatomy, is a medical science basic to the study of psychiatry. The mechanism of emotion is of interest to psychiatry, as is that of hallucinations, for not so long ago, a psychiatrist (Cameron 1963) stated that hallucinations are more of a mystery than delusions and are more difficult to explain. Hallucinations are at present under a cloud. They are often written about in works on metaphysics, magic, mysticism, and the occult. The medium is one who communicates through the use of hallucinations to the "undiscovered country" of Shakespeare—the land after death, the dread of which puzzles the will.

Many factors have prevented the acquisition of scientific knowledge about hallucinations. Often little attention is paid to them by those in basic research, because of the dicta that "voices" are a symptom that is secondary to the disease process and are found in more than one kind of mental illness. Hallucinations have for the most part been looked upon as an epiphenomenon of mental disease, and authors in general agree not to consider hallucinating as a special subject or to class its cause with that of mental disorders. The doctor is taught traditionally that he does not need to discuss hallucinations for they are just a symptom. It is related to the patient that hallucinations are to be denied, because, by definition, they are experiences that have no known, real, or external stimulus. In France, Janet (1925) propounded that hallucinations are an "incommunicable phenomenon of consciousness, concerning which no one has or will have anything to say and this subject of inner consciousness does not concern us and does not concern science." Such attitudes suppress pure research on the subject and make for a subjective analysis of clinical findings.

The well-known advice "Give thy thoughts no tongue" is a law of behavior often followed. Thus, little is known about the content of inner speech, either in regard to thought or to hallucinations of inner speech, because the individual fears the loss of his freedom of expression and action. The tradition to not discuss the content of what one is thinking is very old and very strong, but such discussion would help in clinical situations, for it would lead to restoration and catharsis in dealing with repressed ideas, feelings, and terrible memories of fantasies. Another partial explanation of the lack of available information concerning hallucinations is that there are few cases of psychosis in the higher social groups, who would be the obvious persons involved in making the observations and relating them to others. There are no words, or only a few words, which adequately describe the hallucinatory experience. The German *gedankelautwerden* and the French *echo de pensee* cannot be translated into a single, English, technical term (Fish 1962). No word exists for the patient's subjective experience of hearing the thoughts or hallucinated inner speech of other ill persons in a conversational format of hallucinating.

Throughout history there have been problems associated with epidemics and movements. A contemporary example is the hallucinogenic drug situation. These problems continue in history, because the knowledge necessary for a medical solution is lacking. In order to correct a situation, we must deal with it, for ignoring it is certainly not a solution. If one feels that talking about hallucinations causes contagion, then it would follow that such conversations or written materials are the source of the disease, and this certainly seems impossible. If there is nothing to hallucinations, then why worry about what is said? And if there is something to them, then why not solve the problem?

The silence associated with hallucination is caused by the feeling that it is a dangerous subject. "Voices" have been a serious problem to the hallucinating person. Today they are an indication and manifestation of mental illness and are a common occurrence among inmates of penal institutions (Brierre de Boismont 1855; Davidman 1969). If a person states, "My thoughts come aloud," which is the most common (Modell 1958) but least understood hallucination, he risks being committed to a mental institution (Fish 1962). In the past, "communication of thought" was the most indubitable proof of possession, which was often punished by such agencies as the Inquisition. Under such circumstances, any person would hide his hallucinations. The ignorance, mysticism, superstition, and fear associated with the subject of hallucinations have created a taboo.

In the medical sciences, the physician is dealing with life, and in the case of hallucinations, the patient can die because of hallucinatory orders or he can kill another person because of a delusion, and he may die in the terminal states of the affliction (Malzberg 1949). Full truth with accuracy is absolutely necessary in order to have the means to produce a healthy state for those who are ill. Medical history unequivocally records that the antonyms to truth are the real thing to fear. Problems cannot be solved and correct decisions cannot be made with incorrect information. The absence of factual scientific knowledge and the lack of refinement of thought and action in regard to hallucinations are often the causes of the uncivilized behavior associated with the patient. An apt description of the situation concerning hallucinations is found in the words of Shakespeare: "Ignorance is the curse of God." The patients are in great need of therapeutic knowledge. There is no valid reason for fearing truth, because truth is a basic value of being civilized.

We must look back into the history of medical science for some wisdom to deal with the problem of hallucinations. Dogmatic false beliefs have classically been the enemy against which medicine has had to struggle. The historical literature of anatomy has depicted the many real battles with the superstitions and prohibitions surrounding the procurement and dissection of cadavers. In physiology the situation caused by the antivivisectionist movement has produced trouble. Facing the challenge was well worth the effort, because medical science changed dramatically for the better around 1800 when the supply of cadavers increased (Newman 1957). Instead of hundreds of students studying one cadaver, a limited number could dissect one. While "body snatching," or grave robbing, is of the past, because of anatomical laws, the digging up of the truth is still a dangerous business when ignorance, superstition, and delusions are present. Even today, dissection is done behind closed or locked doors, isolating both the medical students and the research anatomists from those who would place obstacles in the progress of medical research and the advance of medical education. Thus, in regard to the subjective feelings surrounding hallucinations, we must have a closed door, a mature, discreet silence, and an open, objective, civilized mind. Paradoxically, we must have the ability to suppress information to the uncivilized type of person and immature individual of any age, while, at the same time, we must use knowledge of medical science to teach those who have by their acts indicated that they can use facts with wisdom and, as a result, try to cure those who are ill.

The purpose of this work is to search for the available information about the true hallucinations (Claude 1930) of psychosis and their origins, with the expectation that the necessary therapeutic steps to be taken shall be revealed. Statements from leaders in psychiatry emphasize the great need for further research on the subject of psychosis (Bellak 1968; Grinker 1969). Manfred Bleuler (1968), in a twenty-three-year longitudinal study of 208 schizophrenics, compared and contrasted the recovery rate of patients in modern therapy with those patients in treatment at the turn of the century. He concluded that 25 per cent to 35 per cent of all patients had a recovery, which is the same rate as that of the older workers such as E. Bleuler and Kraepelin. In regard to a group of chronic patients, there was an improvement of their residual condition, which might have been due either to the better conditions of confinement or to modern therapy.

Psychotherapy as evaluated by Bergin (1971) has an average effect which is only modestly positive and can be actually harmful or even unproductive. The average hospitalization time for the schizophrenic reaction paranoid type, which makes up about 70 per cent of the functional disorders in the hospital, was 13.1 years in 1958 (Bellak 1958), and 12.8 years in 1969 (Bellak and Loeb 1969) showing that the recovery rate is not changing to any great degree. Karl Menninger (1970) observes that the diagnostic stage that psychiatry is in at the present time is a twentieth-century version of witchcraft.

Pickering (Walsh 1964) states: "The antithesis sometimes made between the science and practice of medicine is false and mischievous." The knowledge presented in this work from the clinical world and the scientific findings confirm each other, so that there is little opposition in ideas and a contrasting of positions. The results of many clinical observations and scientific experiments are given, but this is not a compilation of the literature, for there are a number of new working hypotheses which form the basis of this study, and which are presented with pertinent information and evidence, because the clinical applications are of value. These possible truths are given in the tradition as well expressed by Corner (1969): "Into each of these false temples of the spirit the anatomist has come by turn, but by the very breaking of idols he has helped to win the soul a brighter raiment."

Acknowledgments

At this time I would like to express my gratitude and obligation to the many authorities in the neurosciences who have helped and taught me over the years and to whom I, in turn, have tried to be of service. My first experience in research was with Dr. H. S. Liddell at the Cornell Behavior Farm, where I worked as an undergraduate student for three years and for two years as a graduate student on the subject of experimental neurosis. He had been the Chairman of the Department of Physiology in the Cornell Medical School before it was moved to New York City, and he stayed on in Ithaca as the Acting Chairman of the Department of Psychology, teaching Physiological Psychology and Abnormal Psychology. Professor Liddell worked hard on the problem of neurosis, and he wrote that the bridge between physiology and behavior is a difficult one for students to cross (Liddell 1961). He said, "Neurosis is like a wart and psychosis is like a cancer." Dr. Liddell helped me in so many ways that it would be difficult to list them all, but one was an introduction to Dr. James W. Papez, who was teaching neuroanatomy at Cornell University. I was the last graduate student to receive a degree from Professor Papez.

Although academic tradition insists that my name appear as author on this and other works, it can be said in truth that without his unfailing knowledge, wisdom, kindness, and friendship, this work, or any of the

Acknowledgments

others, would not have been started, much less completed. His counsel, theories, and discoveries guided me for these many years. During the period that I knew him, much of the work in his laboratory dealt with the subject of mental illness, and in regard to the beginnings of this study, he wrote that it was "probably a significant contribution." His researches on the mechanism of emotion or the limbic system, basal ganglia, reticular formation, and cerebral mechanisms have influenced considerably the new era of neuroscience. His wisdom is seen in the words, "Everything for mankind."

Through the consideration and kindness of Professor Griffin, now of the Rockefeller University, a position at the Arctic Research Laboratory with Dr. Per F. Scholander was made possible for me. This experience and Don Griffin's teachings helped me *along* the road of pure science. He introduced me to neurophysiology and to Dr. Galambos, under whom I studied at the Neuropsychiatric Division, Institute of Research, Walter Reed Army Hospital.

I have had many adventures in science and met many neuroscientists with whom I have worked, and I would like to thank them for both their knowledge and help. To mention just a few of them: Dr. Magoun, Dr. Russell, Dr. Schreiner, Dr. Rioch, Dr. Flynn, Dr. Stotler, Dr. Larsell, Dr. Tunturi, Dr. Pearson, Dr. Brookhard, Dr. Livingston, Dr. Nauta, Dr. Truex, Dr. Polley, Dr. Arey, Dr. Gibbs, Dr. Geiger, Dr. Abood, Dr. Bailey, Dr. Lim, Dr. Marrazzi, Dr. Snodgrass, Dr. Israle, Dr. Schwartz, Dr. Mesmer, and Dr. Millichap. Sincere thanks are due to the staff of the Newberry Library, where I worked on the subject of auditory hallucinations and their effect on history, and to the staff of the John Crerar Library for helping me with the medical aspects of the problem. My gratitude to Mrs. M. Ziemer and to S. Bertha Johnson, whose assistance made this work come to term. Grateful acknowledgment is also made to the publishers for their generous assistance.

Traces of hallucinations are found on every page of history.—Brierre de Boismont

1.
Historical Aspects

Religious wars and witch crazes throughout history would have been far fewer in number had hallucinations been known as natural phenomena and had men "possessed by the devil" been considered ill. These seemingly paradoxical observations were made by the late Professor Thorndike (1923) of Columbia University, authority on historical experimental science and Renaissance magic (Trevor-Roper 1967). Evidence shows that hallucinations can be normal (Lindsley 1970) and natural (Johnson 1958), but it also shows that they can be involved with mental disorders (Mellor 1970). Western civilizations have for the most part thought hallucinations to be quite abnormal and, therefore, negatively valued (Wallace 1959). They have been treated morbidly, as in the witch crazes, and yet today they are not considered important enough to be classed as anything more than nonspecific symptoms secondary to the disease process.

The history of hallucinations is ancient, for they can be observed in Greek mythology and in even earlier writings. They are a widely distributed experience, and all cultures provide responses to them. In cultures outside Western civilization, an hallucination is most often regarded as a communication that contains significant information and that is controlled by the will (Wallace 1959). Subjective observations of the communications are valued in most societies; yet the content of the hallucinations can be frightening and disturbing, because the hallucinated suggestions often deal with the commission of fearsome acts

1

such as murder and incest. Learning about a community disaster by means of hallucinations, even if they are delusional in nature, often causes panic. The hallucinations may deal with the anxiety of being captured and killed in a future war. The hallucinatory content is the "focus of interest and the fulcrum of action" in primitive as well as in more advanced societies (Wallace 1959).

ANCIENT VIEWS

The ancients had no unanimity of opinion about "voices" or demons. A demon as described in the dialogues of Plato, according to the speaker Socrates, is wise or knowing. "Every wise man who happens to be a good man is more than human in life and death and is rightly called a demon. When a man dies he becomes a demon which is a name signifying wisdom. A demon is a shepherd or leader who assists in the government of the country" (Hamilton and Cairns 1961). Socrates said that the cause of the moral influence which had improved him was his demon. He stated that a voice warned and advised him.

Having been warned by the demon of a murder about which only the killer knew, Socrates tried to prevent the crime. He said that before his time others had not considered madness as disgraceful or a cause for reproach, and had called mental illness "the noble art." At the time of his trial he said: "You have often heard me speak of an oracle or sign which comes to me, and is the divinity which my accuser Melitus ridicules and sets out in the indictment. This sign I have had ever since I was a child. The sign is a voice which comes to me and always forbids me to do something which I am going to do, but never commands me to do anything, and this is what stands in the way of my being a politi-, cian" (Jowett 1909; Tredennick 1969). The inclusion of hallucinating in the list of his offenses may well have been the beginning of a tradition in Western civilization.

Plato, Pythagoras, and Plutarch expressed the concept that while demons were mediators between gods and men, they were mortals as well. Although they were subject to passions and feelings, they were also capable of reason. Some were good, but others were considered bad (Thorndike 1923). Plato saw mental illness as a lack of intellect brought on by madness caused by prophetic inspiration. Aristotle wrote that men illustrious in poetry, politics, and art were often mad, melancholic, and misanthropic, characteristics that he noted in Socrates, Plato, and others, including Empedocles. Aristotle's attitude caused a stigma to be associated with madness. Because of his hallucinations (Kirton 1660) Aristotle was forced into voluntary exile where he died, perhaps by poison.

ROMAN VIEWS

During the Roman period of history, a prohibition against demons was ordered as they became more and more associated with evil. Albertus Magus (Thorndike 1923) expressed the opinion that demons were evil beings who performed black magic, and Roman leaders, although much involved with magic and mysticism, turned against magicians (Christian 1952). In Rome, Augustus ordered more than two thousand books on magic to be burned, even though he was friendly with Tiburian Sibyl and the astrologer Theogenus. "He did not doubt the value of the science, since he continued to use it; but he feared lest his subjects might find in it some means of overthrowing him" (Christian 1952). Tiberius banished anyone convicted of practicing magic.

Anxiety over the interrelationships of those in authority and those who were involved with hallucinations led to a persecution mania. Nero, for one, did not want his enemies to be able to divine. He visited the Oracle of Apollo at Delphi where the voice of its Pythia said, "Go back, matricide; your presence outrages the god you come to seek." So Nero, in a fit of madness, aroused by the oracle's reproach, had the hands and feet of the ministers of the temple cut off. The Pythia was buried alive with the mutilated bodies in the grotto, and the door was walled up. Vitellius thought he could assure his safety by decreeing the general banishment of magicians from Rome. "In the following reigns, the same prohibitions were repeated against most classes of soothsayers" (Christian 1952).

Many of the Roman Emperors who prohibited hallucinations were mentally ill. A considerable amount of literature dealing with their madnesses has accumulated over the years, accompanied by a continuing controversy over specific diagnoses. A few historians feel that they were just acting like the rest of the population and, therefore, were not ill, but most medical historians do not concur. Emperors and leaders of Rome who had mental disorders were Tiberius, Claudius, Gaius (Caligula), Nero, Augustus, and Caesar (Moss 1963; Sandison 1958). During the Roman period various statements were made that indicate the major feature of mental disease. Celsus, for example, noted that madmen lose reason; and Caelius, from Soranus' work, wrote that mania is a chronic impairment of reason. The Roman definition of *hallucination* contained, as it does in Western society, the factor of unreal presentations, or *inania via,* caused by the imagination, the influence of wine, and the state of insanity (Moss 1963).

The interdictions or bans continued as Charlemagne ordered astrologers and witches driven from his states. He issued several edicts forbidding every sort of magic, and he resorted to punishment by death of those who were possessed by the devil. Pope Gregory IX, in 1233-34, because of a request from an archbishop of Bremon, carried on the tradition by relating that the Stedingers were heretics. He then preached against them and wrote letters to various leaders. This led to war; 8,000 were killed on the field of battle, and the land, with its people, was laid to waste (MacKay 1841).

MEDIEVAL CHURCH CONCEPTS

The elaboration of demonology to supply a social stereotype for persecution and prohibition was in large part the work of the medieval Catholic church (Trevor-Roper 1967), and was used later by Luther and Calvin, who were hallucinists. St. Augustine, regarded as the founder of demonological science, was at first inclined toward the study of magic and astrology, but after his conversion he utterly abandoned and condemned it. St. Thomas Aquinas, the second founder of demonology, wrote that the practitioners of magic were generally criminals who perpetuated illicit deeds, thefts, adulteries, and homicides (Thorndike 1923). The opinions about evildoers and demon magic ultimately developed into the concepts of various kinds of demons, and finally to the concept of the devil (Carus 1900; West 1939).

From a lowly place in the hierarchy of vices, mental illness moved up to head the list, and the denouncing of madness became a general form of criticism. Mental disorder became a complex phenomenon whose concepts were rooted in religion and tradition rather than medicine. Madness became related to sin and temptation; hallucinations had more power of attraction than the temptations of the flesh (Foucault 1967).

Extensive confinement for mental illness started in 1656 when Louis XIII founded the General Hospital, which was then semijudicial rather than medical in nature. Houses of correction, or bridewells, became homes for the insane, the poor, the unemployed, and prisoners of common law. All were confined under the same roof largely because of the belief that "idleness is the source of all disorders" (Foucault 1967). Mental illness was perceived at that time as the incapacity to work and the inability to integrate with a group. Idleness was condemned as a moral sin, and forced labor and instruction in religious and moral duties were used as cures for unemployment (Foucault 1967). The registries of arrest indicated no difference between the mentally ill and the others confined with them; yet they were set apart semantically as the alienated, deranged, or demented.

Delirium, with its moving away from the proper path of reason, was significant in the notion of mental illness. The concept of alienation of reason implied just error and moral fault, leading to the notion of guilt and making a purely psychological medicine possible. Treatment involved reasoning with the afflicted individual, giving solid solutions to correct the fault. Teaching the patient, it was thought, would correct the unreason. The doctor would point out the correct path for the patient to take, thus treating the false principles that had caused him to lose reason. By slow teaching and authoritarian invasion, reason was imposed on the deranged mind, and the patient then yielded to the truth. The departure from reason was said to be cured by fear and by strong and painful sensory impressions upon the body. Cultivating wheat and vegetables was also said to be a good way of restoring reason, as was obedience and blind submission (Foucault 1967).

RIGHTS OF MAN: 1790

The Declaration of the Rights of Man in 1790 led to the separation of criminals from the mentally ill and to the birth of the asylum and the end of confinement of the poor. The mentally disturbed continued to be confined; it is a myth that near the end of the eighteenth century Pinel and Tuke changed this. "It is there [in confinement]—let us remember —that they would leave them" (Foucault 1967). The concept that the origin of madness was the family occurred within the milieu of the asylum, which was arranged by Tuke to contrast with the situation of the family, that is, the most human possible, but the least social. Social failure became degeneracy, and under Pinel, the asylum became an instrument of social denunciation and moral uniformity. Various opinions were voiced. It was believed, for example, that mental disorder was the penalty of liberty, that religious beliefs were favorable to hallucinations, and even that civilization caused the development of the disturbance (Foucault 1967).

A serious ambiguity surrounds mental illness. So-called progress in understanding mental disorders over the years has not resolved this ambiguity (Foucault 1967). An analysis done in the middle of the twentieth century showed that studies pertaining to schizophrenia reveal statements of theory and observations which are obscure and difficult to integrate, and that data lack adequate precision and definition (Grinker 1969). Though there is extensive medical literature dealing with schizophrenia (Bellak 1958; Bellak and Loeb 1969), it has been concluded that hardly any worthwhile studies exist (Bellak 1968).

Over the centuries many descriptions of patients' actions have been made, and various speculations have been put forth as to the cause of their illnesses. Changing values and attitudes have produced confusion about the subject of mental disturbances. The variety of opinions indicates that the truth of the matter is not as yet known. Western history records the evolution of the concept that hallucinations are not a natural phenomenon, and that men and women who are mentally ill are to be stigmatized. Because of these views, hallucinations and unsoundness of mind have become part of the pathology of history.

HISTORICAL HALLUCINISTS

Lelut (1836, 1847) used a psychological interpretation of history when he wrote about historical leaders: "They were not madmen, but they were hallucinists." Noland (1966) noted that at least seventy-five chiefs of state in the last four centuries had led their countries while they suffered from severe mental disturbances. Whilhelm Lang-Echbaum's (1956) work includes clinical literature on Hitler, Mussolini, Whilhelm II, Stalin, and other leaders who were involved with tragic events in history. Although the common man has long considered wars to be madness ("Hitler was insane." "Mussolini was terribly sick." "The Japs were nuts." "It's a rich man's war and a poor man's fight."), this popular idea has not been studied to any great extent. Perhaps the problem is diagnosis; that is, the records may lack the details necessary for a differential diagnosis of, say, the various schizophrenic reaction types. Or perhaps the problem lies in the feeling that the strange behavior of people of a past period was normal for that time in history. Historians state that they are not trained in psychiatry and therefore do not understand the various disorders.

Whatever the reason might be for the lack of knowledge, that either neurosis or psychosis is an important aspect in the initiation of war seems a good working hypothesis. In support of this hypothesis is Toynbee's (1947) conclusion that the active form of the production of war is aberration or unsoundness of mind of the individuals making up the creative minority. Their moral and mental balance is lost, and the unbalanced soul swept along by ungovernable impulses causes disasters. In the production of war, the passive form of aberration in the creative minority is a failure of the creative power which prevents solutions to problems. Impossible obstacles not of this minority's making and not under their control also prevent needed creative acts.

In his classic work *The Pursuit of the Millennium*, Cohn (1957) has written that totalitarian movements have been inspired by the psychic content of fantasies, such as those commonly found in individual cases of paranoia. Hallucinations form the content of delusions and are common in paranoia (Retterstol 1966), which, although an individual disorder, nevertheless helps bind people together and, like delusions, stimulates them to collective action. The central fantasy of revolutionary doctrines throughout history has been that the world is dominated by evil, which is imagined not simply as human but as demonic. The delusions of paranoia are relevant to the growth of twentieth century totalitarians "with their messianic leaders, their millennial mirages, and their demon-scapegoats" (Cohn 1957).

Hofstadter's (1967) historical essays dealing with the paranoid style confirm Cohn's study, and others have noted the significance in our time of the influences of paranoia and its delusions. The relationship of such fantasies to twentieth-century events is emphasized by Oxford historian Trevor-Roper (1967), who in discussing the European witch craze states that the delusion which enlightenment had dispelled returned in the grotesque mythology of anti-Semitism and the barbarous fantasies of Nazi Germany. In 1950, historian Meinecke (1950), writing about the pursuit of the millennial kingdom in Germany (which became an ideology and gospel for the revolution), noted that spiritual factors are of primary importance in history. These are not abstract notions, but facts, for in his first and most important speech before the general public, Hitler talked on a high spiritual level about the imminent Nazi millenium rather than about the delusion of anti-Semitism, which, of course, he dealt with later after he had been well received (Ludecke 1938).

HITLER AS HALLUCINIST

The earliest record of Hitler as a hallucinist is a report that at the end of World War I he had heard a voice in the air telling him to save Germany (Bychoswski 1969). Herman Rausching (1940), in his observations and accounts of Hitler, states: "He hears voices, I have met him when in this mood. He recognizes nobody then; he wants to be alone. There are times when he flees from human society." Another eye-witness told Rauschning: "Hitler stood swaying in his room looking wildly about him. 'Ha! Ha! He's been here!' he gasped. Suddenly Hitler began to reel off figures, and odd words, and broken phrases, entirely devoid of sense, using strangely composed and entirely un-German word formations. He shouts confused and totally unintelligible phrases. 'There, there! In the corner! Who's that?' He was shown that there was nothing out of the ordinary in the room. He stood quite still, only his lips moving."

Hitler's success was based on the technique of suggestion (Bychoswski 1969; Cartwright and Biddiss 1972), which in *Mein Kampf* he described as the "magic influence of what we call mass suggestion." Hitler had a genuinely demonic power to make men his instruments (Devel 1942; Rauschning 1940). The elements of his spell were like hypnosis; Kris (1940) reported that Hitler used mass hypnosis. Devel (1942) observed that Hitler's mesmeric powers of suggestion were most striking and that he reinforced the power of suggestion over others by his hysteria, which occurred often and which Hitler called "my haunting hysteria."

That hallucinations play an important role in hysteria (Janet 1906; Janet 1925) is dictum, having been observed often in the course of history (Charcot-Schules 1885). This hysteria extended to high dignitaries of the Reich, to officials, to officers, and to a whole nation: "National Socialism is the Saint Vitus' dance of the twentieth century" (Rauschning 1940). Many Germans had mass hallucinations (Robsjohn-Gibbings 1947), and the people finally became irrational (Meinecke 1950).

Hitler had delusions of persecution and grandeur (Trevor-Roper 1953); on occasion he lost control of his emotions, chewed on the rugs and drapes (Lange-Eichbaum 1956), and said that he wanted to commit suicide (Devel 1942). He could not sleep: "It is the nights which I find a torment" (Trevor-Roper 1953). He often repeated himself and jumped from subject to subject, unable to concentrate on one concept; moreover, he held compulsive views on certain topics. He would sit apathetically for long periods of time without speaking a word, and he employed people to help him to stop thinking: "I must do anything but think." Like Stalin, who had grotesque fantasies (Lange-Eichbaum 1956; Bychoswski 1969) and was a despot, Hitler converted his morbid hallucinations and delusions into tragic realities.

One of the best of German historians, Friedrich Meinecke (1950), gives a reason for the German catastrophe: it occurred because a person like Hitler who wanted to reform the world lacked equilibrium between the rational and irrational. Meinecke observed that Hitler was psychopathic, primitive, and completely amoral, a demonic person who had a fantasy-swollen mentality. Meinecke notes Hitler's hybrid metaphysics, and he believes that this suppressed metaphysical desire, when not brought to the individual's attention, changes the person into a fanatic and a monomaniac. The neglected irrational impulses of the spirit react violently with the one-sided rational training of the intellect. In Hitler's case, he was an irrational artist at first, and then he reacted to rational experiences, while most fanatics are at first rational and then meet the irrational. Meinecke's historical description is much like that observed in the development of a mental illness (Bleuler 1968).

It has been noted that various persons around Hitler, (who formed his small group of uncivilized assistants) were paranoid and had serious mental disturbances (Swanson, Bohnert, and Smith 1970). Simmel (1946) found that national anti-Semitism in Germany was a genuine mass paranoid psychosis formed under conditions of pathological leadership and post-World War I stresses on the ego systems of the population. In comparing and contrasting the mental state of the Nazi party members with the German people, scientific tests reveal that the narratives from the Nazis indicated systematized delusions of paranoia, while the narratives of the citizens were more normal (Peak 1945).

Hitler is not an isolated case in history. The Japanese militarists during World War II were addicted to heroin, a kind of hallucinogen (Huxley 1952), and Benito Mussolini had syphilis as well as delusions which were hallucinatory (L'Etang 1970).

POWER TO MAKE WAR

Before discussing other leaders and abnormal events which have manifested themselves throughout history, we should note that the power to make war is in the hands of kings, emperors, dictators, and presidents. In all history the majority of the people did not will war (Johnson 1935); wars are declared without representation of the people. In theory the initiation of war is in the power of the citizen, but in practice such restrictions as treaties, policies, and doctrines demand sanction of war, irrespective of parliamentary actions (Johnson 1935). Leaders and small minorities determine war policies, which often assume a pseudopopular character because of propaganda and the force of the situation; so people are influenced to support war by language and symbols rather than by events and conditions (Wright 1935; Wright 1942; Wright 1968). The pattern of despotic wars has been observed as fairly uniform throughout history (Johnson 1935). Albert Einstein (1937) wrote to Freud: "How is it possible for this small clique to bend the will of the majority, who stand to lose and suffer by a state of war? Experience proves that it is rather the so-called 'intelligentsia' that is most apt to yield to these disastrous collected suggestions. Is it possible to control man's mental evolution so as to make [him immune to] the psychoses of destruction?" Freud replied in the famous "Why War" letters that a terrible weapon was needed, but such a weapon has not stopped the small wars, which lead to larger conflicts. In the production of wars, statesmen do not always pause to think; hence, the rational or irrational motives for preventing a conflict which depend on thought and come from deterrents are absent (Wright 1968).

University of Chicago Professor Quincy Wright (1942), a great scholar in the study of war, states that throughout history most people have regarded war as a human problem. Scientifically observed economic factors have been found to be insignificant among the causes of world wars, as are population pressures or demography (Wright 1968). Wright emphasizes (1968) that war springs from "irrational illusions or unreasonable fears." Ignorance, political ambitions, legal claims, ideological convictions, and irrational psychological complexes are important factors. Among the psychological aspects in the initiation of war, noted in the literature, are ambivalence, frustration, projection, fears, and anxieties (Wright 1942, 1968). Lack of thought, such as was observed in Hitler, eliminates the image of the total situation, which is needed to control governmental decisions. Wright (1942) states clearly that wars in the modern period do not grow out of a situation, but rather out of a highly artificial interpretation of a situation, possibly because of an unsoundness of mind that causes defects in intelligence, thought, and judgment, and that leads to factitious explanations.

Wright (1942) relates that the outbreaks of war are never based on actual phenomena, but rather on language and words related not to facts, conditions, or grievances, but to potentialities, hopes, and aspirations. These words deal with wishes, desires, and power, and seem related to the emotional mechanism in the brain, which motivates other aspects of the nervous system, leading to gratification in motor acts. Pseudocivilized needs are translated into high-sounding words, with subjective emotional color and no objectification, thereby causing behavior with abnormal means and ends. The leaders, when not thinking, lack reason, which is necessary to the control of emotional desires and wishes. War has no natural causes; it is a human creation because it is more determined by words (Wright 1942) than by events, and the language used does not describe human reality. Some feel that the normal animal aggressiveness in man is the basic cause of war, but in contrast, Karl Menninger (1963) observes that aggressiveness in man is a serious symptom of mental illness.

WAR AND MYSTICISM

The influential psychologist Gustave Le Bon (1916) elucidated the theory that mysticism plays an immense role in the origin and evolution of war, and hallucinations have always been basic to mysticism. Le Bon (1916) wrote: "Mystic beliefs are induced by suggestion or mental contagion. . . . There is an explosion of mystic frenzy from which even the most celebrated scholars have not been able to escape, because of the influence of mental contagion has prevailed over reason, to such an extent that their utterances are enveloped in a whirlwind of madness. . . . The modern world deems itself free from their sway, and yet humanity has never been more enslaved by them." He wrote that reason has had little to do with wars, and that, therefore, wars could not be foreseen by reason. War is rather of mystic origin, and acts as the strongest of mankind's various incentives. Further evidence for the hypothesis that war may be contingent on the morbid and uncivilized behavior of leaders and small groups of individuals interacting with larger populations comes from a conclusion of Madden (1857) that hallucinations of various kinds ensue in fanaticism. He states: "The madness of the various forms of fanaticism is not confined to individuals; it extends to communities, at times and intervals more or less widely separated, and seizes on the minds of nations at periods, of greater intervening distances, that have been terminated by great wars, or other grievous public calamities. Such fanaticisms have all the distinguishing characteristics of epidemic mental disorders."

Hallucinations are associated with the eight great wars of ancient history and with modern wars as well as smaller conflicts. Alexander the Great, Caesar, Attila, Muhammed, Charlemagne, and Joan of Arc are examples of earlier leaders who were hallucinists. The people of ancient Greece, as compared with those of other periods, were just as inclined to mysticism, magic, and hallucinations (Thorndike 1923). The term *panic* takes its origin from the battle of Platgea, where the air resounded with a "voice" that the Athenians attributed to the god Pan. The Persians were so alarmed at the "voice" that they fled, hence the word *panic* (Brierre de Boismont 1855). Alexander the Great, it is reported, had hallucinations (Kirton 1660) and visions (Dendy 1847); he received orders from "voices" to invade other countries.

As mentioned earlier, many Roman leaders were mentally ill. The following description of the origin of the war of the Jews against the Romans comes from an eyewitness (Brierre de Boismont 1855). "Earlier in the day there appeared in the air, throughout the whole country, chariots full of armed men, traversing the clouds and spreading round the cities, as if to enclose them. On the day of the Pentecost, the priests, being at night in the inner temple to celebrate divine service, heard a noise, and afterwards a 'voice' that repeated several times, 'Let us go out from hence.' The misfortune that followed this was the war which confirmed these hallucinatory signals." Visual hallucinatory signals were present when Antiochus was preparing to carry war into Egypt. Hallucinations were associated with the war of the Romans against the Cimrians and in the fight against Tarquin. Caesar is said to have taken orders from "voices" to invade countries. Drusus was said to have been deterred from crossing the Elbe by the sudden appearance of a woman of supernatural size. The Barbarians brought not only devastation and death to Rome, but also religious creeds based on hallucinations, illusions, and superstitions, some of which were spread by Mohammed (Brierre de Boismont 1895). Attila's march on Rome was checked by a vision of an old man in priest's raiment, who threatened his life with a drawn sword, and by the entreatings of Pope Leo I and Lupus. Constantine fought a battle in the year 312 because of hallucinations and was converted to Christianity by "voices."

Mohammed had auditory and visual hallucinations (Brierre de Boismont 1855; Lombroso 1891; Parish 1897), which were used by him in his calling as a prophet (Brierre de Boismont 1855; Kirton 1660). As he walked in solitary meditation in a lonely valley near Mecca, he was greeted suddenly by a "voice" that said, "Hail to thee, O messenger of God!" He looked right and left to discover from where the voice had come, but saw only stones and trees. Soon afterward, on Mount Hira, the Angel Gabriel appeared to him in a vision and delivered to him the message that God had chosen him to be a prophet. He even thought of ending his life by throwing himself off Mount Hira. Many of Mohammed's writings were derived from the inspiration of his hallucinatory visions, in which were also developed the erotic sensibility that gives his religious system a sensual cast. He brought a code of laws when there was none, and he gave God to his followers. "Allah had commanded Mohammed to make war against nonbelievers" (Abercrombe 1972). Mohammed acted on the command from the "voice" and promised the conquest of the world in wars that would continue after his death. Hallucinations are common to the Middle East, where they are called reverie (Brierre de Boismont 1855).

The Christian emperor Charlemagne was thought to be directly inspired by the angels. He was also considered a great champion of Christianity against the creed of Mohammed. Charlemagne's wars in Italy, Spain, and Saxony formed part of the common epic material, and it is difficult to separate the Charlemagne legends from the truth about Charles the Great who, some fearless medieval chroniclers asserted, rose from the dead to take part in the Crusades (Bryant 1910). Elaborate visual hallucinations occurred during the time of Charlemagne (Brierre de Boismont 1855).

APPARITIONS AND THE CRUSADES

Two million died during the Crusades. "The records of the crusading sermons show that there was a strong element of 'revivalism' in the Crusades, and that thousands were hurried into taking the cross by a gust of uncontrollable enthusiasm, which is excited by revivalist meetings today" (Barker 1910). Even today the hallucinatory enthusiasm of revivalist meetings has been observed. Such inspirations were set in motion by Urban II, when at Clermont in France on November 26, 1095, he delivered the speech that preceded the First Crusade. Urban II used delusions in his speech (Cohn 1970). About such individuals Constantine Africannus wrote in *De melanchoia* that "many religious persons who live lives to be revered . . . fall into this disease . . . and become drunk, as it were, with their excessive anxiety." A great number of people during the Crusades experienced hallucinations, and it is written that kings, generals, soldiers, and civilians were in the daily habit of witnessing apparitions (Michaud 1852). The First Crusade had hardly begun before "apparitions commenced, everyone related his visions, the words he had heard, the commands he had received" (Brierre de Boismont 1855).

Some historians feel that the origin of the First Crusade should be ascribed to the preachings of Peter the Hermit, but many modern historians believe that he is a figure of secondary importance, even though his sermons of fiery zeal produced five divisions of the people's Crusades. Whatever the final record in historical science shows about him, it has often been recorded (Brierre de Boismont 1855; Cohn 1957; MacKay 1841; Michaud 1852) that Peter the Hermit, who in some ways resembled Hitler, inaugurated the events which led to the First Crusade. The hallucinist Peter gave the "signal" and by his influences aroused the whole West. His "thoughts became imaged. . . . He maintained an habitual intercourse with heaven" (Brierre de Boismont 1855). The situation in history at the time preceding the Hermit was not serious in regard to war, for only one letter had reached Urban II from Constantinople about the persecution of pilgrims, and even that message is in question (MacKay 1841). Peter's suggestions to Simeon that he should write Constantinople later stimulated letters from Turkey to Urban II about initiating a Crusade.

The following has been written about Peter the Hermit (Brierre de Boismont 1855): "The study of letters, bearing arms, celibacy, marriage, the ecclesiastic state offered nothing to him that could fill his heart or satisfy his ardent mind. Disgusted with the world and mankind, he retired amongst the most austere cenobites. Fasting, prayer, meditation, the silence of solitude exalted his imagination. In his visions he kept up an habitual commerce with heaven, and believed himself the instrument of its designs and the depository of its will. The fame of the pilgrimages to the East drew Peter from his retreat." Some historians think that Peter, in fact, attempted to go on a pilgrimage to Jerusalem before 1096, and may have been prevented by the Turks from reaching his destination (Barker 1910), but others believe he visited Jerusalem and observed the persecution of a number of pilgrims. In Palestine, while conversing with Simeon, he first conceived the idea of rousing the powers of Christendom in order to rescue the Eastern Christians and the sepulchre of Jesus. Peter then had a vision that Christ would aid and protect the undertaking. "One day, whilst prostrated before the holy sepulchre, he believed that he heard the voice of Christ, which said to him, 'Peter, arise! hasten to proclaim the tribulations of my people; it is time that my servants should be delivered'" (Brierre de Boismont 1855).

Whether or not he reached the Holy Land is perhaps not the major issue, but he did return to Italy and influence Urban II. He was then sent abroad to preach the holy war to all the nations and potentates of Christendom. "He communicated his own madness to his hearers, until Europe was stirred from its very depths" (MacKay 1841). Historians agree that after the council, summoned by Urban II to make preparations for the war, Peter the Hermit's work was responsible for the crusade of the paupers (Cohn 1957, 1970), which formed the first act in the First Crusade, and that he led one of the five sections to Constantinople. The news of the declaration of war from Urban II's council was spread to the remotest parts of Europe in an incredibly short space of time and was known by people in the distant provinces long before the fastest horsemen could have brought the information (Michaud 1852).

According to Cohn (1957), after the First Crusade various mass migrations inaugurated the tradition of the Crusades, which were started by individuals who, like Peter the Hermit, were mentally disturbed. The "propheta" Fulk of Nevilly was a typical ascetic who was said to have the ability to heal the blind and dumb. The crowds he set in motion perished on the coast of Spain. Next there was the Children's Crusade, headed by youths such as a shepherd boy Etinenna and a child named Stephen, to whom the ambassador of the Lord appeared. The child pilgrimage from France ended disastrously; two ships were sunk and the other five ships were steered to Bougia and Alexandria, where the young crusaders were sold as slaves after having been betrayed by two merchants of Marseilles, Simon the Fat and Peter the Pig.

MADNESS AND WAR

The literature holds many indications that madness is associated with war. The ecclesiastical writers related that when two nations went to war, the celestial spirits, stationed on the limits of the two kingdoms, also waged terrible warfare (Brierre de Boismont 1855). Tamerlane (or Timur Lenk) was a megalomanic and homicidal madman (Toynbee 1947), who was involved with the initiation of many wars. The Vikings, or Norsemen, who plundered the coasts of Europe in the eighth and tenth centuries were hallucinists, as were the Turks in later times. Boismont (1855) observed that hallucinations may affect a large number of persons at the same time, as in the battle of Antioch during the Crusades. Professor Trevor-Roper of Oxford (1967) noted that the epidemic demoniaque is explicitly associated with the Thirty Years War; and again, in the fifteenth century, witchcraft is connected with the Hundred Years War, which Joan of Arc ended. She heard "voices" and gave and took hallucinatory commands (Madden 1857; Parish 1897) during her visions.

Some think that George III's health may be of importance in regard to the American Revolution. "Early in his reign, in 1765, he had been out of health, and though the fact was studiously concealed at the time, symptoms of mental aberration were even then perceived" (Gardiner 1910). In 1788, his insanity was beyond doubt, and Dr. Willis was called in. The king recovered in 1789, but in the year 1811 he permanently lost his reason and died nine years later. Today it is believed that his illness was physically determined and hereditary (Macalpine and Hunter 1969). The mentally diseased and psychopaths play an important role in the development of nations.

Concerning the French Revolution, Le Bon stated (1916): "The secret forces which ruled the actors in the great drama were drawn from quite other sources than rationalism." The advent of the Revolution, which affected all of Europe, is discussed in Robert Darnton's (1968) *Mesmerism and the End of the Enlightenment in France.* He did not write directly about hallucinations, for perhaps he was not aware that they play a role in mesmerism, but he mentioned that many of the revolutionary leaders communicated with one another over great distances, with ghosts, and with remote planets. Mesmeric somnambulism, induced somnambulism, and induced hypnosis are important aspects of mesmerism and are also involved with a hallucinatory state. The French psychiatrist Janet wrote extensively about somnambulistic trances, and drew the following conclusion about the relationship between somnambulism and hallucinations: "The unfolding of hallucinations is incomparable. Except in some crises of alcoholic delirium that are a little like hysteria, we shall never find in lunacy such abundance and such copiousness in the hallucinations of all senses" (Janet 1906). Janet (1925) observed that in the literature, animal magnetism or mesmerism was under a cloud, but Charipgnon, in 1848, gave the first research account of the phenomenon as suggested hallucinations. Colquhoun (1851) observed that hallucinations are a characteristic feature of magnetic somnambulistic phenomena and are the "most notorious and best attended." In addition, Boismont (1855) stated that magnetism belongs in the domain of hallucinations.

MESMERISM AND REVOLUTIONS

Mesmerism, a new scientific vogue to the French people, caused the beginning of the Revolution and ended the Enlightenment (Darnton 1968). Some important revolutionary leaders were students of Mesmer, namely: Jacques Pierre Brissot, Jean-Louis Carra, Andrien Duport, Nicolas Bergasse, the Rolands, Dural d'Epremesnil, and Lafayette. In a letter to George Washington, Lafayette stated that he was an enthusiastic pupil of Mesmer and knew as much about mesmerism as any sorcerer ever did (Darnton 1968). Another active leader of the Revolution was Mirabeau, who believed that Frederick II had produced centaurs and satyrs by experiments with sodomy. Mirabeau was also a hypomaniac. Robespierre was a schizoid psychopath (Kretschmer 1931).

Mesmer wandered alone for three months in a forest before going to Paris, and in an inspired state, he learned to think without using words, which he felt Rousseau had shown to be just social artifices. This fact is of considerable importance because a mental patient thinks less rather than more (Bleuler 1950).

Mesmerism took such a grip on France that it molded interests and attitudes even into the nineteenth century. The radicals utilized mesmerism as an important vehicle for the communication of ideas on political theory. Attitudes were transformed—"Mesmerism remade the world" (Darnton 1968). This was the expressed outlook of many Frenchmen, and some famous persons became interested in it. Alexander Dumas conducted somnambulism experiments and even received material for his written works from mesmerism. Balzac had faith in the vogue and found helpful Swedenborgian mysticism, which again deals much with hallucinations. Hugo "contacted" his dead daughter, Leopuldine, and exchanged verse with Shakespeare and Dante, which lifted his poetry into the supernatural.

Brachet's detailed work on the mental problems of the kings of France, which Robinson (1916) discusses, strongly indicates that a major problem existed in historical pathology even before the Revolution. It has been reported (Madden 1857) that in the revolutionary madness or homicidal frenzy associated with the French Revolution, 900,000 were killed in La Vendee, 32,000 in Nantes, and 31,000 in Lyons, and that 18,613 were guillotined. For much of France, however, no records are available.

The mesmerists were active during the Napoleonic and Restoration periods (Darnton 1968). General Bonaparte had auditory and visual hallucinations (Brierre de Boismont 1855, Lombroso 1891, Parish 1897). He consulted somnambulist Mally-Chateaurengud about his first campaign into Italy and about the Battle of Castiglione before his departure for Egypt, and when under stress he was himself a somnambulist (Clark 1922). He had fits of apathy, and his manuscripts were illegible and undecipherable, an index to an inner speech deficit or a thinking disorder. During the Russian campaign, the military were equally assailed by hallucinations, sometimes gay, sometimes melancholy.

Lombroso (1891) wrote that lunatics or neurotics caused all the revolutions in Algeria and the Sudan. They made their own neuroses and their religious societies instruments for invigorating religious fanaticism and for receiving acceptance as inspired messengers of God. Such were the Mahdi and Omar. Although we have only traces of information, it should be noted in passing that neuroses among the kings of Spain (Ireland 1889, 1893) may have played a role in the Spanish wars. Bismark (Kretschmer 1931) had a "psychopathic restlessness," was constantly ill in bed with "nerve pains," and was neurotic (L'Etang 1970). These observations indicate mental unsoundness, which could have been a factor in the wars associated with his times.

The great T'p-p'ing rebellion in China, during which twenty million people died (Wright 1968), was led by a madman who was involved with drugs, secret societies, and criminal activities. Kwang-si, selfish and tyrannical, with a voluptuary's craving for every kind of sensual pleasure, was in a disturbed state when the oppressed people proclaimed a youth as emperor. The mad (Lombroso 1891) Hung Siut-s'tian then proclaimed himself to be sent by heaven to drive out the Tatars. In China (De Groot 1907) the feats of the spectral warriors, or Kwei ping, are a main feature of the demonology. Hallucinations are also common in Japan (Lowell 1895).

The demonology and hallucinations of the Chinese people are recorded in great detail by De Groot (1907), who wrote that spectres appeared on the side of Shi Wan Sue as his auxiliaries against rebels and enemies in reward for his good treatment of a certain general's bones. In the twenty-third year of the Ching yue period, "the people affrighted each other with spectre soldiers, and all fled, quite at a loss where to stay, here and there thronging, beating, maiming, and wounding each other" (De Groot 1907). When the spectral warriors crossed the Loh River, "a rattling noise was heard in the air as of thousands and myriads of chariots escorted by soldiers and cavalry, and then suddenly the passage was finished. Every night they crossed the river twice or thrice. The emperor was highly displeased at the matter. He ordered his wu and his invokers to subdue them by means of sacrifices, and to set out every evening food and drink for them on the bank of the Loh" (De Groot 1907). De Groot (1907) notes spectre-plagues or spectre-panics as late as 1879, and Thompson (1930) makes note of them in the early part of the twentieth century. Although some Chinese had hallucinations and delusions about witchcraft, broomsticks, and cats (De Groot 1907), they did not treat or subject their citizens to the same persecutions and prohibitions as those practiced in Europe. There were mental hospitals in China, but paradoxically, they had no patients in them until a Western missionary arrived. It seems that mental hospitals may come out of the uncivilized treatment of those who suffer from the thinking disorder.

GERMAN CONFLICTS

In 1916, Le Bon (1916) wrote: "Mysticism is the determining cause of the conflict that Germany has let loose upon the world." Thousands of stories about apparitions were published in the newspapers during World War I (Thompson 1930); a well-known example is the famous "Angel of Mons" that appeared to everybody who fought from Mons to Ypes (Machen 1915). During this time a phantom army was observed in France; spectural bowmen, St. George, and St. Michael all appeared as apparitions. Hallucinations were also found in war neuroses during World War II (Abse 1966).

Wilhelm II's speech declaring World War I calls to mind Lelut's (1836) statement about leaders: "In order to act on the multitude, to seize on the people, to overturn or change beliefs, and to imprint a furrow on the face of nature that ages will fail to efface, it is necessary to think, speak, be deceived, and grow frenzied or crazy with the masses, to believe with them, and beyond them, to be their messenger and their prophet, in order that they may think you the prophet of God, and yield power." When Kaiser Wilhelm declared war, he said, "Remember that the German people are the chosen of God. On me, as German Emperor, the spirit of God has descended. I am His weapon, His sword, and His vice-regent. Woe to the disobedient! Death to cowards and unbelievers!" (Kretschmer 1931). Later, in referring to this speech, Lloyd George stated: "There has been nothing like it since the days of Mahomet. Lunacy is always distressing. But, sometimes it is dangerous. And when you get it manifested in the head of a state, and [it] has become the policy of a great Empire, it is about time it should be ruthlessly put away." That Wilhelm II had a mental disorder is recorded in Lange-Eichbaum's work (1956).

Also important are Lelut's observations in regard to Hitler's statements given at the time of the invasion of the U.S.S.R. by Germany. Part of the Order of the Fuehrer states: "Weighed down for many months by grave anxieties, compelled to keep silent, I can at last speak openly to you my soldiers. . . . The destiny of Europe, the future of the German Reich, the existence of our nation now lie in your hands alone. Not . . . to create the necessary conditions for the final conclusion of this great war, or to protect the countries at this moment, but in order to save the whole of European civilization and culture. . . . May the Almighty help us all in this struggle."

A good working hypothesis seems to be that epidemics grow into movements which lead into wars (Madden 1857). Cohn (1957, 1970) writes about many cases in which multitudes of people acted out with fierce energy a shared fantasy that was autistic and delusional and barely related to the world around them; yet they were willing to kill and die for their psychotic dreams. The first crusade of the shepherds was an anarchic movement started by Jacob "mater of Hungary," an ascetic who claimed that the Virgin Mary, surrounded by a host of angels, had appeared to him and had given him a letter similar to the one Peter the Hermit carried. Jacob's army attacked the clergy and Jews, as did those in the second shepherd's crusade, which was started by an allegedly divinely appointed savior. Heinrich Suso's hallucinations are the clearest written examples of anarchy stemming from an incorporeal image and auditory hallucinations. Men who were inspired prophets were largely responsible for an English peasant rising. Muntzer, who lived fantasies, was a leader of another small war. A typical paranoiac, Boulland, who was obsessed by delusions of grandeur and persecution related to hallucinations, had a six-hundred-thousand-member sect.

LEADERS AND FOLLOWERS

The preceding type of situation is found only in certain social settings (Cohn 1970). Many revolts and urban insurrections stood the common people in good stead, bringing solid gains in prosperity and privilege. Industrial workers have improved their own condition as seen in left-wing revolutions and other social revolutions of the twentieth century. In contrast, the types of persons who follow the mentally disturbed leader have been observed and identified as have their prophetae. The leaders are seldom manual workers, peasants (the poor), or artisans, but rather half-intellectuals, such as the many freelance preachers in the Middle Ages or even the petty nobles and impostors. These leaders were obsessed with eschatological fantasies long before the thought ever occurred to them, in the midst of some normal revolution or social upheaval, to turn to those who might follow them. The followers are people who live on the margin of society, without land, or under the continuous threat of unemployment; not just poor people, but those who can find no recognized or assured place in society. They have no group of their own; even their family life is in a state of disintegration, and they seem to wait for a propheta to bind them together. In the middle of the twentieth century such individuals are found in technologically backward societies and in certain politically marginal elements in advanced societies—a small minority of intellectuals and students and young or unemployed workers. The old religious fantasies are replaced by secular delusions that obscure what would be obvious, for "revolutionary millenarianism and mystical anarchism are with us still" (Cohn 1970). Because these various individuals have been identified, it should be possible to prevent such epidemics in the future.

THE FLAGELLANT MOVEMENT

A serious epidemic that lasted for two centuries was that of the flagellants, which was as destructive a force as the witch craze in Europe. The epidemic was so large and so well organized, with leaders, uniforms, and names, such as the Cross-bearers, that it is called a movement (Cohn 1957). Flagellance, or "the new form of penance," originated with hermits in the monastic communities; Regniew, a hermit of Perugia who was a fanatic preacher, is said to have invented scourging. A motive in penitentiary practices such as fasting, flagellation, and pilgrimage was that a person would find a new path to Heaven and forgiveness of sins. (Maudsley 1886) found that the religious ascetic used stress, flagellance, and exposure to act as a "receipt" for "summoning spirits" and to see visions. Another example of these practices is as follows: "A Mohametan receipt, which is in successful use now for summoning spirits, is to fast seven days in a lonely place, burning such incense as benzoin, aloe-wood, mastic, and other odoriferous wood from the Soudan, and to read a certain chapter from the Koran a thousand and one times in the seven days" (Maudsley 1886). Science has now shown that solitude in the form of sensory deprivation can cause hallucinations.

It seems likely that the flagellant movement has aspects somewhat like the twentieth century hallucinogenic drug movement, in which persons believe that hallucinations expand the mind. Perhaps penance gave the flagellants hallucinations that were gratifying to them in that they could summon spirits and see visions, just as do users of hallucinogenic drugs. The witchcraft situation is also like the hallucinogenic epidemic (Barnett 1965). People who make up movements such as mesmerism seem to find hallucinations fascinating and pleasant, and perhaps this is a motive in the epidemics and even in certain aspects of the pseudoromantic adventure of war and its related hallucinations (note the drug abuse in the Viet Nam war).

EUROPEAN WITCH CRAZE

A morbid situation related to the Hundred Years War (Trevor-Roper 1967) is that of the European witch craze, which has been and will continue to be studied extensively, because two million people died and because it is a perplexing phenomenon. One can agree with Trevor-Roper's (1967) conclusion that the witch craze cannot be seen correctly as a mere delusion, isolated and detached from the social structure of the time, as theorized by the nineteenth century historians. Historical situations involve more than single, simple causes and effects—for example, fantasies or delusions. One cannot negate the importance of mental disorders, however, as a cause of uncivilized behavior in regard to either leaders or followers and the interaction between them, because of Cohn's (1957, 1970) work dealing with delusions as found in history. Firm decisions or even opinions that relate psychosis with morbid history are lacking, for in the brilliant and creative works of many authors, the subject of mental illness plays an extremely minor, if not irrelevant, role in the analysis of witch crazes or movements. Even in his 1961 historical work, which mentions mental disturbances, Baroja states that the theory of contagion can be accepted only with strong reservation; the judges and witnesses at the witch trials are obvious cases, but the psychopathology of the witch remains blurred.

PSYCHOSIS AND NEUROSIS

Psychosis has remained unchanged throughout the ages. The basic problem, the hallmark of mental illness, is the disorder of the intellect, reason, or thinking, as even Plato observed. The differential diagnosis of psychosis as written by E. Blueler (1950), Lehman (1967), and Schneider (1957) is based on hallucinations and delusions, association or thinking disorders, abnormal emotional behavior, such as undisguised aggression (Menninger 1963), and the lack of emotions, described as blunting. Medical diseases do not change; nomenclature changes, but not the disorder. Menninger's (1963) extensive treatment of the ancient classifications of mental disorders as compared to those in the Middle Ages, Renaissance, and modern times clearly shows that the classical syndromes have not changed their basic forms and are essentially the same as originally observed by Hippocrates. A disease described in antiquity is the same disease in modern times, as Moss noted in 1967, and although the resulting behavior in either period may appear different on the surface it is nevertheless a product of the basic disorders. This point of view has been expressed by Professor Mettler (1966), of Columbia University, who has studied medical history as well as neurology, anatomy, and psychiatry.

That the basic problems of psychosis and neurosis do not change is an important concept to keep in mind, because of the mistaken idea that what we think is psychotic today would be considered normal in another period, and vice versa. It is true that the "mind of one age is not necessarily subject to the same rules as the mind of another" (Trevor-Roper 1967), but madness is not a rule; it is a constant and recurring disorder throughout mankind's history. Just because a large group holds a belief that is false—that is, an insane delusion—does not make it truthful or normal. Certain paranoid fantasies and their contents have not changed, for the same autism is found in the Middle Ages and in modern totalitarian movements (Cohn 1957, 1970). False beliefs, such as the master race delusion (Bon 1916) that was held by the whole country of Germany during the two world wars, must be considered only as delusions. Perhaps the problem is that because a certain amount of hallucinatory behavior is normal, historians who treat the phenomenon as a reflection of a changing society, as in primitive cultures, have trouble in their diagnoses of what might be normal or abnormal in that society or that time.

CIVILIZED BEHAVIOR

What is civilized in one time is civilized in any time. Civilized behavior and its product, mankind's artifacts, do not go out of style, but are added to, lost, and rediscovered and added to once more in renaissance periods, such as the one that Lord Clark (1970) observes we are in now. Mankind's behavior has not changed much, according to those who compare and contrast ancient behavior with modern acts (Moss 1967). The problem in history is diagnosis and a definition of what is normal. Perhaps a lack of historical detail obviates a clear diagnosis of what schizophrenic reaction type an individual may have had; yet enough information would be available to indicate that the person or group was at the fourth level or order of ego dysfunction in the Menninger (1963) system—that is, psychotic behavior. In pathology one can observe clearly what is morbid, for one has an idea of what is normal. In psychology normal behavior must be determined, yet it is often written that normal behavior cannot be defined and is an impossible item to equate experimentally (Nathan and Harris 1975).

As a working hypothesis in this study, I propose that to be normal is to be civilized. A civilized person acts normally; an uncivilized person acts abnormally. This should be self-evident. An educated person, however, is not necessarily civilized, for knowledge is applied by some not with the wisdom of men but, rather, with the cunning of brutes (Herrick 1956). In addition tests show that so-called normal individuals have little imagination, limited interest and social activities, limited aspirations, and no ambition (Cole 1970). While these "normal" people were not neurotic and psychotic and would not have been seen by a doctor, nevertheless, their behavior is not that of a truly civilized person. Civilized behavior starts on a scale that is evolutionary in nature, and progresses with the growth and development of civilization in an increasing way towards an open end, which is always expanding.

A person who is morbid, and uncivilized, exhibits many symptoms, some of which can be medically treated. Even in an arrested civilization, such as that of the Eskimos, members of the group who are uncivilized are isolated, and illnesses of a mental nature have been observed. No matter what may be the level of civilized behavior in a culture, there are abnormal individuals who are either so uncivilized or so ill that others try to help them (Benedict and Jacks, 1967). Customs and clothes styles change or are added to periodically in history, but the human problem of mental disorder, described even in the Bible, is just as much in evidence today as in Biblical times. Materialism, like education, does not always bring with it civilized behavior, because the basic therapeutic knowledge necessary to correct the abnormal or uncivilized behavior is not always known.

UNCIVILIZED BEHAVIOR

There can be little doubt that the various individuals involved with the events surrounding the witchcraft situation hallucinated often (Thomas 1911) and that symptoms included nonrational or uncivilized behavior, such as: an alienation of reason, a withdrawal from reality (as observed in the witches' fantasies), and abnormal sexual emotional behavior. Judges, witnesses, and witches all acted in uncivilized neurotic and psychotic ways (Middleton 1967). Agents, such as belladonna, henbane, scopolamine, and mandragora, were used then (Barnett 1965) as well as today among witches in the Basque country (Baroja 1961), and these drugs can each cause hallucinations (Barnett 1965, Brierre de Boismont 1855). Baroja (1961) observed that a clear distinction has not been made between the illnesses of those who are possessed, bewitched, or liable to fits, on the one hand, and the disturbances of the sorcerers and witches, on the other hand. Those who acted as witnesses, who said they were possessed or bewitched often have been diagnosed as having a type of hysteria (Kraepelin 1921), or a psycho-neurotic disorder. Janet (1906), Abse (1966), and Levenson (1966) have noted that hallucinations are found in hysteria. The witches often may have been psychotic (Thomas 1911), but not all of them were mentally ill, which is stressed in historical works on the subject of the witch craze. All the individuals acted in uncivilized ways based on the content of their delusions and hallucinations, which they believed to be reality (Hansen 1966).

The friars created one basic element of the witch craze by initiating the persecution of independent persons in the mountains. According to Trevor-Roper (1967), this prohibition of individuality is the major origin of the problem called witch craze. Independent people's normal dislike of conformity may have been a factor in motivating the friars. The friars started a stream that flowed into a prevailing climate of opinion handed down from Greece and Rome, thereby catalyzing a serious cancerous growth in history.

That the situation is often ripe for such movements is indicated by the following observation that in France (Kirton 1660): "The Magicians, Astrologuers, Sortiarie, Sorcerers, Wizzards, and Witches were so numerous that they began to boast themselves not only for a society, but for an Army; and to professe that if they could get someone in authority to be their commander or leader, they dust wage warre with the king or state; and doubted not of the victory through the verture of power of their art. Like as the Hunnes (by thufe very means) had for merely done against Sigebeut King of France." In this case the people who lived on the margin of society did not have their propheta to lead them. The existence of a paranoid delusion of a vast conspiracy is clearly indicated in the morbid introduction to the English translation of *Malleus Maleficarum* (Sprenger and Kramer, 1951). In one case, there was an abnormal interaction between the disturbed leaders and the larger group of people, leading to persecution. In the other case, the hallucinist led a movement to hostility and aggression. Additionally, because of the prohibition on hallucinatory behavior, citizens reacted out of morbid curiosity to become involved with the movement or with its persecution and prohibition.

No matter how one wants to write or interpret history, it is incorrect to dismiss the salient and catalytic factor of mental unsoundness and the resulting abnormal uncivilized behavior that causes a sociological disturbance. Equally absurd is the belief that all of history is psychotic or neurotic. The major growth, development, and progress of civilization are not derived from the insane obstacle of war and the uncivilized behavior of morbid individuals. Many factors are involved in such historical events as the witch craze; for example, Walker (1968) points out that two sorts of people were thought to be in league with the devil, scientists and the mentally ill. During the sixteenth century scientists were frequently confused with sorcerers. Anatomists were in particular danger because their interest in the human corpse was misunderstood in light of the prohibition and interdictions about the dead body that originated in the taboos of primitive man's negative magic. History is a combination of factors, and in the tragic events of history the abnormal elements are more important than the usual historical features.

INDIVIDUAL PATHOLOGY

Medical history in the past often has studied epidemics (Hecker 1859, Sigerist 1943), and scholars (Barbu 1960, Brown 1959, Muzlish 1963, Frank 1967, Rogow 1968, Wolman 1971) have written on historical pathology, but the studies of individual cases are of great importance. On abnormal conduct, the historian Bernheim (Robinson 1916) wrote: "A theoretical knowledge of mental troubles is quite indispensable in an understanding of the numerous phenomena of character and of numerous actions. I do not speak of the Caesarean madness, now becoming commonplace, but of the phenomena which recurs so frequently in the biographies of historical persons, such as religious exaltation, which passes over into hallucinations and fixed ideas. Here the realms of psychology and psychiatry touch." The situation can at times be serious, for as Keynes observed there are "madmen in authority, who hear voices in the air."

We must examine the mental problems of creative individuals, for Toynbee (1939, 1947, 1961) observes that the basic mechanisms in the growth and the breakdown of civilizations, and in the further disintegrations, are the creative minorities or creative individuals. The growth is dependent, at first, on the achievement of their inspiration or discovery and, second, on the conversion of the society to this new way of life. The major cause of the breakdown of civilization is either the failure of creative power in persons who make up the creative minority or the advent of situations that make it impossible for the creative individuals to continue their work—a problem that is neither under the control of nor produced by the creative minority or individual. Freud (1937-1939) wrote in *Moses and Monotheism*: "How impossible it is to deny the personal influence of individual great men on the history of the world." Although many historians do not believe in all of Toynbee's concepts they do feel that his theory of the creative minority is a valid one.

Toynbee's writings on the breakdown and disintegration of civilizations are of interest because he examines various aspects in the loss of creativity. The active form of abberation is destruction, outrageous behavior, and surfeit excesses in various types of behavior such as in eating, drinking, and orgies. *Surfeit* is also defined as words and plans dealing with murder, and since so many members of the creative minority were psychopathic this interpretation is an important factor. The passive form of aberration or failure of the creative power in the individuals who make up the creative minority is described in part as a loss of elan, a loss of ardor, apathy, indifference, and "resting on one's oars." These symptoms are an important basic element in Toynbee's thesis and are well-known symptoms of mental illness (Greenson 1949). He relates other items which are also seemingly much like derivations of a disorder. They include a continual and progressive feeling of moral defeat and a failure to master and control one's self, a compounding of incompatible values and a loss of a style of living. Toynbee finds a "sick soul" in relation to the loss of creativity.

An intellectual and emotional type of ambivalence exists when the creative individual's lines of action split into a pair of mutually antithetical variations, such as abandon and asceticism. Abandon, a substitute for creativity, found the prophet of its present resurgence first in Rousseau's theories with the alluring invitation to "return to Nature." Abandon is defined as giving free rein to spontaneous appetites, such as immoral practices and abandoned sexuality, through which no civilization has been able to survive (Huxley 1952). Other examples of abandon are included in the political theory of Machiavelli and the sensuous social practices of that circle. Machiavelli believed in prevision dealing with hallucinations, and he gave free rein to his sexuality. Conversely, asceticism is an old form of behavior that deals with individuals who hallucinate (Toynbee 1970) and at times live in the desert, and do odd things beyond what is considered the most psychotic type of behavior.

Martyrdom is another factor in the decline of civilization. Le Bon writes (1916) that to mysticism we owe the martyrs of all creeds—religious, political, and social. Toynbee (1939) gave Socrates and Christ as examples, because according to him, they had the same characteristics of mentality. Of considerable importance is that, at the time of his trial, Socrates intended on two occasions to apologize, but his "voice" or "demon" stayed him both times (Dendy 1847); nor was the acoustic hallucination present at other times, and Socrates took this to mean "don't apologize." Socrates had various loopholes presented to him for escaping death, but his hallucinations in part prevented him from taking these opportunities, therefore making him a martyr.

CREATIVE INDIVIDUALS

The creativity of a genius is not a symptom of mental illness, but creative people can surely become ill. The studies of Roe (1963), Jacobson (1909, 1926), and Kubie (1968) indicate that the ability to create certainly is not facilitated by thinking deficits, abnormal autisms, apathy, ambivalence, neurosis, and other serious mental disorders. A considerable body of literature dealing with the mental disorders and other aspects of creative individuals, accumulated over many years, illustrates and indicates that disturbances can occur to limit continual successful creative responses to challenges. However, hallucinations can be of some importance in the process of creativity (Bauers 1970). Obviously, to diagnose as *non compus mentis* all those creative individuals who have helped mankind would be in error. Nevertheless, of the 113 geniuses that have most helped civilization, 37 per cent to 40 per cent were psychotic, 83 per cent to 90 per cent were psychopathic or sociopathic, and 30 per cent of the most important were committed (Lange-Eichbaum 1932, Stein and Heinze, 1960). One might hypothesize in light of the normal distribution curve that some had many serious medical problems, most had moderate deficits, and the remaining had only some minor disorders.

Because the creative minority plays such an important role in the decline of civilization, the following list of creative individuals is informative. History records them as having hallucinated, and since the symptom is part of the mental illness syndrome one can assume that a disturbance at times might have been present:

Socrates	Galileo	Cowper
Plato	Newton	Pellico
Aristotle	Shelly	Scott
Pythagoras	Poe	Goethe
Rousseau	Swedenborg	Alfred de Musset
Cellini	Van Helmont	Cosway
Tasso	Blake	George Fox
Bryon	Hobbes	Luther
Schumann	Columbus	Calvin
Raphael	Pascal	Descartes
Spinello	Lamb	Roger Bacon
Montano	Engel	Johannes Muller
Mozart	Schopenhauer	Oliver Cromwell
Donizetti	Swift	Brutus
Wagner	Charles IX	Caesar
Rossini	Ben Johnson	Auguste Comte
Warren Hastings	Sir John Herschel	Spinoza
Rossetti	Napoleon	Hugo
Dumas	Balzac	Mohammed
Hitler	Stalin	Alexander the Great
Attila	Charlemagne	Joan of Arc

Hallucinations are always associated with epilepsy; those individuals who had seizures were: Flaubert, Mendelssohn, Wellington, Charles V, Peter the Great, Louis XIII of France, Ferdinand V, Alfred the Great, William III, William Pitt, Tolstoy, Dostoevski, Petrarch, Handel, and Richelieu. A number were chronic alcoholics (and were chronic hallucinists also): Beethoven, Handel, Burns, and Poe. Others were either sick or they were institutionalized, for example: Cowper, Donizetti, George III, James I, Auguste Comte, Engel, Tasso, Swift, Charles Lamb, Southey, Holderlin, Schumann, Romney, Kean, Mozart, Mendelssohn, Chopin, Galileo, and Isaac Newton. Wilhelm Lange-Eichbaum (1956) wrote that Kant, Copernicus, Faraday, Linnaeus, Maupassant, Monet, Dostoevski, and Nietzsche were psychotic. Vico, Comte, and Ampere are thought to have been ill (Mora 1964). Others tried to commit suicide: Schumann, Cowper, Chateaubriand, Lenin, Poe, Alfred de Musset, Hayden, Ken Booth; and some succeeded: Chatterton, George Sand, and Clive. These names as well as the foregoing information can be documented in the writings of Kirton (1660), Wanley (1774), Godwin (1834), Dendy (1847), Colguhoun (1851), Brierre de Boismont

(1855), Lombroso (1891), Nisbet (1891), Parish (1897), Clark (1922), Kretschmer (1931), Robsjohn-Gibbins (1947), and Lennox (1960). Further literature may be found in Mora's work (1964) and Ireland's studies (1889, 1893) which contain detailed cases.

INFLUENCES OF HALLUCINATIONS

To emphasize the problem further, here are a few examples of creative persons who were influenced by hallucinations. Tasso, under the influence of a hallucination, drew a knife, and was going to attack a servant who had entered the ducal chamber. Tasso was imprisoned. Schopenhauer moved from one city to another because a "voice" ordered him to "break free and lead his steps elsewhere." At sea off Charleston, Junius Booth jumped overboard, saying he had a message for an actor who had drowned himself near the spot some years before. He was rescued with difficulty. In one day Cowper tried to kill himself with laudanum, to drown himself, to cut his throat, and finally to hang himself. He fastened a thong to his bedroom door, looped it round his neck as he stood on a chair, and then threw himself into space. As he did so he distinctly heard a "voice" say three times, "Tis over, tis over, tis over." The "voice," however, was mistaken. The frenzied poet hung by the neck until he lost consciousness, and then the thong broke, and he found himself lying face downward on the floor. He was confined in a mental hospital for eighteen months.

Various creative personalites have suffered greatly. Byron was tortured by his afflicting hallucinations. Keats had mental problems, and his agitation resembled insanity. Alfred de Musset suffered terribly from sleeplessness and had strangely vivid hallucinations. Gustave Flaubert lapsed into a dreamy indolent state. James Watt complained of "stupefaction and confusion of ideas." Loss of memory and giddiness troubled Faraday. During his last years Chopin was "possessed by a melancholy which went as far as insanity." Late in life Galileo fell into a state of melancholy during which he felt "as if he were being incessantly called by his daughter." Some famous individuals had delusions, including Mozart, Rossini, Rousseau, Poe, Victor Hugo, Balzac, and Chopin.

In a letter to his doctor, David Hume described his mental problems. "I found that I was not able to follow out any train of thought, by one continued stretch of view, but by repeated interruption. . . . Yet I have collected the rude materials for many volumes . . . but in reducing these to words I found impracticable for me. . . . I had not hopes of delivering my opinions. The French Mysticks and our Fanatics, their case and mine, were pretty parallel. . . . All my ardor seem'd in a moment to be extinguished." At this point in his life Hume had decided to be a merchant in order to correct his mental disturbance (Hume 1963).

The loss of the power or ability to be creative has affected the lives of many persons. In a stupor of dementia Swift remained for a whole year without speaking, reading, or recognizing anyone. He died in 1745, in a state of complete dementia. Alexander Dumas in his latter years became an "imbecile," but "unfortunately, he did not lay down his pen until he had partly ruined his great reputation." Thomas Compebell in his later years showed mental debility. The genius of Romney degenerated into mental illness, his skill departed, and he ceased to recognize his friends or relatives. The great actor, Edmund Kean, drank heavily, and at thirty-seven his mental health was shattered. He lost his memory and his emotions became blunted. Schumann's depressions stopped him from composing, and Handel in his phases of depression produced little, as was the case of Rossini (Storr 1972). The creative imagination of Neitzsche and Strindberg ceased when the illness began and their productive lives came to a close (Cole 1970).

INSPIRATIONS OF HALLUCINATIONS

One can easily observe from all of the preceding knowledge that many creative individuals have had serious problems and have hallucinated; so it does not seem to be an absurd working hypothesis that a loss of creativity is related to these disorders and deficits. However, creative people at times have been inspired to work because of the reverie and enthusiasm of hallucinations. Cazzamalli's (1937) study demonstrated that hallucinations have influenced and guided the thought of philosophers, statesmen, inventors, scholars, musicians, painters, dramatists, and poets. Many produced in spite of any disorder; some met early challenges successfully but failed as the disorder increased. Clearly, good things can happen because of hallucinations, but morbid situations also can occur, as can failure, leading to a decline and fall of the individual as well as society. The situation is "messy," for the symptoms of a mental disorder and creativity are often similar (Arieti 1959); so considerable clinical judgment and wisdom are required to make a differential diagnosis.

The creative minority leads by means of mimesis, which Toynbee indicates can be defined as magic, dealing historically with hallucinations. This is used as a process for imitation. Leaders who use mimesis as a basic tool can produce much good for civilization, but Toynbee (1961) states that its use is overdone at times and, in fact, can lead to disaster and a disintegration of society. Toynbee also observes that the creative minority fails at times because obstacles not under their control or of their making are placed in their lives, preventing creative work. Hirsch (1931) wrote, "Belittlement of genius has become a favorite avocation for many alienists, doctors, and monographists." In a study of eminent men in England, Havelock Ellis (1926) wrote that it is, "impossible to estimate the amount of persecution to which this group of pre-eminent British persons has been subjected; it varies between mere passive refusal to have anything to do with them or their work, and active infliction of physical torture and death. At least 160 of the 975 eminent men were imprisoned, and many others escaped by voluntary exile." What is wrong with those who build these obstacles? The answer may be ignorance, uncivilized behavior, and a lack of elasticity in their views of those who are working and producing, views brought about by "academic jealousy" or some other subjective emotional problem.

The tradition of looking at the eminent person as merely a sick individual is old. Often the feeling is that the genius is an abnormal being, and this feeling can arouse an instinctive animalistic hostility and aggressiveness. Perhaps, like the various primates such as baboons that have hierarchies, everyone wants to be top dog, and in order to move up, less intelligent persons destroy the genius. Emotions and uncivilized attitudes that arise from the older evolutionary parts of the brain make individuals subjective about eminent individuals or creative leaders. These comparative neurological behavior problems, such as aggressiveness, if not civilized in nature are classified as neurotic or psychotic. The persons who obstruct progress are unhealthy and uncivilized.

ACHIEVEMENTS OF HALLUCINISTS

Some are cynical about those who suffer from hallucinations, but persons who were hallucinists created more for mankind than we know of at the present time. Although religious aspirations are an important aspect of being civilized many groups have seriously attempted to destroy religion and the good works achieved in other fields. Reputations, too, have been destroyed by the stigma of mental illness. The foolish fear of mental patients and the evil criticism of the geniuses and their products may in the long run be far more dangerous to man's progress than anything else, for it undermines the historical works that form the foundation of civilization. Lange-Eichbaum's (1956) exhaustive work devotes more pages to Jesus and his clinical background than to any other person. Albert Schweitzer (1948), whose doctoral thesis considered the psychic disturbances of Jesus Christ, found that Jesus's spiritual nature made him an ethical religious leader. Jesus had hallucinations at the time of his baptism, but he did not appear to be wandering in a system of delusions. "He is never out of touch with reality," wrote Schweitzer. Many individuals are not familiar with the history of that period and do not understand the logic of the teachings about the Messiah at that time. Many authors have stated that Jesus had a paranoiac mental disturbance, with morbid ideas about his own greatness and about being persecuted. The writers succeeded to varying degrees in throwing doubt on his mental soundness (Loosten 1905).

Woodrow Wilson, whom historians include among the five best presidents of the United States, has come under considerable psychiatric criticism. A person who disliked President Wilson enlisted Freud's aid in writing a psychoanalytical study that showed him to be of abnormal mind (Freud and Bullitt 1967), but historians state that the study is not valid because of its subjective nature. In 1972, Stefan Lorant, in discussing President Lincoln, observed that the president had a severe depression and had consulted with a Doctor Henry, who said the symptom was a "nervous debility." Milton Shutes, who studied Lincoln's periods of depression, observed that although the disturbances invaded the border of the pathologic, his common sense would and did lift him up whenever an emergency arose. Dr. Shutes concluded: "After all, a large share of the world's work, and much of its best work, has been done by psychoneurotics" (Lorant 1972).

The observation that Vesalius was a schizoid (Lange-Eichbaum 1956) is no reason to negate his fine work in anatomy. In fact, Charles Singer (1952), a world expert on the history of medicine, anatomy, science, and technology in England, wrote that the *De Humani Corporis Fabrica* is the first work of modern science because its medical art permitted others to confirm the findings in the field of gross anatomy. Others in America have confirmed this theory about Vesalius's writing, which represents the findings and efforts of many anatomists. Vesalius is known as the father of modern anatomy, modern biology, and modern teaching methods. Medical history records that gross anatomy ushered in the first Renaissance.

Sir Isaac Newton was quite interested in magic and with such concepts as the "philosopher's stone" and the "water of life." The dream of changing elements came true with atomic physics, and the dream of maintaining life is an inspirational goal. The observation that Newton was mentally ill at home for a year and a half and had much trouble in writing after the experience does not nullify his fine work. Thorndike's conclusion after writing eight volumes of history on the subject of experimental science was that Newton was the father of modern experimental science (Thorndike 1923-58).

STIGMA OF MENTAL ILLNESS

Mental illness has been scientifically found to be the most stigmatic of all diseases (Tringo 1972). That Walt Whitman (Lange-Eichbaum 1956) and Freud (Keup 1970) hallucinated or that Hemingway and Ezra Pound were in mental hospitals certainly does not justify criticism of their works, literature, and poetry. Even if a person is mentally unsound, his work is not necessarily unsound. Stein and Heinze (1960) indicate that many famous men became ill before they accomplished their best efforts or they were disturbed during the times when they were doing their finest works (Monet, Maupassant, Rousseau, and Holderlin) Some, of course, did their best works when they were well (Jacobson 1909, 1926), yet others did nothing of importance after becoming ill, or even after leaving the mental hospital. One must help the geniuses to be well, for the morbid function if not corrected is eventually reflected in structure and expressed habitually (Dickinson 1949).

An important aspect of wisdom is discerning and judging soundly what is civilized and true. What would happen to Freud's work if he were classified as unsound of mind because he hallucinated? Would his work then be unsound? Freud, needless to say, produced a number of truths. Knowledge is additive, but many people seem to want to subtract truths by destructive criticism. The lives of geniuses can be considered as a long examination paper: some of the answers are, to be sure, not correct, yet most of them are both helpful to mankind's progress and truthful in nature. The facts must be judged on their own merit, and should stand on their own as either sound truths or false information. Personalities no doubt influence products, but even when delusions or uncivilized ideas are produced, we must be patient and try to correct the unsound learning. A good example is Harry Stack Sullivan, who left a fine legacy to psychiatry and the social sciences. In regard to Sullivan's personal life David Elkind (1972) wrote, "Many people, myself included, would gladly be labeled alcoholic, schizophrenic, and homosexual if they could give a similar accounting of their life work." Destructive criticism and defamation of character added to the deficits already associated with mental illness create an obstacle that limits the creative individual just as much as the disease and lasts long after spontaneous remissions of the symptoms. The stigma of mental illness (Tringo 1972) makes persons so subjective, both intellectually and emotionally, about a member of the creative minority that their minds close to the knowledge that is so basic to civilization.

In his classic work on the history of insanity, Foucault (1967) presented the thesis that the role of unreason in civilization is a creative force. There is a brilliancy of mind and a force of images, which he calls "reason dazzled." He states that unreason is the "center of the great cosmology which animates all classical culture." Unreason "gives a *droit de cite,* and a hold on Western culture which makes possible all contestations as well as total contestation." This unreason makes truth possible and confirms it. The works of art explode out of madness, and "unreason has belonged to whatever is decisive for the modern world."

The extremities of unreason are, on the one hand, tragedy and, on the other hand, the confused murmur of madness (Foucault 1967). It was observed that melancholia and madness belonged to the works of creative individuals. The madness of the writer was for other men the chance to see the truth of the work of art being born. The extremes of unreason caused a situation where many "succumbed" to mental illness and this caused them to annihilate their works of art. "Yet by the disorder which interrupts the work, the art that would have drown in the world is revealed and engages the times, masters and leads it. The dissolution of Neitzsche's thought took his work from him, but offered it to mankind. . . . The disorder is contemporary with the work, and inaugurates the time of its truth, yet when there is a work of art there is not madness, although the work is engulfed in the disturbance. . . . The task for others is from the unreason; reason is restored to it through a critical explanation" (Foucault 1967).

In the mid nineteeth century, De Boismont wrote: "Hallucinations present no obstacles when they have not exercised any influence on conduct, have not perverted sentiments of affection nor prevented the person from always fulfilling with propriety his social duties." He stressed that hallucinations can be consistent with reason and can coexist with reason. Reverie is eminently favorable to the production of physiological hallucinations; "Hence poets, painters, sculptors, whom genius has touched with his wing, have all perceived before them the form of the ideal of their dreams. . . . Moreover we do not believe that there are immortal creations without his materialization of the idea" (Brierre de Boismont 1855). Hallucinations, he found, are so closely connected with the artistic and with creations of genius that he associated them with the physiology and psychology of great people.

NORMAL ELEMENTS OF HALLUCINATIONS

To emphasize the normal element of hallucinations further, I. Disraeli (1818) wrote: "Unaccompanied by enthusiasm, genius will produce nothing but uninteresting works of art. Enthusiasm is the secret spirit which hovers over the production of genius. A great work always leaves us in a state of musing." Disraeli defined enthusiasm as Tasso's lofty hallucinatory conversations held with a spirit, and also as the young Descartes' hearing of a "voice" in the air, calling him to pursue the search for truth. Disraeli (1818) also wrote: "A state of mind occurs in the most active operations of genius, which the term reverie inadequately indicates, meta-physical distinction but ill describes it, and popular language affords no terms for those faculties and feelings which escape the observation of the multitude who are not affected by the phenomenon."

Max Weber (1946), in discussing the importance of "Plato's mania," stated that unreason entices or forces the idea and that enthusiasm is also a prerequisite of inspiration, which is decisive to creative work. Lange-Eichbaum (1932) stated that this type of experience sensitizes the genius to aspects of the environment. Maritain (1953) writes about the importance of mania in creative intuition. The historian Meinecke (1950) noted that the irrational forces of fantasy nourish the reason and guide the way to beauty and to what is good. Possibly the intellectual faculties become more developed and the character more improved during some hallucinations. This latter idea is confirmed by inspired persons and ecstatics such as De Boismont (1855). One day a lady said to him: "Voices suggest expressions to me with which I am not familiar; they give me words much superior to those I have been in the habit of using, or which my education justifies. Their conversations often run on geography, politics, and on domestic economy, questions to which I am a stranger, but which I perfectly comprehend when the voices suggest them."

"It is to this exaltation of mind, to enthusiasm, to the choice of words, eloquence, and the nature of the organization, that we must refer the great influence some hallucinated persons have exercised over their fellow creatures. To this cause, Mohammed doubtless owed his immense influence over a large portion of mankind" (Brierre de Boismont 1855).

PRODUCTS OF HALLUCINATIONS, MAGIC, AND DEMONS

One must always keep clearly in mind that, out of magic, hallucinations, and demons came science, medicine, art, religion (Frazier 1911), law, mathematics, astronomy, chemistry, art, and music (Thorndike 1923-58). This does not pertain only to primitive man and his magic, for in this century modern art and writing, some elements of modern architecture, and the new period of enlightenment had roots in the occult, magic, and mimesis. Kandinsky often painted in a trance, and Paul Klee produced drawings while under hypnosis. Henri Rousseau painted according to the dictates of his dead wife. Yeats, D.H. Lawrence, Gertrude Stein, Oscar Wilde, Miro, and Picasso were all much involved with mysticism (Robsjohn-Gibbings 1947). Doctor Maudsley (1895), a British specialist in mental disorders, wrote: "Little as we like the notion, it has been so willed in the mysterious counsels of creation that the best work of the world should be done under illusions." The challenge is to correct the uncivilized situation that surrounds hallucinations and to leave the "good things" that history has shown can happen.

RECENT HISTORY

In 1967, Columbia University professor Hofstadter wrote *The Paranoid Style in American Politics,* as well as essays that consider contemporary history. His study and that of Thrupp (1970) confirm Cohn's study (1957) on early uncivilized times and includes a computer-like projection or prognosis of the future, unless the situation is corrected by humane medical methods.

Hofstadter (1967) observes that the paranoid style is found in fascism, frustrated nationalism, and the Stalin purge trials. In America the paranoid style is the preferred ingredient of minority movements that deal not so much with class struggles, as in Europe, but, rather, with ethnic and religious problems. It is a strong style among the middle class (Sheppard 1970). In United States history the style of paranoia has been observed in: (1) the anti-masonic movement, (2) the anti-Catholic movement, (3) anti-Mormonism, (4) abolitionism as a slaveholder's conspiracy, (5) the conspiracy of international bankers, (6) the conspiracy of the munitions makers during the First World War, (7) the popular left-wing press, (8) the contemporary American right wing, and (9) the race controversy.

The paranoid is observed as a militant leader who does not see a compromise in social conflicts because the conspiracies create a conflict in his mind between pure evil and good, and he is thus motivated and has the will to fight, or to go to war. The enemy of the paranoid is an active demonic agent, which is easy to observe in the introduction of the English translation of *Malleus Maleficarum* (Sprenger and Kramer 1951), for there is a delusion that the Russian people are demonic. The leaders of movements are afflicted by fantasies and have a megalomanical view of themselves. The syndrome is most likely to be elicited by the fear of catastrophe. A minor or insignificant conspiracy is by pathological imagination deluded into a vast conspiracy. Professor Hofstadter (1967) observes that movements come in successive episodic waves that are mobilized by social conflicts involving schemes of values that bring into the political life of the nation fundamental fears and hatreds rather than negotiable values and interests. The situation becomes worse when the paranoid leader and those on the margins of society cannot make themselves felt in the political process in which power is seen as omnipotent and sinister (note the present hallucinogenic movement).

L'Etag (1970) notes in his history of the effects of disease on twentieth century leaders the "terrifying hallucinations and torturing delusions" of Forrestal, the Korsakow's psychosis of Kamal Ataturk of the Ottoman Empire, the hypomanic character of Nikita Khruschev, the sleepwalking of F. D. Roosevelt, the manic depressive aspects of Church-ill, and the pathology of other leaders, many of whom helped our civ-ilization and others who failed.

HALLUCINISTS TODAY

Hallucinists exist today, as they have over the centuries, some with visions of reason, others with morbid delusions. One can interpolate that a partial answer to the more abnormal aspects of history can be found in the deficits associated with mental illness and the uncivilized behavior related to the moral insanity of the psychopathic leader. The hallucina-tory content of the delusions is elaborated into pseudowisdom, just as the dreams of Hitler and Stalin became reality. Solutions to problems and challenges of government cannot be found because of the significant decrease in intelligence associated with the sluggish thought process. Be-cause the individuals are thinking less rather than more, checks and bal-ances are absent, and ideas which might be incorrect receive little cri-tical thought. The creative minority does not pause to think, and this omission leads to false solutions and the elaboration of delusional theo-ries that produce uncivilized situations. The emotional motives are not idealistic but are a comparative neurological behavior problem. Exces-sive hallucinating competes with the time needed to think, even in those who have not developed faulty patterns of thought. When the symptoms remit, the intelligence returns to normal, making it difficult to diagnose those involved with historical mistakes. The masses are taught delusions, and many on the fringes of society believe in them and follow paranoid leaders. The minority of leaders can no longer create the answers to chal-lenges, and excessive mimesis leads to the disintegration of mankind. The medical history of today seems like that of yesterday, but tomorrow must be different.

Time shall extricate truth from the
deadly embrace of sophistry.—I. Disraeli

2.
Auditory
Hallucinations

Descriptions of hallucinations have historically conveyed an impression of mysticism. If a person were asked what he considered the most common hallucination, he would usually reply that it was hearing external "voices." Unfortunately, this concept is not accurate. Medical literature has emphasized that hallucinations form the "first rank symptoms" and are often diagnostic of schizophrenia (Mellor 1970, Schneider 1957). Yet, many investigators have not given much weight to these symptoms, and little has been done to investigate them experimentally. Auditory hallucinations are a central feature of schizophrenia, and investigations of the symptoms would lead to a better understanding of the nature of this illness (Fish 1962). Arieti (1955) wrote that he, for one, does not approve of the present tradition of not interpreting hallucinations. Modern textbooks of psychiatry do not fully describe hallucinations.

In the quest for knowledge about hallucinations, we must first turn to the medical literature. By surveying the past, we can remove the ambiguity and obscurity surrounding the subject and arrive at a correct view of hallucinations. Although medical historians have written that the term *hallucination* was coined by Esquirol, the word is also documented in Vesalius's (1543) book *De Humani Corporis Fabrica* when he wrote, *verum Arabes hallucinatur,* or "but the Arabs are hallucinated." The factor of inaccurate presentations in the definition of hallucination can be traced back to Rome (Moss 1967). In 1531, Donat (Bryant 1906) first published an account of a case dealing with auditory hallucinations. Arnold (Brierre de Boismont 1855, Parish 1897) described hallucinations in 1782 as follows: "Ideal insanity is the intellectual state of a person who believes he sees and hears what no other person sees and hears; who imagines he converses with spirits, perceives things impalpable to the senses, or that do not exist outwardly such as they appear to him; or who, when he sees external objects in their reality, has false and absurd ideas of his own form, and of the palpable qualities of objects." In 1795, Crichten (Brierre de Boismont 1855, Parish 1897) defined hallucinations as errors of the mind, by which ideas are taken for matters of facts and illusions as real objects falsely represented.

Esquirol is worthy of the honor of being called the father of modern psychiatry (Menninger 1963). Thus, it is appropriate to present a number of his ideas. He was the first person in France to give a definition to the term *hallucination* and states:

> The professed sensations of the hallucinated are images and ideas, reproduced by memory, associated by imaginations, and personified by habit (Esquirol 1838). . . . That illusions lead the judgment astray respecting the nature and cause of the impressions actually received and urge the insane to acts dangerous to themselves and to others (Esquirol 1833). . . . There are insane persons who hear 'voices' speaking to them very distinctly, and with which they have regular conversations. These voices penetrate through walls, pursue and weary those who hear them both day and nights. They assume the accent and tone of the voices of their parents, their friends, their neighbors, their enemies, they discourage them from purpose, and counsel them to abstain from actions. . . . These voices speak in all the languages of Europe which are familiar to him; he hears them as distinctly as if the persons themselves were present. Still he has more difficulty in comprehending them when they express themselves in the Russian language, which he himself speaks with difficulty. These voices hinder him from going to sleep in the evening, sometimes they throw him into a state of anger, and they repeat that he must kill himself. . . . One who was laboring under melancholy and to whom I had made some observations on the illusion of hearing, said to me one day, "Do you sometimes think?" "Undoubtedly," I replied. "Well then, as to myself," says he, "I reflect in a loud voice."

Esquirol's (1833, 1838) clinical observations are basic knowledge concerning the hallucinatory conversational phenomenon and hallucinated suggestions. His concepts of the causes and the maintenance of mental illness are also fundamental. "The causes of mental alienation are as numerous as its forms are varied. They are general or special, physical or moral, primitive or secondary, predisposing or exciting (Esquirol 1838). . . . If insanity is characterized and maintained by errors of sensation, by illusions and hallucinations; it is also, by the multiplicity of sensations, by the abundance of ideas, the versatility of the affections, which are produced in melancholy confusion, without order, end, or coherence" (Esquirol 1967). Esquirol's idea about the maintenance of mental disorder by the hallucinations, illusions, and thinking disturbances is rather important because we are dealing in large part with a functional disorder. Unlike structural disease aetiologies, when the cause is removed or cured, the functional illness is still maintained by the new abnormal functions and habits, which are not reversible.

In a famous study, Baillarger (1846), who was a student of Esquirol, classified hallucinations into two groups, one called psychical and another named psych-sensorial. He made a distinction between the acoustic sensations of auditory hallucinations or the psych-sensorial, which "strike on the outward ears of the body," and the psychical, which are produced by the mind of the patient. Baillarger (1846) stated, "The voices are, the one intellectual and produced in the interior of the soul, the other which are corporeal strike the exterior ears of the body. . . . One of the patients assigned to his thoughts two different seats: the one for those thoughts which belonged to him, the other for those which he attributed to his interlocutors. . . . They hear not voices, but thought." The experience of the patient is that on one hand, he hears a thought (psych-sensorial), which is not under his voluntary control, and does not knowingly arise from him; on the other hand, the individual uses his thought to converse with the voice heard, and this aspect of the hallucinatory experience is under the control of patient's will. Although the terms that Baillarger coined are not used today, the concepts are most germane.

Further information in the literature concerning hallucinations is found in the observations of Henry Maudsley (1886), who stated:

> The insane person does not always hear the voices as distinct articulated utterances; he is careful to explain they are in his head

and are interior voices, thoughts which he hears rather than words actually heard with his ears. They are distinctly apprehended and clearly understood even when they come to him, as sometimes they appear to do, mysteriously from great distances; they oblige him to listen, seem to answer his thoughts before he himself conceives them, comment upon his conduct, instigate him to words or deeds that are odious to him, vex and embarass him continually, and in the worst even drive him to despair and suicide, because of his inability to escape from their importunities, or of the fear that he may obey their injunctions.

Another series of pertinent observations was made by E. Parish, who in 1897 stated: "The phenomenon with which we are now concerned, so-called auditory hallucinations, which however, consists merely in the unnoticed articulation of one's thoughts, which becomes audible and takes the form of an auditory hallucination. . . . From all this, it would appear that the greater number of the 'voices' if not all, are caused by automatic speech on the part of the participant." The conversations were not made in articulated language, but by an exchange of thoughts, quite as clear and intelligible as if the thoughts had been spoken aloud. By their soundlessness, the voices are clearly distinguished from the more highly externalized acoustic sounds of overt speech in which the sound element is more or less strongly marked. Parish noted that a patient felt that other persons produced auditory hallucinations and that his own were "induced" by some of his fellow patients. Parish (1897) made mention of the "ghostly" counsellors and the persecutors of the patients.

In his clinical descriptions, which are fundamental to modern psychiatry, Kraepelin (1919, 1921) stressed hallucinations in the statement:

It is especially peculiar to dementia praecox that the patients' own thoughts appear to them to be spoken aloud. In the most varied expressions we hear the complaint of the patients constantly repeated, that their thought can be perceived. . . . People speak to the patient in his thoughts. . . . Strangers send him thoughts silently. . . . On the other hand the patient sometimes knows the thoughts of other people . . . carries on conversations, dialogues, with his companions. . . . His thoughts become loud, so that others know them. . . . Hallucinations are almost never wanting in the acute and sub-acute forms of the disease, and often enough they accompany the whole course of the disease. . . . The sympton is peculiarly characteristic of dementia praecox. (Kraepelin 1919)

Eugene Bleuler (1950) in his classic work *Dementia Praecox or the Group of Schizophrenias* observed the important role that hallucinations play in differential diagnosis and explained:

> The described combination of auditory and body-sensation hallucinations permits the diagnosis of schizophrenia—the diagnosis, but not the delimitation of the concept of schizophrenia . . . the previously described disturbance of associations, and also probably the type of hallucinations are characteristic and sufficient for a positive diagnosis; in addition, a general flattening of affect may serve this purpose. . . . Where auditory hallucinations continually dominate the clinical picture, one can practically always conclude that one is dealing with schizophrenia. . . . When a person continually produces entirely illogical ideas of persecution in a state of full clarity of consciousness, he is nearly always a schizophrenic; if the characteristic hallucinations are also present, the diagnosis is certain. . . . Jahrmarker also includes the disposition to hallucinations among the primary manifestations. He is probably correct. . . .

E. Bleuler (1950) wrote that the hallucinations make the psychosis manifest, requiring psychiatric help, which makes the stay of the patient at home impossible. Delusions and particularly the hallucinations stand in the forefront of the hospitalized schizophrenic. The consequences of the hallucinations and delusions were the patient's peculiarities of behavior—agitation, seclusion, despair, and outbreaks of anger. "Almost every schizophrenic who is hospitalized hears 'voices' occasionally or continually. Almost equally as frequent are the delusions and illusions . . . . The 'voices' of our patients embody their entire transformed relationship to the external world."

In 1930, E. Bleuler stated that hallucinations are characteristic of schizophrenia, and that there is a pronounced preference for auditory hallucinations in the form of words, while those without words are not prominent in the clinical picture. As a rule, the patients ascribe the voices to people talking, and, as a result, all their thoughts suddenly become voices. "The acoustic component may be expressed in the following sentence: 'The voices are unlike spoken voices, but are as if thought!' That which are called 'voices' by the patients are 'audible thoughts' or 'soundless voices' " (Bleuler 1950). E. Bleuler frequently found the patient's thoughts becoming audible and "thought-dialogues, be it with God, a protector or a persecutor" (Bleuler 1950). The patients hold a conversation with their voices while their attention is concentrated on the hallucinations. "In the case of the thoughts becoming loud, on the contrary, what is thought at the moment by the patient is spoken out. Not so rarely the hallucinations are dependent to a certain extent on the will: the patients ask questions in thought; they are answered for them" (Bleuler 1930). The patients believed that everyone around them could hear the 'voices', and that people far away perceived them. Many patients did not have a single moment free of hallucinations, and they indulged in their hallucinations because the practice was pleasant (Bleuler 1950).

Paulus (1941) wrote a historical review of the literature dealing with hallucinations in which he summarized the findings of clinical observation since Esquirol. In this review, he stated that auditory verbal hallucinations are only an extreme form of surrealization transforming simple thoughts. Lelut (1847) considered hallucinations to be spontaneous transformation of thought into sensation. Boismont (1855) and Parish (1897) cited various older works by Szafkosy, Falret, Leuret, and Betty, who agree in general with the description that hallucinations are thoughts or ideas converted into sensations. Sully (1886) observed that the patients frequently complained of having thoughts spoken to them and it was not uncommon for them to imagine that they were addressed by a number of voices at the same time, and that they could converse successively with three, four, or as many as a dozen individuals. A description imparted by Mendel (1907) states that the patient's internal speech can be observed as, "there is thought-speech," and the talking is attributed to certain persons, for example, "Meyer speaks to me." In many cases the person answers the voice and carries on a conversation with it.

In the more recent medical literature are observations which confirm the older findings. Ariete (1955) asserts that hallucinations are thoughts, and that every normal individual can hear his own thoughts which are generally expressed internally by verbal auditory images. In the patient, however, the perceptual quality of the thoughts is increased, producing hallucinations. Ariete observes that this phenomenon is common in schizophrenics. In one case, the person knew that his voice was expressing his own thoughts in Italian, while the other people around him and his clients were talking English. Ariete (1959) states that the most important fact about hallucinations is that an abstract thought has been perceptualized; that it follows the laws of perception rather than those of thought; and that the experience is externalized. Arieti (1974) states that the closer one examines patients, the more one becomes convinced that they actually experience perceptions. Concerning the problem of whether or not hallucinations are imagery or perceptions, Arieti (1974) believes that hallucinations are mental processes which use some of the mechanisms of perception, and do not originate from sense organs. Fish (1962) observes that the patient hears his own thoughts spoken and hears people around him reply to his thoughts. In a modern textbook of psychiatry (Redlich and Freedman 1966) it is written that the patient's thoughts become vocal statements, which the patient believes others can hear. He also believes that he can hear the thoughts of other individuals.

Modell (1958, 1960, 1962) observed in three important papers on the subject of hallucinations that the most predominant aspect of the hallucinatory experience is the process by which the patient's own thoughts are attributed to voices. He stressed that nearly all auditory hallucinations are of this type, with a close relationship existing between hallucinations and hearing one's thoughts. Modell stated that this takes the form of hallucinatory conversations, and he proposed that verbal hallucinations be termed *hallucinated inner speech*. There are two aspects to auditory hallucinations: first is the perception of the acoustic *voices* and second is the production of the voice by the patient who uses hallucinated inner speech. We have a problem with words and their definitions, but perhaps *hallucinations of inner speech* might convey both aspects of a patient's experience.

Various references in medical literature provide evidence for Modell's concept of hallucinated inner speech. Arnow (1952) found in a research work that verbal hallucinations are the most significant form of hallucination. The clinical indication is the patient's discussing the hallucinated inner speech with the doctor, which denotes an improvement in the patient's mental condition. In 1963, Grant wrote that hallucinations are a kind of inner speech, like silently "talking to ourselves," and that others can hear the voices, which the patient, in turn, hears as coming from another person. Morel (1934) stated that the necessary condition of all verbal auditory hallucinations is verbal thought. The French psychiatrist Ey (1934) observed that verbal hallucinations are a disturbance of internal speech, and Janet (1936, 1947) described *hallucination psychomotrice verbale* as a major group of auditory hallucinations and observed the relationship between interior language and hallucinations.

Scattered in the medical literature are various other observations concerning hallucinations of inner speech or thought. Freud said that hallucinations are thoughts turned into images (Jung 1906) as voiced thoughts, or a condition in which the patient hears his own thoughts spoken out loud. Lehermitte (1949), in one of his works on the subject of hallucinations, wrote that verbal hallucinations are disorders of thought and inner language. Conrad (1950, 1958a) observed that the patient's thoughts are heard as voices. McKeller (1957) described the hallucinations of a schizophrenic: "This patient declared that these 'voices' had the tendency to repeat his own thoughts, but were quite distinguishable from his own voice." In a review of inner speech, Rudolf Pintner (1913) states: "Only in cases of insanity does this inner speech detach itself from the individual." The term *thoughts out loud* and used by Lange (1938, 1939a, b, 1940) for "hallucinoid, minimal automatic subvocal speech." He emphasized that there is an overwhelming immersion in hallucinoid verbal communication with others and that the hallucinating disrupts the functioning of both language and thought. Klimes (1941) reported on audible thoughts in hallucinations. Hallucinations were observed by Cossa and Martin (1951) as an external projection of an internal thought. From the preceding, there seems to be clinical evidence that hallucinations of inner speech are the most important feature of auditory hallucinations.

Many books have been published in France on the subject of hallucinations. In 1934, Lagache published a monograph on verbal hallucinations with over a hundred references cited from French medical literature. Quercy (1930), in two volumes on hallucinations, came to the conclusion that the concept is still a point of much controversy. Mourque (1932) believed that there is an intensification of the image with a dissociation of the personality. Ey (1934, 1935, 1967), in his various works, reviewed the theories dealing with hallucinations, and his conclusion was that many people believed that hallucinations had an organic origin. The problem continues, however, as to whether hallucinations are a form of sensation. This forms the focus of the controversy. There are indications that transcendental psychology believes hallucinating is a peripheric stimulation, and Fischer (1969) reported that hallucinations are an intensely active sensation. Various monographs have been published in France, such as one in 1946, by Agadjanian, another in 1951, by Lhermitte, and another in 1952, by Hecaen and Ajuriaguerra, and in 1973 by Ey. De Mousier (1930) recommends that adherence to explanations about hallucinations be based on the methods of experimental science.

Inner speech as the expression of thought used in hallucinating has been found to be documented in clinical literature (Klimes 1941, Sedman 1966). What is the experimental evidence for these clinical observations? Gould (1948, 1949, 1950), in the first experimental studies of the hallucinated inner speech of patients, used the stethoscope and a microphone with amplifiers. He found that the subvocal speech is inaudible with the unaided ear, and from these findings he stated: "It was obvious that the patient experienced more than was recorded." His work using a microphone and amplifiers was confirmed by Arnow (1952) and Freeman and Williams (1952). Arnow (1952) noted that the experiment enabled him to find a marked correspondence between the content and character of the subaudible speech and the content of the "voices." Gould (1948, 1949, 1950), who used electromyographic techniques, observed that there is an extreme degree of activity in the vocal musculature of the hallucinating patient as compared to both the normal control group and the nonhallucinating patients. He concluded that inner speech forms the basis of hallucinations.

Gould's electromyographic work was only partially confirmed by the study of Roberts, Greenblatt, and Solomon (1952), who found that the evidence of electromyographic activity in the vocal musculature did not always occur when the patients made note of auditory hallucinations. This finding may be due to the difference between the patient's hearing acoustic inner speech of others and the patient's production of inner speech. Gould did mention that the patient was experiencing more than that which was recorded. Electrophysiological studies of verbal hallucinations were made in Czechoslovakia by Cerny (1964, 1965), whose work confirmed that of the original observations of Gould on inner speech used in hallucinations. McGuigan (1966b), in a careful work on a patient, recorded muscle potentials from the vocal musculature during periods of verbal hallucinating, with respiratory muscles and other muscles acting as controls. He also used a microphone, tape recorder, and amplifiers to record and play back the subvocal speech produced by the hallucinating patient. MacGuigan (1966) compared what had been recorded on the tape recorder and then amplified it so that subvocal speech could be heard aloud with the overt statements of the patient in regard to his hallucinations. Both were found to be similar. Another electromyographic study of verbal hallucinations was made by Inouye and Shimizue (1970) using nine patients as subjects. The EMG activity of the speech musculature increased at the time of verbal hallucinations, demonstrating the production of subvocal speech during the auditory hallucinations. The EMG was not always present when the patient reported acoustic hallucinatory phenomena. The experiment supported the previous findings that a hallucination is an expression of subvocal speech. Inouye and Shimizue concluded that verbal hallucination is a manifestation of the patient's thinking using a kind of undifferentiated speech. The content of the verbal hallucinations showed condensation and sense domination.

Lindsley (1956, 1960, 1961, 1962, 1963a, b) observed vocal hallucinations by direct measurement. A microphone operated a voice key, which was adjusted to emit a brief pulse whenever the sound level caused by the hallucinating in the room rose above a preset intensity. The frequency range was set for human vocalization only. Hallucinatory behavior was correlated with the recordings. The vocal psychotic symptoms were under the internal control of the patients and were responses to "voices." Acoustic and electromyographic studies were made by Johnson (1958, 1967), who observed that the subvocal speech of the patient could be recorded by a microphone and a cathode ray oscilloscope, and that EMG activity was present in the intrinsic vocal musculature of the hallucinating person. That the muscles of vocalization are employed during the process of hallucinated inner speech, and that sound is produced and can be recorded are scientific findings. All of the preceding experimental observations verify definitively the clinical studies that have found that inner speech is used in hallucinating.

In the past it has been thought that "hallucinations are described as 'inner voices' although their character is entirely unlike the inner speech of the subject with himself" (James 1890). As time went on, hallucinations came to be observed differently: "By far the great proportion of auditory hallucination consists of verbalizations . . . auditory verbal hallucination is when the patient hears his own thoughts expressed aloud" (Cameron and Margaret 1951). Then, in 1964, Landis stated:

"Many patients have described the experience of hearing their inner thoughts whispered or spoken aloud by some outside agent" (Landis 1964). One of the great problems in the history of the study of hallucinations has been the selection of words used in describing the phenomenon. Various phrases have been employed; for example, the communication of thought, an interior voice of location, a thought transformed into a voice, an invisible spirit which is accustomed to converse with "me," the interior voices of mystics, the audible perception of the voice of conscience, a spiritual or soul-language, an audible thinking, a mute communication audible only in mind, conversations in thoughts, speaking mind to mind, the process of materializing thought and hearing internal voices. The experience has been described by St. Theresa as, "I hear a voice of exceeding gentleness, speaking as it were in a whisper. . . . I hear it with my bodily ears." In one of his writings Swendenborg states: "The speech is heard as the speech of one man with another. . . . Speech flows at first into man's thought and by an internal way into his organ of hearing. . . . It affects the organs of hearing as much as speech from without." Landis (1964) has written that the many names given to hallucinations by different patients are legion, but that the descriptions have so many elements in common that it may be safely concluded that hallucinations constitute a common class of experience.

The observation has often been made that people conceal their hallucinations in order to avoid being institutionalized or judged insane. Kraepelin (1919) stated that hallucinations are, at first, usually kept secret by the patient, and that the patient exposes his hallucinations only after they have existed for a long time. Kraeplin felt that it was generally difficult to get trustworthy accounts of the occurrences of hallucinations from the suspicious and reserved patients, who usually denied that they heard voices. E. Bleuler (1950) observed that in spite of the fact that the schizophrenic constantly complains about the annoyance of his hallucinations, it was not easy to obtain exact information as to the content of the hallucinations. Patients are afraid to reveal experiences which might be considered pathological. Another investigator (Goldstein 1944) stressed that it is difficult or impossible to find out, in either direct conversation or investigation of isolated capacities, something about the hallucinations that govern the patient's behavior. Because of the difficulty in getting information about hallucinations, it is of considerable importance to take stock of what is available in the literature.

In order to obtain information from the patient, it is necessary to understand the various possible reasons why the person does not give a clear depiction of his hallucinations. The factor of hallucinating being taboo may be important, as is the anxiety caused by the tradition of silence surrounding the subject of hallucinations. Voices are a manifestation of mental disease, which has a stigma and is held to be shameful (Maslow and Mittleman 1941; Tringo 1972). Thus, the patient will not discuss his hallucinations. Individuals in Western civilization are not accustomed to revealing the content of their thoughts or inner speech to other persons. This has been seen clearly by Ernst Dimmet (1928), who relates the old story about asking a person, "A penny for your thoughts," and receiving the negative response, "Oh! I'm thinking of nothing." One must circumvent the problems of tradition and taboo in order to make accurate observations.

The issue at hand is to find the means to make a truthful and accurate description of the hallucinatory experience in order to understand the problems maintained by the phenomenon. Critical to the problem of making observations is finding the correct words, for the term *inner speech* is not known to the patient. Thus, the doctor has to teach the patient the meaning of the words. The definition of inner speech is best based on common knowledge about silent reading. Such terms as *inner speech, silent speech,* and *subvocal speech* can then be employed as a description of the voice used in hallucinating. One of the most important aspects of communicating is the need for terms that can be used to talk about the subject, and, in this case, *hallucinations of inner speech* is excellent provided one clearly indicates what one means by the phrase.

The basic premise in transference is friendliness, kindness, and compassion. Understanding the difficult problems and the unpleasant situation the patient faces is necessary for honest empathy and rapport between doctor and patient. In talking with patients, doctors often relate that even when they are able to get information, the experiences of the schizophrenic differ so widely from those of the normal person that the ordinary channels of verbal expression are neither sufficient nor suitable for understanding these experiences. The problem is so common in England that if the doctor does not comprehend the content of what the patient relates, he usually diagnoses the symptoms as schizophrenia (Fish 1962). The choice of words is therefore important, as is a deep interest in what the person has to say, even if at first the material does not make sense. To tell the patient that it is just "crazy talk" does not help him to converse on the subject which is causing his suffering.

Another point is that hallucinations are found in many mental disorders, but their content and organization differ according to the type of illness. In the schizophrenic reaction, simple type, the patients are delusional but noncommunicative about their delusions and hallucinations. The delusions and hallucinations are shifting and poorly organized in the hebephrenic type of schizophrenia. The mental content of hallucinations in the paranoid type is composed of delusions and hallucinations often organized into those of persecution. In the manic-depressive reaction the symptoms of illusions, delusions, and hallucinations (Rennie and Fowler 1942) are present in addition to the fundamental affective alterations. The paranoiac has delusions of jealousy. Hallucinations may occur in all groups of paranoid disorders with those of self-reference, as well as those of persecution, being of high incidence (Retterstol 1966, 1970).

The observations to be described in this study on hallucinations are based on interviews with fifty-eight mental patients (Johnson 1958, 1967, 1972). The normals who hallucinated consisted of a doctor (M.D.) who was in charge of a science division, a professor of psychology and chairman of a department, an assistant treasurer of the City of Chicago, two housewives, a retired business woman, a retired secretary, a male professional artist, and a man working in a steel company. That a normal person can hallucinate without psychosis developing has been known for a long time. Extensive studies of normal individuals from England, France, Germany, and America indicate that the range of hallucinating is 10 to 30 per cent as determined by questionnaires (Parish 1897); among students it can be higher (McKeller 1957). A comparative study of hallucinations was made (Mott, Small, and Anderson 1965) showing that 35 per cent of the relatives of psychiatric patients hallucinated, while 34 per cent of medical patients who were not psychotic hallucinated, and 58 per cent of unselected medical students showed evidence of hallucinations. In a study (Dewi Rees 1971) of persons who were widowed, 50 per cent of the women had hallucinations of a normal type, while the number reached 66 per cent among the males.

It is often impossible to tell just by the behavior of a person whether or not that individual hallucinates. At the time one makes the observation, the patient might not be hallucinating, and if he is hearing "voices" or answering them, he may show no outward sign. The preceding is important, for while only about 69 per cent of acute schizophrenics will discuss their "voices" or hallucinate under observation (Goodwin, Alderson, and Rosenthal 1971), there are indications that every schizophrenic has a problem with hallucinations. The clinical observations of Kraeplin (1919) and Bleuler (1950) support the view that all mental patients hallucinate, and 94 per cent of the chronic schizophrenic group have been found to hear "voices" (Goodwin, Alderson, and Rosenthal 1971). It should be mentioned that 84 per cent of the alcoholic group had hallucinations and 60 per cent conversed with the voices, while 70 per cent participated in visions (Mott, Small, and Anderson, 1965).

The conversations with patients were held in the most favorable and friendly place in the mental hospital. They generally took place over a cup of coffee in the canteen. It was found necessary to discuss hallucinations with the patient in the context of the hallucinating life of the person on the ward and to clearly relate that patients subjectively converse with someone else using inner speech. Asking questions and receiving answers are possible after one defines inner speech and hallucinated inner speech. The problem and solution concerning us at this point relates to the questions of whether or not the person uses his silent reading voice to voluntarily hallucinate, whether the person has the experience of hearing the subvocal verbalizations of others, and whether he converses on this subvocal level. To make many long stories short, the answer is yes from all of the patients, thus adding verification to the many clinical and experimental observations reported in the medical literature. The following is a conversation with a patient who was a schizophrenic, paranoid type:

DOCTOR: There's one thing I don't quite get straight here when you say "internal speech," and it seems to me it would be your internal speech you were hearing.

PATIENT: No, that's the point. The patient can hear his own internal speech, his own hallucinations, but he also can hear the hallucinations of other patients, you see. They converse back and forth. You see, they are hallucinating when they are sitting there with this masklike face, poverty of expression and emotion and so on, they are talking amongst themselves through their hallucinations. When they hear voices, they're not hearing their own voices, necessarily. They do hear their own voices, but they hear other voices, you see. And they practice talking. It's something they foster. They actually sit and practice the ability to communicate among themselves.

DOCTOR: That is the auditory hearing, I mean, the hallucinatory hearing.

PATIENT: That's right, that's right.

DOCTOR: In other words, this cuts down the actual common, ordinary noises from the environment?

PATIENT: Apparently, yeah.

DOCTOR: Is that the idea?

PATIENT: So they can hear these other patients speak to them more clearly. And they'll go so far as to try and clean out the wax in their ears, and they'll practice listening. They'll be very quiet, so they can hear somebody speak, and what have you. You see, this society is built up primarily on these conversations between the patients and ummm. . . .

DOCTOR: Well what happens to the patient who or the person who has been a member of this society and then gets well and has lost the power to hallucinate?

PATIENT: Well, as I said before, some of them, I won't say they actually lose the power to hallucinate, Doctor, they control it. When they start controlling themselves better they get well. They, most of these patients, can still hallucinate at times, if they really want to. It comes sort of voluntarily, you know. Turn it on and off.

DOCTOR: Is there much communication between the patients on the various wards?

PATIENT: You mean through the hallucinations?

DOCTOR: Yes.

PATIENT: Very seldom do they relate. Of course, there is quite a long distance, and most of them don't, aren't, haven't the ability to speak that far.

DOCTOR: Well, then, is communication always intrahospital? Or is it between hospitals, too, sometimes?

PATIENT: Well, of course I told you about these interlopers. People do come in from the outside.

DOCTOR: Wait a minute. Do they come in their actual persons?

PATIENT: No, their presence is through these hallucinations and illusions and things like that.

DOCTOR: Yeah.

PATIENT: They sort of project themselves. They learn how to do this and, well, they manage sometimes over what would seen incredible distances, miles, literally. And they come in, and they dominate the ward often. They actually set up their own base of operations, so to speak, and through suggestions, order the patients around, and tell them what to do.

DOCTOR: Yes.

PATIENT: Hallucinations are a rather puzzling sort of thing, and it is certainly a puzzlement at first. In fact, the patients are totally mystified by this whole business, initially. They're not too well aware of what's causing this. They don't think very clearly, because they are not thinking, and so often you run into patients who are trying to figure out where these so-called voices are originating from. They are not sure. They think it might be the radio, television set, or it might be something to do with the telephone. Often I run into patients who are hunting up and down the hall, looking, trying to locate the source of the hallucinations. And the patients pretty much at times are mystified by the whole business.

DOCTOR: One thing occurs to me. When there would be a hallucination, could you tell the difference between that and when somebody was actually communicating in a normal fashion, or usual fashion?

PATIENT: You mean aloud?

DOCTOR: Ahuh.

PATIENT: Oh, certainly.

DOCTOR: I mean, there was no mixing up of these two things?

PATIENT: No.

DOCTOR: How could you tell the difference?

PATIENT: Well, words spoken aloud sound differently than words spoken through hallucinations, or by hallucinations, or internal speech. Quite different. Different sounds to them, physically, from the point of view of physics, much different, you know.

DOCTOR: How can a person tell hallucinations from a dream, or can he?

PATIENT: Well, of course dreams have a great deal more visual effect to them, you know. Hallucinations aren't similar to dreams.

DOCTOR: They aren't at all?

PATIENT: I don't think so, no. These are definite conversations. They're, of course, the things are pretty far-fetched, I admit. They verge on the context of a dream; some of them are quite unrealistic.

The subjective experience of the hallucinated person is employing voluntarily silent speech in a conversational format instead of using internal language to reflect to one's self as in the process of reasoning and in the controlling of voluntary movements. The words forming these verbalized hallucinatory conversations do not have the quality of sound like those words spoken out loud. In contrast, they are identical in nature to the sounds made while reading silently. The quality of the sound is quite like the internalized sounds created when one composes a letter, and these sounds are soft and smooth in contrast to the rather harsh raspiness of the sounds heard when speaking overtly. In normal thinking the sounds are confined within the tongue and oral cavity, but in the process of hallucinating the words are detached from the patient's oral cavity and externalized as if he were talking to someone out loud at a distance. What the person says and hears covertly forms the content of the average hallucination.

The patient voluntarily produces the silent hallucinated speech, which is termed hallucinated inner speech, and he hears the hallucinated subvocal utterances of other people, which is the acoustic hallucinatory experience. The hallucinated inner speech of other persons is clearly differentiated and distinguished by the patient as not coming from his inner vocal mechanism, and this aspect of hearing another person's silent speech is not under the control of the patient but is totally involuntary. A male patient may hear a woman speaking or someone silently talking in a foreign language, which he does not know or has never heard before. The patient spends most of his time either passively listening to the hallucinatory conversations of others or actively participating in these discussions. Constant hallucinating can completely monopolize the inner speech mechanism, and the patient may develop the bad habit of hallucinating. E. Bleuler (1950) observed that hallucinations can dominate the entire thinking, feeling, and action of the patient. Hallucinations can cause a disability (Lerner 1964).

The man who cannot think and see; but only hallucinates,
and missee the nature of the thing.—Carlyle

3.
The Pathology of
Hallucinations

Once, some time ago, Sigmund Freud explained that "hysterical symptoms spring from fantasies, and not from real events (Freud 1924-1950, vol. 5)." "If the fantasies become overluxuriant and overpowerful, the necessary conditions for an outbreak of neurosis or psychosis are constituted" (Freud 1956). He taught that the thought content is regressively transformed and worked over into the fantasy, which is conscious as a sense-perception, and which undergoes a secondary revision to which every perceptual concept is subject (Freud 1924-1950, vol. 14). For some time the psychoanalysts have been correlating the serious thought disorder of mental illness to destructive and regressive fantasies (Monchaux 1962). Concerning the normal thought of the adult, or secondary process thinking, it is theorized that the nervous excitation is transmitted from the perceptual system through unconscious and conscious memory systems, as well as through a censorship system, to the action of the motor mechanism. In mental illness and sleep, the excitation was said to move in a backward direction. In secondary process thinking, the hallucinatory attempt to establish perceptual identity is abandoned and replaced by the establishment of normal thought. For the secondary process to function, the hallucinations must be inhibited. "One can love or hate an internal imago, but one cannot think with it" (Monchaux 1962). A strong ego is free of ties to imagos.

Many pioneers of psychiatry wrote about the thinking disorder, which is a basic symptom, and about the effect that hallucinations have on mental behavior. The German psychiatrist Kraepelin (1919) stressed that sooner or later the patient's train of thought suffers, for "there is invariably at first a loss of mental activity, and a certain poverty of thought. . . . The patient can no longer think. . . . Thinking is difficult for him." He also observed the patient's mental condition as an incoherence of thought, and this state might go on to a complete loss of connection, and then, even to confusion. The patient cannot think because of his hallucinations. "There is a painful interruption in a series of ideas (sudden blocking of thought). This interruption of a series of ideas is involved with 'voices' which 'pull a thread' so that the patient has to think stupid things; reading is interrupted and thoughts are influenced by suggestion, which act on the patient or are forced on him. . . .They complain that they are 'dark in the head,' often in confusion, and cannot grasp a thought, cannot understand anything, for their thoughts have flown away. They begged to be free from spirits" (Kraepelin 1919). One of the most basic ideas in psychiatry is Kraepelin's concept of the blocking of thought, and its origin in hallucinations is of considerable importance.

Eugene Bleuler (1950) presented a working hypothesis in his monograph, which has remained a classic in the medical literature (Arieti 1955). He wrote about the development of the association disorder. "We found that a complex had been touched upon. In our patients the affectively charged complexes are generally connected with delusions and hallucinations. Therefore, we get very little information about these processes from the schizophrenic even though they generally dominate the entire thinking and feeling of the patient." In discussing the production of the disconnected thinking, E. Bleuler (1950) observed that "Nothing was said to the patient to stimulate this production; it seemed as if he reacted to hallucinations." E. Bleuler explained that it is quite common to find the association disorder attributable to hallucinatory influence. He gave some examples: "Thus, while one of our patients was asked to sing songs, he was suddenly unable to continue. The 'voices' told him, 'See, you have again forgotten.' But these 'voices' were those very agents who, according to the patient, provoked his lapse of memory. . . . A usually attentive and naturally intelligent patient was unable to get a simple little tale into his head, although he strained his attention so intently that he got red in the face, perspired, and breathed heavily. The voices interfered too much." In addition, E. Bleuler stated that the complexes appear as fully developed delusional systems. One example he gives is of a patient who would not speak to other individuals because of the delusion that she knew "that certain people are possessed" (Bleuler 1950). E. Bleuler explained that the hallucinatory and delusional complexes may involve the major part of the thought processes. The distortions of logic are caused by the splitting off of the complexes. The patient then forms a world of his own without taking reality into consideration. He thus impedes conceptualizations and determines disturbed associations.

The term *complex* was coined by C. G. Jung, who worked at first under the direction of E. Bleuler until they had a falling out. Jung observed that the schizophrenic disturbance of thought is the result of a complex. "We could only establish that this breakdown of ideas is distinctive of schizophrenia. It was this peculiarity in common with a quite normal phenomenon, the dream. . . . Dreams, which are the hallucinations of normal life, are nothing but hallucinatory representations of repressed complexes" (Jung 1960a). In the cases about which Jung writes, the patient's hallucinations play a major and important role. Jung felt that the primary symptom was the same condition which Pierre Janet termed *abaissement due niveau mental* and which is caused by *faiblesse de la volente*. This concept explains the condition in which a train of thought is not carried through to its logical conclusion or is interrupted by strange contents that are insufficiently inhibited because the willpower of the individual is lowered. E. Bleuler (1950) considered as being schizophrenic the same patients which Janet described as having a lowering of mental level.

In order to recognize the importance of the thinking disturbance, one must understand E. Bleuler's (1950) view that the patient is thinking less, rather than more, and that the thought process can simply come to a complete halt for long intervals. This E. Bleuler called the arrest of thought or the blocking of thought. He stated that it is the "most extraordinary formal element of schizophrenic thought process" (Bleuler 1950) and emphasized that this arrest of thought is particularly characteristic of the disease, that it is the most striking consequence of schizophrenic activity. The disturbance of thought is of fundamental significance in the diagnosis and symptomatology of schizophrenia. The reduction of thought is what causes the lessening in the associations, which is the primary and fundamental disturbance. As E. Bleuler (1950) observed, thinking stops in the middle of a thought and may cease altogether. Ideas are only partially worked out; these fragments of ideas are then connected in an illogical way to constitute a new idea. Therefore, the concepts lose completeness, and the process of association works only with the fragments of ideas and concepts. The results are incorrect, bizarre, and unpredictable associations. The patient is forced to operate with fragmented ideas leading to "displacements, condensations, confusion, generalizations, clang associations, illogical thinking and incoherence" (Bleuler 1950). E. Bleuler also states that the ego may undergo the most manifold alterations. "Loss of the feeling of activity and particularly the inability to direct one's thoughts robs the ego of some essential components" (Bleuler 1950).

The thinking disorder causes other disturbances, for when ideas are not well expressed, they are accompanied by just a moderate amount of feeling tone. Thus, the emotional expressions are not adequate, and there is a blunting or muting of the emotions (Bleuler 1950, Harris and Metcalf 1956). On the other hand, the weakening of the logical functions with the hallucinations (Mellor 1970) can result in the relative predominance of the affect. The thinking disturbance is then conditioned by the emotional disturbance, so that a vicious cycle is established. E. Bleuler (1950) observed that ambivalence is a direct consequence of the association disturbance. In addition, the thinking process can be so completely fragmented that it will not produce a complete idea for a motor action, but just vague movements. The patient remains silent and motionless, more or less without thoughts, with the associative activity at an abrupt and complete standstill. When all threads between thoughts are torn, and when excessive hallucinations are present, the result is stupor (Bleuler 1950).

A serious thought defect occurs in all schizophrenics (Ewalt, Strecker, and Ebaugh, 1957, Fish, 1962), in the manic depressive (Kraepelin 1921), in the depressed patient (Payne 1961), in the case of paranoia (Glueck 1925, Schweitzer 1948), and in the neurotic (Bellak 1970). Modern clinical psychiatry agrees with E. Bleuler (1950) that the presence of a thought disorder is a diagnostic sign of the first order (Linn 1967, Mayer-Gross, Slater, and Roth 1960). As expressed by E. Bleuler (1950), when the arrest of thought or blocking of thought is present, "one can very well make the diagnosis of schizophrenia with a considerable degree of certainty. At least, we have not found any exception to this conclusion as yet." He stated that the appearance and disappearance of the arrest of thought are dependent on psychic influences and interests, as well as the complexes based on hallucinations and delusions. This is a basic consideration, because the patient has a deep interest in the content of the hallucinations and is influenced by hallucinatory suggestions, which, when present, can determine conduct and dominate thinking. E. Bleuler's important hypothesis concerning the effect that hallucinations have on thinking has, for the most part, been passed over in the literature. We shall find that various clinical and experimental studies support his hypothesis. For example, evidence for the concept is expressed as a final conclusion in Lagache's (1934) *Les Hallucinations verbal et le parole*, and this conclusion was that verbal hallucinations explain the progress in the dissolution of higher psychic functions whose exercise is the main function of vigilant thought.

Clinical observations on the subject of the thinking disturbance were made by Harry Stack Sullivan (1954), who stated: "First I might mention what can be described as 'loss of thought,' the person suffers an oblation. Sometimes one is able to discover that a markedly autistic process swept in a dominated attention with a result that what was there before is gone really completely." Of relevance is that E. Bleuler (1950) defined one type of autism: "To a considerable extent reality is transformed through illusion and largely replaced by hallucination." In 1944, Sullivan stated: "Social communication is gradually crowded out by fantasy; and fantasy itself, because of its own participation in the relation in action, becomes in turn less and less influenced by social patterns. The result is a progressive loss of organized thinking." The usual dictionary definition of fantasy is hallucination, which is how Freud often used the word in his writings. Sullivan (1954) explained that there is a more severe manifestation of "loss of thought" which is "blocking," and he noted that this refers to a state in which a contradictory impulse predominates over the progression of thought. The term *blocking* was first used by Kraepelin, who, as already noted, stated that the interruption of a series of ideas is involved with hallucinations.

Linn (1967), in a detailed description of the clinical manifestations of the thought disorder, observes that autism connotes that the forces which destroy the flow of associations are derived from within the patient, and that these forces are the fantasies, delusions, and hallucinations. Thus, the speed of the associations is reduced during the preliminary stage of the withdrawal in schizophrenia. When the schizophrenic is making efforts to recontact the world in the restitutional phase, the associations are speeded up, but even in this phase the intrusion of auditory and visual hallucinations may be intermittent. "These hallucinations are responsible for the seemingly haphazard and unpredictable nature of the thought disturbance" (Linn 1967).

Another observation concerning the subject is that of Manfred Bleuler (1968), who characterized schizophrenia as a tendency to form a fantastic inner world. He found that this form of fantasy life is hidden in the healthy and overwhelms all obstacles in the schizophrenic. The schizophrenic psychosis is therefore characterized by a loss of equilibrium, for this "fantastic inner world" forms a picture of conflicting, contradictory human wishes and human fears. It is a picture contradictory to human nature.

Mellor (1970) demonstrated that there is a significant statistical association (5 per cent level) between the hallucination of thought insertion and thought withdrawal, and the formal thinking disorder of schizophrenia. Thought insertion was defined as thoughts ascribed to others and not having the quality of being a patient's own thinking. Patients invariably complain of some external agency imposing the hallucinated thought by varied means upon their passive minds. Mellor gave the following example from a patient: "I look out of the window and I think the garden looks nice and the grass looks cool, but the thoughts of Eamonn Andrews come into my mind. There are no other thoughts there, only his. . . . He treats my mind like a screen and flashes his thoughts on to it like you flash a picture" (Mellor 1970).

In thought withdrawal, the patient describes his thought as being taken from his mind by some external force. The formal thought disorder was observed as a meaningless mixture and fusion of all parts of speech, a driveling with incomprehensible content and derailment of thought. The theory that there is a valid casual relationship between the hallucinations and the thought disorder is an important contribution.

The view of Mayer-Gross, Slater, and Roth (1960) is that more pathognomonic than the hallucinations in themselves is their effect on the thinking of the patients. This is an example given by them: "All sorts of 'thoughts' seem to come to me, as if someone is 'speaking' them inside my head. When in any company it appears to be worse. I don't want 'thoughts' to come but I keep on 'hearing' them. . . . These 'thoughts' do not mean anything to me and cause a lack of concentration in whatever I am doing at work." Ewalt, Strecher, and Ebaugh (1957) maintain that when hallucinations appear, they are in close connection with disturbed thinking. The "voices" interfere with the patients' ideas and even present contrasting ideas. The patients report that the hallucinations are the cause of the incoherent thoughts.

The English psychiatrist Maudsley (1895) stated: "Whether the hallucination begins first in disorder of sense, as it may do, or in disorder of thought, as it often does, there is no question that disordered senses cheat the understanding and are in turn cheated by it." Another English psychiatrist, Fish, (1962) writes: "The phonemes (voices) may be continuous and obstrusive so that the patient may become incoherent, because the phonemes (voices) continuously interfere with directed thinking. . . . Auditory hallucinations are extremely common in schizophrenia, and in many cases their severity is roughly proportional to the severity of the formal thought disorder. . . . The control of thought is affected by auditory hallucinations inserting alien thoughts into the mind of the patient." Fish discussed the work of Conrad (1950, 1958a, b), who has correlated the thought disorder with hallucinations and delusional phenomena. Disorders of thought manifested in responses from the Bender Gestalt test were associated with hallucinatory experiences (Fish, Forrest, MacPherson, 1960).

Evans (1972), in an analysis of Henri Ey's concepts of the disorganization of consciousness in schizophrenia, states that hallucinations are involved in the confusion of a pathological dream state with a loss of synthesis and coordination of ideas. Consciousness loses its ability to confront the world of reality. Objectivity fails, and imaginary fantasies flood into consciousness. There is a failure of reason, which is the capacity to integrate reality into a logical system of values. The patient, because of fantasy, is at the deepest level of the disorganization of consciousness.

Further observations indicating a relationship between hallucinations and the thinking disturbance can be found in the clinical literature. Carl Schneider (1942) has associated the hallucination of thought withdrawal with the verbal derailments, the blocking and the breaking off of thoughts. Vermeylen (1934) observed in twenty-one cases a lowering of the mental level, which he considered a result of the hallucinations. The intellectual factors most affected were judgment, reasoning, analysis, and synthesis. In 1949, Chtopicki stated that there was a disintegration of sentences and a confusion of speech in auditory hallucinations. The associations between hallucinations of a given sense and disorders of conscience, as well as the disintegration of personality, have been considered (Scoppa and Fasullo 1970), and it has been found that the auditory hallucinations, and above all the verbal ones, are involved with marked changes in the personality. Agadjanian (1946) made a study using physiological conditioning techniques and found that the defects in perception and association are connected with the origin of hallucinations. When he is hallucinating, the person's perceptions and associations are lowered, and he has serious trouble with his judgment. In 1971, Ushakov proposed that hallucinations produce functional excitation which leads to the fragmentation of the thought process.

Professor Landis (1964), of Columbia University, wrote at some length about the mental confusion arising from "voices." He put forth the conclusion that the auditory hallucinations were experienced more or less continuously by patients and that the hallucinations interfered with the patients' normal ability to think and to observe. He stressed that frequently the mind of a patient would be so filled with hallucinatory voices that any attempt the individual made to answer questions put to him by outside observers was interfered with and that his replies became garbled. Landis's final conclusion to an extensive study of the written works of many patients is as follows: "In the preceding pages one cannot but be impressed by the bewildering disorganization of the thought processes as the afflicted sufferers have struggled to express themselves" (Landis 1964).

The most direct studies concerning the effect hallucinations have on cognitive functioning are those of Lindsley (1970) at Harvard University. He studied hallucinations by using experimental methods which included scientific measurements and recorders. A hidden microphone, set to respond to hallucinations, operated a voice key, which was adjusted to emit a brief pulse whenever the sound level in the room rose above a preset intensity (Lindsley 1956, 1960). The frequency range was set for human vocalization only. In this experimental situation, the patient was tested by the operant method, which involves giving reinforcement after a behavioral act. The patient would respond at a high-normal rate, and then hallucinations, as experimentally recorded, would affect the rate with a low erratic response as the result of the hallucinating. The patient was bluntly told to stop listening to his "voices"; at this command, the person stopped hallucinating. He then responded at the high rate of a normal state, rather than the low rate observed while he was hallucinating (Lindsley 1963a). After a period of time the therapist left the patient, who, as a result, started hallucinating again. This caused a low erratic rate.

The differences between the nonpsychotic who hallucinates and the psychotic who hallucinates were observed by Lindsley (1962, 1970). The hallucinogenic drug Benactyzine was given to individuals who then reported having auditory hallucinations, and carried on psychoticlike vocal hallucinatory conversations. This group of normal individuals and another consisting of psychotics were tested by free-operant conditioning methods. The nonpsychotics did not hallucinate for as long a period of time as did the psychotic patients. The vocal hallucinatory symptom in the normal individuals did not compete with their operant responses. The after-discharge of the drug-induced and experimentally stimulated hallucinatory phenomena in the normal hallucinist is much shorter than the after-discharge of the "spontaneous" or experimentally stimulated hallucinatory episodes in the psychotic. In the patients, the vocal hallucinatory symptoms have an abnormally long after-discharge and an abnormally high degree of competition with normal cognitive behavior. The pauses in the operant responding of the patients with vocal hallucinatory symptoms are due to the functional competition from these symptoms. The hallucinatory symptomatic reflex functionally dominates other systems of behavior. In summary, Lindsley (1962) stated: "What defines this form of psychosis is having the symptomatic response of talking to no one last long after a non-psychotic would stop, and being unable to do anything else demanded of him while this talking is going on that defines the psychotic."

There can be no doubt that these scientific studies of Lindsley clearly demonstrate that the patient who uses hallucinated inner speech excessively in dialogues and who listens to the acoustic component of the hallucinations develops a serious disturbance of cognitive behavior. In comparing and contrasting the normal and abnormal hallucinist, one finds that the basic difference is first in the amount of hallucinating. The normal hallucinates a little, while the abnormal hallucinates a lot. In the nonpsychotic this hallucinating does not compete with thoughtful behavior, while in the patient that does hallucinate persistently, this hallucinating competes with cognitive acts, and then functionally dominates other systems of behavior. When the patient no longer hallucinates, his behavior can return to normal.

One dyscontrol of the nervous system's mechanism involved with thinking is overinclusion. The basic importance of hallucinations as a cause of the disorder was stressed by Norman Cameron, who discovered overinclusion. The observation was made (Cameron and Margaret 1951) that in many schizophrenic disorders a clear separation between fantasy and social fact is not achieved by the patient, and overinclusion is the typical development. The hallucinated person or object is commingled with the various components in the social operation so that confusion and chaotic responses result. The hallucination can appear as an addition to the social context in that the hallucinated figure is projected against the objectively shared background.

Overinclusive abnormalities are attributed first to a distraction in the line of reasoning caused by an interpenetration of some personal theme, and second to the overinclusive generalizations. In the former, it appears to be hallucinations and delusions causing the interruptions. In the latter, there is an inability on the part of the patient to develop inhibition. A lack of attention occurs, causing the person to include such a variety of ideas at one time that the result is an extensive inclusion of material and also a less precise concept than in the case of the normal who preserves the boundaries of an idea. An important aspect of this situation is again the interference from the hallucinations, which interrupt the train of thought, preventing the proper focusing on the relevant stimuli. In the normal adult, inner speech is employed in attention as a tool to focus the mind on a particular stimulus and to inhibit or neglect other stimuli (Neisser 1967); but in the patient, for long periods of time thinking comes to a stop and is uncoordinated and nonvolitional. Because of the lack of thought used in the process of inhibition, which is employed in attention, the thinking becomes even further distracted, leading to vague and imprecise thoughts with errors of reasoning. It has been demonstrated that hallucinatory individuals in the acute phase of the illness show a significant difference in attentional and perceptual behaviors marked by a greater tendency to completion effects and greater degrees of attention error as compared to the normal individual and the nonhallucinating patient. This difference is not attributable to set (Caston 1969).

In an extensive review of the literature concerning the thinking disorder and the dysfunction of cognition in mental illness, Payne (1961) concludes that the disorder of perception is basic to cognitive abnormalities, and that this disorder may be related to misperceptions such as hallucinations. He states: "It is tempting to relate them to the tendency in psychotics to develop hallucinations and to feelings of unreality in neurotics" (Payne 1961). Payne also put forth the hypothesis that delusions are involved in causing overinclusion. He observed that overinclusiveness occurs much more in the schizophrenics who have delusions and ideas of reference than in the formerly deluded patients who do not differ greatly from normal controls in the degree of overinclusion (Payne 1964). Symptom-free patients are not overinclusive nor retarded in thought. Craig, (1965) using objective measures, found that overinclusiveness is correlated with the thought disorder and delusions.

In psychosis there is a general intellectual deterioration, which increases as the patient gets worse, and the longer the disorder continues, the greater the I.Q. drops. Using raw data, Payne (1961) calculated figures which indicated that there was a progressive general deterioration in psychosis. Rappaport and Webb (1950) presented direct proof of the impairment. In their longitudinal experiment, they worked with ten schizophrenic patients, who had been given I.Q. tests in high school before becoming ill. They were given the same tests after being hospitalized. The mean of the I.Q. tests at first was 97.60, but during the psychosis the same test showed a mean I.Q. of only 63.90, which is a difference of 33.7 points and is significant at the 1 per cent level. Other longitudinal studies which have been carried out show a decrease of some ten points (Foulds and Dixon 1962). The average I.Q. of the patients when first entering the hospital is 104.3 (Nathan and Harris 1975).

When the symptoms of hallucinations and delusions remit in the patient, the intellectual functions improve. The beneficial effect caused by the absence of symptoms on the cognitive disfunction have been observed by a large number of scientists (Glass 1956, Haywood and Moelis 1963, Mahesh 1960, Schwartz 1967, Schwartzman, Douglas, and Muir 1962). Further observations of Davidson (1938, 1939), using the Binet test, indicate that the score improves when the patient improves clinically, for both the manic-depressive and the schizophrenic. Other tests show that the vocabulary deficit improves, as does the associative interference. This was studied by pairing the associated learning of the remitted schizophrenic with the unimproved hallucinating patient (Spence and Lair 1965). Schwartz's study (1967) indicates that the improvement can be less in the person with just a grade school education than in a patient who has gone to college. Perhaps this is because the habit of thinking may still be defective in some patients. When the hallucinations were extinguished by use of an experimental procedure, the other aspects of behavior showed improvement, and there were no remissions during a six month period (Rutner and Bugler 1969). Self-administered, aversive stimulation causes a decrease in hallucinating with resulting improvement, the most central being in the conscious cognitive factors (Weingaertner 1971). The preceding studies show an interrelationship between the symptoms of hallucination and delusion, and the intellectual behavior of the patient. The experiments all indicate that certain aspects of the illness are reversible, particularly the most serious symptom which is the thinking deficit. A reversal of this symptom is possible only when the patient controls hallucinations and delusions.

In a study on hallucinations and the intellectual deficit, Bessette (1955) found that hallucinations have an injurious effect on learning, with the control group differing significantly from the hallucinatory group on all tests given except one. A demonstration has been made (Finkel 1956) showing that hallucinatory individuals are less socially oriented than the nonhallucinatory delusional persons. Another study (Taylor 1956) points out the serious effect hallucinations have on the psychological measurement of field dependency, using a comparison of hallucinating with nonhallucinating patients who still had residual false thoughts. In an experiment (Powell 1970) comparing persons who were in varying states of hallucinating, it was observed that there was a difference between the control subjects who were less field dependent and the patient group. A correction of the role of verbal intelligence should be made in such tests. Witkin (1965) reports that control subjects are less field dependent than patient groups. A study (Rogers 1959) has been made on the effect of hallucinations on learning with the patients showing a maximal retroactive inhibition under all experimental conditions, while the nonhallucinating schizophrenics showed minimal retroactive inhibition in learning as compared to the normal individuals. The characteristics of persons who were hallucinating were contrasted with those who were not hallucinating by using the MMPI as a measure. The data showed a difference between the two groups, and the result was a greater disorganization in the hallucinating patients, with an inability to pursue constructive plans. Also, the ego strength of the patients was low (Lewinsohn 1968). Auditory hallucinators show a poorer performance on learning and perceptual tasks than nonhallucinatory patients, even though the latter still have delusional thoughts (Johnson and Miller 1965). It was found that there was a significant overall impoverishment in descriptive language skills in the hallucinating patient as compared to the nonhallucinator. In those patients who had higher cognitive abilities, the reports of hallucinations concerning them were significantly less common (Miller, Johnson, and Richmond, 1965).

McKeller (1957) states that the distraction caused by the hallucinations is one determinant in the discontinuity of psychotic thinking. The content of the hallucinations may in turn evoke thoughts that are different than the associations previously operating in the patient's mind. These thoughts, which are initiated by the "voices," may be quite irrelevant. Using performance tests, Zucker (1939) studied schizophrenics in whom he deliberately evoked the reconstruction of hallucinations. He detected a relationship of the hallucinations to the various degrees of thought disorder. At first, there was the experience of thought-withdrawal, which continued to the breaking of thoughts on the one hand, and to talking past the point of incoherence in thinking on the other hand. Arnold (1948) observed a relationship between hallucinations and the incoherence and withdrawal of thought. He stated that if one finds acoustic hallucinations, then the thought disorders follow and are to be expected.

Studies on experimental isolation have produced not only various hallucinatory experiences in the subjects, but also difficulties in ordered thinking (McReynolds 1969, Solomon 1961, Zuckerman 1962). That the hallucinations caused by sensory deprivation can be similar to the mental patient's hallucinations has been noted; (McReynolds 1969) and that the hallucinations produced by LSD (Payne 1966) and amphetamines (Angrist and Gershon 1969, Connell 1958) can lead to a serious disorder of thinking has been reported in the clinical literature. In cases of sensory deprivation and pharmaceutical agents, the important point is that the hallucinations precede any serious thinking disturbances. A great deal has been written about the psychological effect of drugs. The net result on the individual, for example, was written about by Shakespeare in *Macbeth*: "Have we eaten on the insane root that take the reason prisoner?" Fleming (1953) made a historical study on the insane root, mandragora. The other agents used in Shakespeare's time were henbane and hemlock. A good discussion of hallucinations and pharmaceutical agents can be found in Baldwin and Hofmann (1969), West (1971, 1975) and Logan (1975).

The formal thought disturbance falls into two major categories (Fish 1962). The first is the patient's inability to produce any thoughts and the second is the person's production of unusual thoughts. In the latter case, either the ideas do not emerge or they emerge only in an incomplete way, so that a derailment into other concepts takes place. Then there occurs a mixing up of different memory images, producing unusual thoughts. The most important dysfunction in the stream of thought happens when the train of thought stops, and after a period of time a new one begins, one which is not connected to the previous thought. The control of thought is affected by thought deprivation and by auditory hallucinations inserting thoughts or preventing thoughts. With the loss of clear thinking, the planning and anticipation of the future become impossible. The system and order in life vanish as does a sense of values. In the medical literature there are many nuances relating hallucinations to the thinking disorder. Direct observations and scientific experiments all lend evidence and support to the working hypothesis that hallucinations affect the thought process.

It has been emphasized that schizophrenic behavior includes a group of reactions characterized by many varieties of defects in the thinking and associative processes. Is there anything tangible about abnormal thought or normal thinking? Is there something about thought that is definite, or is this phenomenon so mysterious and obscure in nature and so inexplicably enigmatic that one cannot scientifically study the problem? How do we come to grips with this situation in order to develop a precise approach and definite knowledge? To be cognizant of the normal thought process is a prerequisite and is indispensable to any clearer or deeper understanding of the pathology of thought in its relationship to hallucinated inner speech.

Philosophers have studied thinking from the time of Plato, but their body of knowledge is so complex that it presents a dilemma in its application to medical problems, as is also true of the psychological literature. The most serious problem that exists in both psychology and philosophy concerns the relationship between the mechanism of inner speech and the process of thinking. This relationship has been the object of much controversy, and many views concerning thought prevail. Plato stated: "In thinking the soul is conversing with herself." Kant felt that thinking was the activity of bringing ideas and concepts before the mind, while Hume and Berkely considered thinking as basically involved with a sequence of images. Locke felt that thought is an abstraction of sensory experience, and Hobbes emphasized that it involved the use of verbal images or mental words. The view of Dewey (1933) is that while language is not thought, it is necessary for thinking, and Adler relates that thought is discursive and that it involves language.

Many of the preceding views have been summarized and criticized by various authors (Aune 1967, Copleston 1950-1966, Ryle 1967).

Bruce Anue states: "To most it seems plainly false that inner speech occurs whenever one can correctly be said to think *in foro inerno*. . . . For while silent thought need not be inner speech it may still be an activity that is at least formally analogous to speech." Blanshard (1939), using the logic of philosophy, refutes the idea that thinking concerns talking with inner speech, for language may vary while thought is the same; and thought may vary while language is the same; speech may be present without thought, and thought may be present without speech. He states that it is no help whatever to be told that thinking and nervous process are the same: "Thus, to say that our thought of an object is an excitation of a nervous trace, if meant as a statement of present knowledge, is false, and if meant as what would seem to be true in the end, is at the best a pious wish" (Blandshard 1939).

The influential work of Ryle (1967) presents the observation that rational behavior can be carried out. This is not always rehearsed in thought, but rather done in accordance with certain principles of inference and evidence in the mind. He states that thinking can occur when talking out loud, and yet he emphasizes that there are certain special thinking activities which certainly do seem to require our saying things in our head, *sotto voce*. We need to examine what there is about these special activities which require the inward production of words and phrases. Ryle (1958) states: "Thinking runs on the wheels of words, phrases, and sentences." His belief is that thinking's proper place is in all departments of behavior, and thinking is not a rival occupation to any human act.

The psychologists do not doubt the importance of knowledge about the central nervous system in regard to understanding thought, but there is nevertheless a real dispute. They battle over the conflicting arguments which sociologists state is in many ways similar to the battle of ideas in philosophy. Experimental psychologists have studied thinking for many years, and many controversies have existed concerning the introspective method, the role of imagery, synesthetic thinking and imageless thought.

The dispute that exists today is between those psychologists who support the central theory and those persons who support the motor theory, which is also named the peripheral or central peripheral theory. The centralist believes that thinking goes on inside the brain with the muscular movements being merely accompaniments, and that words are not necessary for thought but only for conveying it. The peripheralist's position is that all thinking goes on in actions such as inner speech and other acts of mediation. The former states that thinking takes place only in the brain, while the latter believes that the body is involved. The peripheralists hold that responses are necessary conditions for thinking, while the centralists state that responses are unnecessary. Vinacke (1952), in a fine study on thinking, discusses in considerable detail the two theories along with their histories. The reader observes an impasse, for at one point, Vinacke agrees with Watson (1924), who emphasized that the term *thinking* should cover all word behavior of whatever kind that goes on subvocally, and that as adults we behave as though verbal conditioning were of the primary order with manual or visceral conditioning being of the secondary order. An impressive weight of evidence in favor of the motor theory is presented, yet in the conclusion, it is mentioned that while the motor or central peripheral theory is more convincing than the central theory, one cannot conclude that it is the correct one.

In philosophy there is an expressed theory about silent thought in which inner language does not play a role. In psychology, this would be called the central theory. In contrast, another theory of philosophy states that in special thinking activities an inward production of words is necessary. Psychologists named this theory the motor, peripheral, or central peripheral theory.

From the view of comparative neurology animals such as the chimpanzee can clearly solve problems and thus, in a real sense, can think. This type of thinking has been called thought in images (Chauchard 1962), has been termed nonverbal reasoning, and is common to both animal and man. An experiment reported in a summary of the literature (McGuigan 1966) demonstrates this concept for man. In this study a pharmaceutical agent was used to block neuromuscular transmission, and the muscles which would have been used in subvocalization were paralyzed. The case reported that the subject was conscious, and that he inferred some process which was described as thought.

Experimental psychology (Woodworth 1938, 1960) has demonstrated that the determining tendencies or sets, which act or serve to evoke a sequence of cognitive events, are nonverbal or imageless thought processes in the brain, and would be described as unconscious thought. The latter evidence for unconscious processes would be in addition to dreams and slips of the tongue. That human infants and infrahuman animals, neither of which have an actual language, are able to perform delayed reactions and develop simple concepts, suggests that these processes are not solely dependent upon linguistic ability (Munn 1965). Under normal conditions, nonverbal reasoning is often accompanied by inner speech, but it is probably independent of subvocal speech (Brain 1955a). Thinking without language is observed in persons who cannot speak or hear (Furth 1966). Vision plays an important role in motivation and in nonverbal reasoning and is used inordinately by the mental patient who has a serious thought disturbance.

In contrast to the preceding studies, there have been a number of investigations of the laryngeal muscles, which function in the process of covert vocalization used in thinking. The experiments support the concept that subvocal speech is used in the thought process. The older observations of Jacobson (1932) and Max (1937) have been confirmed and extended (Faaborg-Anderson 1957, Luria 1960). In Faaborg-Anderson's (1957) extensive work, individuals were asked to think about the phonation of the vowel "e," and their inner speech produced was accompanied by an increase in electrical activity and action potential amplitude in the vocal muscle and the cricothyroid muscle, both of which deal with speech. Electrical activity was associated with the laryngeal muscles during silent reading (Faaborg-Anderson and Edfelt 1958, Edfelt 1960). Also, electromyographic recordings of the action currents in the muscles of vocalization have been made in the subvocal reactions of the child (Luria 1960).

Many studies have been made on the development of thought and verbal regulation of behavior in the child (Hodges 1954, Piaget 1929, Vygotsky 1962). During the normal development of thinking there is a gradual transition from overt to whispered and then to implicit speech in the child. Speech is interiorized and the child then uses the internal subvocal speech for reasoning. Children give no clear evidence of reasoning until after some language activities have been acquired (Munn, 1965). Using a microphone, scientists have been able to record covert language responses made during silent reading in a few young children (McGuigan, Keller, and Stanton 1964). Thus, from the literature dealing with the muscles used in covert language and from the study of human growth and development of behavior, it can be observed that langauge does play a role in thinking (Reed 1916).

The "experiments of nature" as found in clinical neurology demonstrate that lesions in the brain can produce serious defects of inner speech. Various types of aphasia result in a disturbance or even a loss of inner speech (Brain 1955a, Goldstein 1948), and a serious thought problem is observed in such clinical cases by using psychological tests (Goldstein and Sheerer 1941, Zeigarnick 1965). A serious defect in abstract thinking has been found, and the tests used for abstract thinking depend on the ability to use inner systems, while the tests for concrete reasoning depend more on sensory reflexes. Goldstein (1944) showed a disturbance in abstract thinking in the mental patient. Writing is one of the best tests for determining the functioning of inner speech, and the process of writing is disturbed in the mental patient (Jasper 1963, Mayer-Gross, Slater, and Roth 1960). When certain parts of the brain are damaged, a defect termed *agrapha* is clinically observed. Any person can copy words or take dictation, but the mechanism of inner speech is absolutely necessary for a person to write creatively.

The preceding studies show definitively that inner speech can be used in the process of thinking. These experiments support the motor theory of thinking as expressed in psychological terms, or in philosophy, the concept that language is an important tool in thought. Paradoxically, we now have scientific evidence for both schools on the subject of thinking. What does this mean? In the view of Church (1961), the "either-or" concept in regard to these two theories is incorrect, because one should distinguish those kinds of thinking activities which are contingent on language, and try to determine how language contributes to the types of thought in which it plays a role. This is similar to the idea of Ryle (1958), who stresses that we need to examine the language activities used in the process of thinking. The facts at hand indicate that one could argue from either point of view. Osgood (1953), however, believes that a compromise is in order—that one uses inner speech when young, but that it is not necessarily needed as an adult.

The evidence strongly supports the hypothesis that man can think centrally without language and that he can also think using language, depending on the situation and his needs. Animal experiments demonstrate that problem solving can take place without language, and that rational behavior can be carried out by the human, who does not rehearse it in silent speech, but who acts in accordance with mental principles of inference or set (Ryle 1967). The evolution of this mechanism of unconscious thought may be advanced in *Homo sapiens*, but the clinical findings of neurology and psychiatry unequivocally demonstrate that this kind of nonverbal reasoning is not enough by itself to maintain a high level of intelligent behavior over long periods of time. The idea that there is only nonverbal reasoning and that subvocal speech is never used either in the process of thinking or in the expression of thought does not receive the support of experimental science.

In the mechanism of thinking there can be silent unconscious thought, which at times is not expressed as language, and yet there is at times nonverbal thought, which is expressed and created by inner speech through the feedback of perception, as in the act of hearing the flow of language. Vygotsky (1956) states: "Thought is not expressed but created in a verbal process." Inner language plays an important role in determining the character and course of the nonverbal thinking and can casually influence the total mechanism of unconscious thought. Silent talking is a shaper of ideas, and it acts as a guide for mental activity by channelling the thoughts of its users. Unconscious thought gives rise to inner speech which, in turn, feeds back influences and formulates images, making the ideas expressed in language.

Both nonlanguage and verbal neurological systems are interdigitated in the adult human, and they act together in the process of thoughtful behavior. At first in primitive man, the main function of language was to communicate ideas or feelings such as are observed in the vocalizations of a child. By the process of perception (Lenneberg 1967) the tool of language was slowly added to the nonverbal silent thinking mechanism, thus improving the performance of man. When one adds a new aspect to a living mechanism, this is not a product of the system, but is rather a part of the total biological apparatus. Like any new machine tool or die this can be a feature which increases efficiency and purpose. Inner speech is a motor mechanism in part. One of its features is the production of intrinsic sound confined within the tongue and mouth. The sound is a part of the total apparatus in that the sound flows back over auditory circuits. This is a motor-sensory system or a verbal motor acoustic mechanism that deals with the control of behavior and that must be viewed as an integrated intrinsic series of functioning structures. Should one remove a part of the system, this would be like taking away an important tool from any machine, living or not, thus subtracting from the operation of that instrument. The mechanism can still function if inner speech is removed on a nonverbal level, but performance without inner language is an abnormal operation, and the resulting behavior is not as correct as it might be.

The most important tool mankind has is language, which can be expressed either overtly or covertly. Freud (1934) states: "The voice of the intellect is a soft one, but it does not rest until it has gained a hearing. Ultimately, after endlessly repeated rebuffs, it succeeds. This is one of the few points in which one may be optimistic about the future of mankind." The terms used for talking covertly are interior monologue, implicit speech, silent speech, subvocal speech, internal language, and inner speech. This type of conscious thought has been described by Goldstein (Brain 1955a), who states: "This central internal experience, specifically verbal, thanks to which the sound heard, uttered, read or written becomes a fact of language, the common verbal attitude, which we adopt toward this event." Inner speech is used in many different human acts, for voluntary movements are initiated and controlled through the vehicle of internal language. An interior monologue is employed in man's learning process. Inner speech can be utilized in various ways such as in observing, commenting, recollecting, anticipating, contemplating conduct, daily planning, ordering experience, solving problems, and organizing daily work and creative labors. Language plays an intimate and indispensable role in the awareness of reality. Without the use of language, thinking at the most abstract level seems impossible (Brain 1955a, Thomson 1959), because it involves learning which is dependent on the use of language and the employment of complex signs. Thinking with inner speech makes the thought process more efficient and accurate.

We can conceive of the serious disorder of thought that is present in the schizophrenic as a basic disturbance of inner speech. This removes some of the metaphysical aspects surrounding the concept of thought. While thinking is a difficult situation to come to grips with, a person's inner speech is not mystical, nor is his hallucinated inner speech. On the subject of the pathology of all internal speech, we have the observations of Kraeplin (1919), who states:

> But much more significant are the disorders of internal speech,
> of the transformation of ideas into linguistic movements of expression.
> . . . The variety of such errors is very great. Unfortunately, in
> dementia praecox, there have not been as yet any satisfactory inquiries
> into the corresponding phenomena; nevertheless it seems to me
> that we find here the most important of the anomalies observed . . .
> but especially do the disorders of inner speech find their place
> here, which may likewise be understood from the point of view
> of a relaxation of the relations between idea and actual speech.
> By this destruction of inner concatenation and causation, the whole
> of active life receives the stamp of the incalculable, the
> incomprehensible, and the distorted.

Cameron and Margaret (1951) noted that acquisition of a system of interpersonal communication of inner speech is essential for effective socialization and is responsible in large part for the organization of valid thinking. This system is used less and less in the course of the disorganization of the schizophrenic and becomes subordinate to, and often replaced by, the products of fantasy. Another observer notes that the clear distinction between fantasy and reality-ordered action is blurred in the mental patient, and inner speech is no longer used for good self-direction, but becomes autistic, unrealistic, and incomprehensible. The patient is thinking less rather than more, and his thought can come to a complete halt. Thus, one can present a hypothesis that inner speech, which is observed as an index to the mechanism of thinking, will, quantitatively speaking, not be used to the same degree as it is in the normal person. Evidence for this proposition comes from the extensive studies reported by Werner and Kaplan (1967) in *Symbol Formation*. In comparing and contrasting the inner speech of schizophrenics with normal individuals, they found that the number of word units produced is low in the output of the schizophrenic's inner speech. In the case of immediate personal reactions, few subvocal words are used by either the normal or the schizophrenic. In the normal person, when he is communicating to himself about other items, the number of words increases as does their explicitness. In contrast, the schizophrenic patient has no increase of inner speech, or only a slight one, for all items. The schizophrenic's inner language was less objective than the normal person's. In regard to the inner speech of the normal, more than half was communal, but in the schizophrenic it was less than one-fifth communal in amount. The schizophrenic's silent speech is less differentiated in explicitness, for there is a lack of differentiation between circumscribed word-meanings and comprehensive sentence meanings. What little inner speech is expressed by the schizophrenic has a much greater amount of idiomatic material (55.8 per cent), as compared to the normal (33.6 per cent). In summary, the inner speech of the schizophrenic is, quantitatively speaking, much less than the normal, and it is much more subjective in nature.

Further experimental evidence for the lack of inner speech comes from the electromyographic study of Gould (1948) on the activity of vocal musculature in hallucinating and nonhallucinating patients as compared to a control group. The results were that 28 per cent of the normal group had muscle potential recordings, while there was only about 8 to 15 per cent in the nonhallucinating group, indicating less activity in the muscles dealing with inner speech. The amount of microvolts recorded was much less in the nonhallucinating patients than in the control group, or in the group of hallucinating patients, whose recorded amount of microvolts was high. These findings were confirmed and explained (Johnson 1967) as relating to an absence or deficiency of normal inner speech. The results indicate that when the patient stops hallucinating, there is a low level of inner speech activity, and the patient does not always go back to thinking when he stops hallucinating.

One might ask if it isn't possible that the major factor in the disturbance comes from nonverbal thinking mechanisms in the central nervous system rather than from the inner speech system. In regard to set, dealing with the totally silent cerebral thinking mechanism, a study (Raskin 1967) on thirty-four schizophrenics with a recent history of auditory hallucinations showed that they had an impaired reaction time as compared to the control group. In this experiment, the individuals were subjected to a manipulation of events, which might have affected the reaction time depending on the symptom of hallucinations. It was felt that a significant factor underlying the impaired set of the schizophrenics was the idiosyncratic thought processes associated with hallucinations interfering with their attention. The failure to maintain "major sets" was due to the intrusion of minor sets which represented attention to both irrelevant external and internal stimuli with the transitory hallucinations acting as the minor sets. The study indicates the importance of the idiosyncratic nature of inner speech and the role that hallucinations play in disturbances of set. An analysis of the literature found that language disturbances bear upon nonlanguage processes in the central nervous system (Lhermitte and Gautier 1969).

The question presents itself as to how the patient becomes defective in the use of inner speech, which would affect many of his behavioral acts. One idea comes from clinical psychiatry: "Patients report that their thoughts break off and are withdrawn from them. Their thoughts become vocal and hallucinated. Others can hear them and they can hear the thoughts of others" (Redlich and Freedman 1966). The description, of course, indicates that the person's thoughts are no longer used in thinking, they are used in hallucinating. The hypothesis is that hallucinations of inner speech affect normal inner speech with a resulting disturbance or loss of the normal inner speech habit. What we know about the effect that hallucinated inner speech has on the use of inner speech as a tool in thinking has come from interviews with fifty-eight schizophrenic patients. In twenty cases, inner speech was defined using silent reading as a method, and the association problem was discussed in terms of the arrest of thought, and then waiting for the patient to voluntarily relate his problems. In eighteen of the cases, it was stated that there was a problem with thinking and using common knowledge about silent reading. Thinking was defined in terms of subvocal speech, as was hallucinated inner speech. In the rest of the cases the individuals related their problems without questions after the definitions were made.

In regard to thinking, every patient stated that he had a problem with thought, and that inner speech as used in normal thinking was absent often for long periods of time ranging from hours to months and even years. In all these cases, the hallucinatory mechanism was inner speech, which the person used in conversations instead of using silent speech to reflect to himself as in reasoning. All of these cases stated that they had an arrest of thought, which was due to the hallucinations of inner speech (Johnson 1967). One person who was working in a long-term mental hospital said that the problem with thinking was so severe that it was necessary for him to ask his foreman what he should do, and then, after finishing that job, he would have to ask what to do next. The patient was devoid of thought, due to excessive hallucinating. Another patient, who was a graduate of Amherst, stated clearly that the hallucinations and the subsequent lack of thought were his problems. A person with a master's degree in philosophy said that in the course of the development of his illness, it had been the overuse of hallucinations which had affected his thinking by causing him to think less rather than more.

The knowledge that the process or mechanism dealing with thought is involved with hallucinations is most critical to keep in mind in order to comprehend the significance of the morbid effect that excessive hallucinating by inner speech can have on normal inner speech. The finding that the patient is using inner speech to hallucinate with is basic to understanding what happens to the normal subvocal language mechanism. An unequivocable observation is that the patients are hallucinating to such a degree on the wards of the mental hospital that all of their time is occupied in hallucinatory behavior. The schizophrenics hallucinate extensively, and their thoughts become vocal, with hallucinations completely monopolizing their inner speech and inner life. For inordinately long periods of time, the patients are no longer thinking, but are either listening to auditory hallucinations or using their hallucinated inner speech to converse with another "voice." They develop a bad habit of hallucinating, and lose a good habit of thinking, excluding the use of their thoughts for normal purposes.

Interviews with the fifty-eight patients produced information concerning the development of the thinking disorder. The person, during even the first hallucinatory experience, can hallucinate to such a degree that his thought process is affected. This has been observed as overinclusiveness, while in the chronic state it can be seen as retardation (Payne 1966). In the beginning, the fact that the sounds of the acoustic hallucinatory words are the same as the sounds produced while thinking makes for a perceptual interference in the act of thinking with inner speech. The neurological mechanism used in normal silent speech is now much involved with hallucinated inner speech. This produces a difficult problem in the patient's differentiating and controlling the two different acts. Hallucinations act as an interference, for they are irrelevant external auditory cues, and they provide internal interference as stimuli of hallucinated inner speech. Both distracting stimuli prevent the patient from mediation and maintaining a clear focus of attention on the task at hand. The result is a psychological deficit leading to overinclusiveness, for a set cannot be maintained or changed quickly.

The patient develops an excessive interest in hallucinating and is influenced by the content of the hallucinations. The ideas expressed and heard while hallucinating form the basis of hallucinatory delusions and complexes, which motivate and facilitate hallucinating, while suppressing and inhibiting the act of normal inner speech. The hallucinations become a reflex act. The habit, or conditioned reflex, of continually using inner speech in thought and behavior is now interrupted by the hallucinations, and the normal inner speech is no longer reinforced because the patient is spending much of his time listening to the auditory hallucinations. Thus, there occurs an external inhibition of the flow of inner speech. The patient, in addition, uses his inner speech extensively in the hallucinatory dialogues rather than in thought. The extinction of the normal inner speech habit takes place because of the lack of reinforcement, and the condition reflex, therefore, becomes defective, idle, inactive, or lost. A state of internal inhibition develops, making it difficult for the patient to start the process of normal subvocal speech. The schizophrenic, instead of being able to fluently use the internalized silent vocal language, now has only a sluggish flow of internal speech, which is termed *retardation*.

The hallucinist can externalize inner speech to such a degree and for so long a period of time, as speaking in hallucinatory conversations, that he loses the ability to internalize the sounds within the oral cavity (localized in the tongue). The patient can become devoid of thought, and this can reach the level of a total disuse or functional paralysis of the normal mechanism of internalized subvocal speech (Johnson 1967). The serious loss of the habit of inner speech makes it difficult, and even impossible, for the patient to execute silently in his mouth the words and sentences employed in thinking, writing, and silent reading. The person can still hallucinate afar but cannot think internally with his inner speech. The faculty of inner language becomes defective much as in the case of deaf and dumb individuals.

The disorder of thought could be helped by retraining and re-education (Payne 1966), and it could be prevented by therapeutic instruction for the patients often have no idea of what they should do in a hallucinatory situation. The hope is that, with the growth of scientific knowledge on the subject of hallucinations, a change in attitude will weaken the force of false ideas, battle cries, and prohibitions from the past which have made the direct treatment of either the thinking disorder or hallucinations of inner speech an impossibility until this time.

4.
The Influence of Hallucinations

The history of taking orders and suggestions from "voices" is ancient, and the phenomenon of being controlled has not changed with the passing of time (Linn 1967, Wallace 1959). E. Bleuler (1930) believed that the association disorder came about in part because of influences and hallucinated suggestions which dominate the thinking of the schizophrenic. As a result of "voices" giving commands, behavior is possible without willed thought. A serious problem arises, for these actions can be morbid, and taking orders from hallucinations "is almost pathognomonic for schizophrenia" (Linn 1967). Hallucinations play a major role in the "way of life" of the schizophrenic. From the subjective point of view of the hallucinating individual, the silent voice conversations form a basis for a hallucinogenic society, which at times is largely run by the "voices." The person is dominated by the commands which are interpreted as coming from other people. These suggestions can cause abnormal behavior and are symptoms that produce much suffering, both to the patient and to others.

Although little has been written on hallucinated orders, they have, at times, been briefly noted as a serious problem. Kraepelin (1919) states: "In a series of cases, the voices give commands which in certain circumstances are very precisely obeyed. They forbid the patient to eat

85

and to speak, to work, to go to Church; he must run barefoot. 'Go on, strike him, beat him,' it is said." Brierre de Boismont (1855) has observed that the patient is obeying some superior order which tells him to remain motionless or to take a certain position. Frequently, the person's actions are influenced by hallucinations, and he blindly follows all of their dictations. Brierre de Boismont (1855) found that the conduct, actions, and whimsicalities of the affected are explained by hallucinations and illusions. Maudsley (1895) states that the hallucinations may instigate destructive violence in the patients, and he gave the example of such a person who saw angels whose voices commanded him to commit homicide, "and he, obeying their commands nearly killed a companion who was lying near him. . . . Another suddenly split open with an axe the skull of a laborer who was working near him." Brower and Bannister (1902) found that voices are a direct incentive to actions, and that they give rise to assaults and crimes. E. Bleuler (1950) states: "The commanding 'voices' give no order, which for some reason the patient does not wish to obey. . . . Patient obeys commands with or without resistance" (Bleuler 1950). He gave illustrations, such as a person's opening the window a hundred times a day in obedience to commands, or making a special journey to a river in order to jump in. The "voices" can continuously tell the person to do the opposite of what he should do, and when a patient does do something, the "voices" declare that it is not right, with the result being, "many patients are brought to a point of despair by these things" (Bleuler 1950). Bleuler noted that the influence of hallucinations can cause the patient to curse profusely, become violent, and suffer spells of excitement and agitation. Noyes (1953) found that the hallucinations that convey commands are convincing and compelling, and that they lead to direct and dangerous actions. Many patients have the feeling and belief that they must do as the "voices" tell them, and they disclaim any personal responsibility for thoughts, words, and actions (Ewalt, Strecker, and Ebaugh 1957). English and Finch (1964) stated: "The patient is capable of acting on the 'command' of the voices." Mayer-Gross, Slater, and Roth (1960) made the clinical observation that auditory hallucinations may accompany every action of the patient with their comments and that they influence the person's actions. Linn (1967) observed that the "voices" may order the patient to commit acts of violence, self-mutilation, and self-destruction.

The relevance of the preceding literature can be clearly seen in the case of John Perceval (1840), who was the son of a prime minister of Great Britain. In a narrative about his experiences as a patient, he stated: "I began to hear voices. . . . These voices I obeyed or endeavored to obey and believed almost implicitly; especially after my mind was entirely deranged. . . . Those voices commanded me to do and made me believe a number of false and terrible things. I threw myself out of bed. I tried to twist my neck. I struggled with my keepers . . . in short for a whole year I scarcely uttered a syllable, or did a single act but from inspiration. . . . [I] was told to throw myself over a steep precipice but refused to do so for fear of death. . . . I replied in thought to these voices. . . . [I] fancied the voices were sent to try and instruct me and that I was bound to respect and pay attention to them."

Perceval's experience shows that mental illness deals largely with commands and a state of confusion of understanding. He changed from a "dangerous lunatic" into the first stage of recovery when he rejected the control by the "voices" over his actions and thoughts. He states: "Thus my mind was set to rest in great measure from another delusion; or rather, the superstitious belief that I was blindly to yield myself up to an extraordinary guidance was done away with."

To verify that patients are in mental bondage, Landis (1964) states: "Lastly, many, indeed most, persons who have had auditory hallucinations are of the conviction that the 'voices' are all related to some outside central controlling agency which can take charge of their minds and does indeed do so much too often." He confirmed Kraepelin's observation that "voices" have a greater power of convincing the patients than anything said by those around them. In regard to compulsion, it was observed that some patients, particularly those suffering from auditory hallucinations, attributed the impulses to certain statements or commands given by these "voices." The voluntary control of the patient's thoughts and behavior is seriously affected by hallucinations. The persistence of the "voices" will compel the person to realize that the mysterious outside governing forces are far more powerful than any self-generated internal control, and that he is no longer responsible for his mental life and social behavior. Landis (1964) gave various examples from the literature illustrating this type of abnormal behavior. In Lange's case (1939a): "Exercising their asserted Divine Authority, the thoughts-outloud demand that I take off my clothing and go around in the nude." In another case (Landis 1964) the patient was ordered by a "voice" to walk into the ocean. The voice said, "Just walk in, and keep walking." The person did so and even struggled against the lifeguards who came to his rescue.

The information to be presented concerning "suggested hallucinations" is drawn from interviews with twenty schizophrenic patients. For long periods of time, the patients can behave as if they were slaves to a "voice." A person heard a "voice" telling him to burn his skin with a cigarette. The auditory hallucination related that the burn, much like a tattoo, symbolized a certain event. If the patient burned the skin in a particular part of the hand, the resulting scar would represent life everlasting; if he burned a certain part of his leg, the scar would indicate the individual's commitment to try to stay alive. The hallucinatory conversation at times is more involved than just a simple order. One person was involved in hallucinatory behavior and believed falsely that a blood vessel had been broken. A "voice" said that burning the skin in a particular place would stop the internal bleeding. This patient burned himself eleven times.

Coprophagia, or smearing, is another type of behavior caused by hallucinations. In this case the person is told to disrobe by "voices" and then to defecate and eat the excrement or smear it on his skin or on the wall. Arieti (1955) observed that it is not rare to find coprophagia in a mental hospital.

Fights are often started by voices telling the patient to strike another person. One individual heard a voice which he identified subjectively as coming from a nursing assistant. The individual then proceeded to hit the person whom the voice had told him to strike. In this case, the person was another nursing aide. Subsequently, after a single light blow was struck, the attendants took the patient to a room, where the four aides, after a considerable amount of beating, subdued the patient and placed him in restraints. The person followed the hallucinogenic order to strike a nursing aide every day for several months. The patient did not stop until he no longer felt the effects of the beatings and told the aides that he was immune, that he had never heard a voice from an orderly giving a command. His face needed plastic surgery, and X-rays showed a broken sternum. Perhaps it is that "as elsewhere, rough usage (often amounting to brutality) was believed to be the most suitable treatment for those suffering under this the greatest of human misfortunes, mental aberration" (Campbell 1902). Although this latter practice is not observed in the mental hospitals as much as it used to be, it must be stated, according to the personal communication of a forensic psychiatrist, that it still exists in prisons today as an almost preferred treatment.

The clinical literature reports that "voices" catalyze suicide. Boismont (1855) states: "Suicide is frequently the result of hallucinations; suicide and murder are commanded by invisible voices." Mendel (1907) observes: "Hallucinations, especially auditory hallucinations, may often lead to suicide. These command the patient to destroy himself." Fish (1962) reports: "This may lead to suicidal and homicidal action in response to phonemic [voices] instruction." A patient who survived an incident reported taking an overdose of medication while he was following the directions of an auditory hallucination. Another case also told about a "voice" that commanded him to take an overdose of medication. He identified this "voice" in his mind's eye with the doctor in charge of his case. Two other persons said that they had cut their wrists because of hallucinatory orders. In a case reported by a minister, a man had cut both wrists and his throat because of hallucinatory commands in which the "voices" told the patient to refuse help. During one weekend in Chicago, a *Tribune* health columnist reported, sixty persons had cut their wrists. A man who lived after his suicide attempt stated that he had taken an overdose of drugs and alcohol as a result of "voice" orders.

One patient under the influence of hallucinations behaved almost as if in a hypnotic trance while he was on an airplane. The person said that a voice used the hypnotic expression, "Relax, relax—get tense, get tense," and the man followed the guidance of these and other orders. He obeyed every command, even to the act of opening the door of the airliner and starting to jump out. He was saved at the last second by another person on the plane. The hallucinating individual was then placed in a mental hospital for three and a half years. A female case was urged to suicide by disagreeable, painful, and frightful voices about which she said, "They make me act; they make me speak; they drive me."

Another case of attempted suicide is that of a man in his forties who had graduated from a university and had considerable success in life. Under the influence of voices one morning, just as he was waking up, he jumped out of a window. He broke his legs and his jaw, and almost died. The voices talked to him about a fire in the building. He believed that the fire existed and, therefore, jumped out of the third-story window under orders from the hallucination. Yet another case is that of a man who lived in Washington, D.C., worked in the Treasury Department, and knew many important figures in the government. He said that he heard the voice of the president telling him to visit the White House. He had a serious problem with hallucinatory suggestions and once tried to take an overdose of medicine.

A number of cases which were observed by Schulz and Kilgalen (1968) showed that voices played a role in many abnormal acts. In one such case, the patient made many attempts at self-destruction during the early period of his hospitalization. He heard voices telling him to castrate himself, and he almost stabbed himself in the abdomen with a knife. He also thought, at one time, that his therapist's voice was telling him to jump out of a window, and he attempted to do so. The importance of hallucinations in causing behavior is not mentioned in the many books that have been written on suicide. Arieti (1974) has observed that suicides of schizophrenics are largely caused by acting out commands or ideas suggested by a hallucination, delusional ideas, or new ways of thinking. In many cases the suicidal act is the result of the acting out of commands combined with a depressive syndrome or episode and a disinhibition of masochistic trends.

Motor behavior of patients can be controlled and regulated by hallucinations. Voices ordering a patient to drink water at a fountain is a common occurrence. Persons are sometimes commanded not to eat and are often told to walk to some point on the ward, or are instructed not to visit the restroom. Mendel (1907) states: "In catatonic stupor the arrest of motion depends here upon an 'obstruction' (Kraepelin). This obstruction proceeds from hallucinations and delusions." That hallucinations play a role in the catatonic schizophrenic has been observed by Lidz (1968), who states: "Frequently these patients are in the midst of some mystical experience, believing themselves in heaven or hell; they are often immobile and refuse to speak, because they believe any movement or word can produce a universal catastrophe." A patient related that he was under the domination of a voice, which he felt was that of a scientist. This person's neck was bent in a strange manner. After the individual stopped taking the various orders from his "voice," the problem with his neck largely disappeared, and he was discharged from a long-term hospital. In the case of another catatonic, the patient stated that a voice had informed him to stand still in a strange position, and that he could not think. In still another case of a catatonic who stood like a statue, a therapist was able to conclude that his strange pose was the result of hallucinations.

In 1970, the experiment of Mellor demonstrated a statistically significant relationship, at the 1 per cent level, between the abnormal motor activity characteristic of catatonia and the hallucinations of "made" impulses and "made" volitional acts. The definition of "made" impulses is that a powerful impulse made by an extenal agency, and imposed upon the person from without, overcomes the patient. In "made" volitional acts the patient experiences his actions as being completely under the control of an external influence. The difference between the two is that the "made" impulse to carry out the motor action is not the patient's, while the performance of the act is the patient's. In the second case, the movements are initiated and directed throughout by the controlling influence, and the patient feels that he is a passive observer of his own action which becomes something like automation. The resulting abnormal motor activities are akinesia, excitement, mannerism, and stereotype. The catatonic symptoms of perseveranction, abitendency, and cooperation in body movement, after the patient was told to resist, were tested in the investigation. Mellor (1970) observed that hearing voices arguing is significantly associated (1 per cent level) with the hallucinations of "made" impulses.

Thorndike (1923), in his extensive work on magic and the development of experimental science, wrote about numbers used in the occult. There is a strange hallucinated order code made up of numbers and their meanings which is associated with abnormal behavior. This code goes back historically to pre-Christian times. In Egypt during that time the number three meant love, as it does today. In hallucinatory episodes patients are told by "voices" to make up false stories about their lives. In hallucinatory jargon this is expressed as "to is," or to lie about one's vocation, birth, name, or to relate a fantasy to the doctor. The patients are told that by doing this they will stay alive. This is named number one in the code, while number two means that the patient should tell the truth. Some patients lie to such a degree that it is impossible to gather any truthful information from them. A patient from the Chicago State Mental Hospital said that he was a street cleaner, born in a mental hospital, from the planet Pluto, an admiral and a captain in the Navy. This person did understand that in part he was making up a story.

Perhaps the recorded observations of a patient shall throw some light on the situation:

PATIENT: But, ah, of course you have this whole problem of the patient and the old classical definition of the person thinking he is somebody else, like the classic one about Napoleon Bonaparte that is ridiculed. This is sort of interesting because this comes up from time to time. The patient of course lies about his identity. He says he is somebody else through this "is" business.

DOCTOR: But he knows that he isn't.

PATIENT: That is right. But he sits there and verbally portrays himself as somebody else. In addition to this, you have these interlopers that come in, and they seem to pretty well take over the point of space where the patient is sitting, and so you have this problem with the patient now being supplied with information and with another person talking, so that you are never sure whether it is he or this interloper, this outside form or entity or voice. And then you have these patients, because the knowledge is handed down for years, and you have information that they utilize on historical figures and things like that, and at night particularly they'll enact the story of Henry the VIII or something like that. You know, they will romanticize and imagine what was going on at the time. So you have the patient thinking he is somebody else either through lying or because somebody has come onto the ward with his voice from the outside or because of knowledge that is handed down and acted out.

A number of excellent cases of hallucinations causing the formation of another personality in the patient are given by Jasper (1963) in his fine study of psychopathology.

The words of a schizophrenic patient give some idea as to the condition of suggested hallucinations and their meaning to the person who is involved with them:

> Well, the hallucinations, of course, give them instruments at their
> hand; instruments of power and force, which make it possible
> for them to control the environment through suggestions leading to
> violence and what have you. They actually set up, as it were,
> a little society of their own. Now the purpose of this, of course, I
> suppose is actually. . . . I admit it is a little hard to give a broad purpose
> to it. Sometimes, of course, you run into individual purposes, but
> I hadn't thought too much about what the general overall purpose of
> the thing is. Generally it is to utilize somehow this method of
> communication and to put it to work. They put it to work with this
> falseness of the whole environment the resultant. Of course, they
> don't have a valid purpose at heart, for most of the time it is
> definitely one of those things that leads to harm and to misfortune
> and tragedy. These suggestions are the tool with which these people

move around other people. Of course, as I said before, I think
most of these things obviously are quite sick basically. I mean they are
not a normal way of behaving. They go against all of our
knowledge and certainly all of our ethics.

Over a century ago, Brierre de Boismont (1855) wrote a chapter
in his book about the subject of hallucinations and criminology. He
states: "How often, indeed, have we had an opportunity of remarking
that men, charged with vagrancy, robbery, breaches of the peace and
murders, were only unfortunate persons who had yielded to the suggestions of hallucinations and insanity. . . . A fatal destiny seems to pursue
the hallucinated. If he escapes from the hospital, he finds the gates of
the prison closing on him. Such is, in fact, the nature of his disease, that
he is regarded as a guilty man if he does not pass for a crazy man"
(Brierre de Boismont 1855). In 1970, the investigator Frances Smart
(1970) discussed a number of cases in which hallucinations played an
important role. In one case, there were voices of numerous young boys
telling the patient to do destructive things, and he was unable to resist
them. They told him to damage his eyes, and he tried to do this. They
also told him to steal; his attempt to do this was what had brought him
to prison. The "voices" told him to kill his mother, and he also attempted
to do this. In another case, the auditory hallucinations had begun when
the patient was fifteen years of age. A "voice" which was always the
same one had told him to attack his mother. In a third case, the "voices"
had urged the person to kill his homosexual friends, and on more than
one occasion he actually had tried to kill the boys he knew. Halleck
(1967) noted that hallucinations are found in homosexual individuals,
who often have a fear of being seduced by the hallucinations.

Many legal reports demonstrate the influence of hallucinations on
behavior; for example: "Employee in course of employment was killed
by fellow employee laboring under an hallucination or delusion that de-
ceased employee had improper relations with fellow employee's wife"
(American Law Reports 1948). Walker (1968) had studied the subject
of law and insanity; concerning the subject of irresistible impulse he cites
the case of an individual who attempted to murder his sister-in-law because, as he told the police: "The man in the moon told me to do it. I
will have to commit murder, as I must be hanged." This situation was
also observed in a case of infanticide, where a woman gave as the reason
for her act that the devil had tempted her to kill it. In a famous case, it
is noted that Hadfield threatened to kill his own child because God had

told him to commit the act. M'Naghten made the following statement to the police: "They follow and persecute me wherever I go, and have entirely destroyed my peace of mind. They followed me to France, into Scotland, and all over England; in fact they follow me wherever I go" (Walker 1968).

Winslow (1866) states: "Under the irresistible influence of an imaginary voice, many a person is driven to acts of violence and homicide." One person heard a voice telling him to molest children, which he did, and related that the voice was highly educated and perhaps that of an industrialist. In another case, it was a person's opinion that, by using hallucinated inner speech, he had ordered a murder of someone who had murdered an important person through a voice who was a member of organized crime.

Fires are often started by individuals being influenced by hallucinatory orders (Brierre de Boismont 1855). The Manson case in California is an example of the use of hallucinatory influence to cause a crime at a distance. Karpman (1944) wrote in great detail about the case of Walter Manson, who told about his many hallucinations, in a study on the psychopathology of crime.

Not until 1838 were the mentally ill in France transferred from the prisons and workhouses to aslyums especially constructed for patients (Ives 1914). The fact that both the inmates of the prisons and the patients of the mental hospitals were under the same roof indicates that certain features are common for both, and even today the name for a room in both structures where the individuals can sit and talk is called the *day room*. Another feature common to both concerns hallucinatory phenomena. Both experience psychosis, which in the inmates' case is termed *prison psychosis*. A good review of the older literature dealing with prison psychosis was written by Nitsche and Wilmanns (1912), and the indications are that this psychosis may be observed among the inmates long before they enter prison, but that the penal situation exacerbates the symptoms, making the disease apparent to all concerned.

Hallucinations are found in prison psychosis (Bachet 1947), and in a clinical study of one hundred cases of auditory hallucinations in prison psychosis, the investigator Schwarz (1936) observed that hallucinations are an outcome of a previous psychological experience, because of their peculiar content. In the inmates who had a psychosis and a psychopathic personality, the hallucinations often told them that they had "squealed" and that they would be subjected to serious harm or might even be killed. This, in turn, produced delusions of persecution, leading them to the mental hospital. In addition, the individuals reported receiving, from hallucinations, commands which were often succeeded by contrary commands. The "voices" would talk about the inmate's sexual life in morbid critical ways, producing feelings of guilt (Schwarz 1936). In prison psychosis, the individuals do not feel in control of their own thoughts, a condition which is similar to that of schizophrenia (Jasper 1963). The "voices" might say, "Today we shall finish him off." In time, the voices multiply and call the patient by name, with the content elaborated into a delusion-like idea, and the person is convinced that he is really being persecuted and about to be killed (Jasper 1963).

Glueck (1925), in a fine analysis of the literature dealing with mental illness and criminal law, presents evidence that at Sing Sing Prison some 18.9 per cent of the prisoners were psychopathic, while 12 per cent showed deterioration or a distinct mental disease, and 21.8 per cent were feeble-minded. Similar findings were observed at the Massachusetts State Prison, the Indiana State Prison and the Detroit State Prison. In the Chicago courts, it was found that dementia praecox plays the highest role, and is the criminal psychosis par excellence. The following evidence was given: in the criminal branches, out of 270 males 107 had dementia praecox, and out of 152 females, 84 had dementia praecox, while in the Morals Court, out of 359 cases of males, 107 had dementia praecox and out of 464 cases of females, 260 had dementia praecox. As to the problem of hallucinations, Glueck (1925) states: "Hallucinations may result directly in illegal conduct; their vivid reality and compelling force may lead the patient to commit the most serious crimes, in carrying out a supposed command from the Deity, or in redressing supposed insults and threatened injuries."

The Illinois Crime Survey (1929) presents findings from 1,700 inmates studied at the Joliet Penitentiary, and of these, only 34 persons, or 2 per cent, were found to have no demonstrable abnormality. Even though many of them are reported to be suffering from psychosis, the great majority are not considered in need of transfer to a state hospital, and only the more striking types of abnormality were listed in the figures constituting only 22 per cent of the total. The Municipal Court of Chicago's laboratory found that out of 3,257 cases, dementia praecox was diagnosed in 1,145 individuals and 294 had a psychopathic constitution. A recent study by Davidman (1969) indicates that hallucinations are present in prisons, and in addition to his own observations, a study by

Snow is discussed concerning six different women's houses of detention. Of the women interviewed, 45 to 105 cases, or 43 per cent, were overtly psychotic, "based upon definite symptoms of disturbed inappropriate effect, disorders of production and progression of thought, referential and delusional content of thought and gross perceptual disorders such as hallucinations" (Davidman 1969). Twenty of the 105 women had elicitable histories of previous hospitalization. Male prisoners have almost as high an incidence of psychosis as is reported among the women, and the good majority of prisoners are involved if the submanifest schizophrenics are included. Today only 0.5 per cent to 10 percent of the inmates are listed as mentally ill in official statistical reports; the reason is that, in general, the more cursory the examination, the lower the percentage of serious mental disorders, which can reach 50 per cent with careful observations on the inmates' mental and emotional aberrations. This observation is the finding of Doctor Satten (1963), of the Menninger Foundation, where doctors have observed the highest degree of suggestibility among the inmates of the prisons. Often, the diagnosis of male inmates is that they are sociopathic, alcoholic, or drug dependent, and women are diagnosed as hysteric (Guze, Goodwin, Crane 1969, and Guze 1976). All have hallucinations (Hill 1936; Mott, Small, and Anderson 1965).

As a working hypothesis, it is proposed that the vast majority of inmates hallucinate before they enter the penal system, and that there is a tragic social injustice surrounding hallucinations. The term *prison psychosis* is used to cover up the situation by dogmatically stating that the illness is derived from the confinement, rather than being present before the person becomes an inmate. This is like saying that the mental hospital produces the mental illness. From all of the literature which has been given, it is obvious that the inmates are diagnosed as schizophrenic, psychopathic, alcoholic, and drug dependent, none of which depend on the prison as a cause, but which start before the penal situation. To dismiss the whole problem by calling it prison psychosis is in error. Long ago, Brierre de Boismont (1855), who studied criminology most of his life, observed that the major morbid crimes are caused by hallucinations, indicating that the person involved hallucinated before he entered prison.

An old argument exists in the courts concerning whether or not inmates are mentally ill. Legal insanity is a disorder of the intellect, while moral insanity is a disorder of the moral affections such as feelings, will, and propensities dealing with emotional motives, and is a type of insanity not recognized by the courts. Although most of the inmates hallucinate before they enter prison, they may not have as serious a defect in thinking as is found in the schizophrenic. It seems likely that persons "get something from their hallucinations," and at times this can be uncivilized. Eysenck (1970) has studied crime and personality. In 1973 it was concluded that female prisoners (and males to a lesser degree) are psychiatrically ill to a marked degree. The scientific tests of the prisoners (both male and female) are not very different from those of the neurotic and psychotic hospital populations (Eysenck and Eysenck 1973).

Brierre de Boismont, who was a student of Esquirol, spent all his life working in jurisprudence as related to mental illness. His summary is as follows:

Recepituation—Hallucinations, single or combined with illusions, may be the cause of a number of reprehensive, dangerous, and criminal resolutions. Suicide is frequently the result of hallucinations, which exist in the form of apparitions, menaces, and chimerical fears. Blows, wounds, even assassinations are often occasioned by the sight of imaginary enemies, by insults, grimaces, and injuries, which only exist in the imagination of the hallucinated. Challenges to a duel have often been caused by these errors of the mind. Hallucinated monomaniacs, who believe themselves the objects of plots and persecution, are dangerous. Many murders may be referred exclusively to them. It is not unusual to see persons, thus hallucinated, make several successive attempts. In some cases suicide and murder are commanded by invisible voices.

Dangerous actions incited by hallucinations are often the results of illusions. Maniacal delirium, acute delirium, and that which accompanies febrile affections, may occasion both suicide and homicide. Resolutions and actions, into which individuals are drawn by hallucination, sometimes occur quite suddenly. Night, darkness, and solitude appear to favor the disposition. Hallucinations may be the exciting causes of theft, incendiarism, and other reprehensive actions. The hallucinations and illusion of delirium tremens merit much attention; they are almost always the motives of actions committed during drunkenness. Hallucinations and illusions are the key to a great many incomprehensible actions (Brierre de Boismont 1855).

The illusions which Brierre de Boismont wrote about are visual hallucinatory illusions external to the person, who subjectively believes them
to be caused by another individual.

In many cases, it is not at all a simple thing to tell the person to
stop taking hallucinatory commands, with the result that the patient is
no longer influenced by voices. Often the behavior is not overtly morbid.
The person may be drinking water, walking about, looking at a book,
and appearing normal, while behind this behavior there is an auditory
hallucination. One patient who had been in the army intelligence during
World War II, and who was in a long-term VA hospital, said that to him
the orders were important because they had often helped him out of situations during his war-time work and even in peacetime. This patient
would not give up taking orders because of his strong feeling as to the
worth of the hallucinatory commands. He had a pseudorational reason
for his behavior.

Another patient said that since other people would take his hallucinatory inner speech orders, he in turn felt that he must take their "voice"
commands. This person had taken orders to cut his wrists on two occasions and to take an overdose of drugs on another occasion. It was
strange that these morbid events in his life did not cause the patient to
stop taking further orders. He was Phi Beta Kappa with much success
early in life, notwithstanding the fact that he started hallucinating in high
school. In his thirties he developed the habit of excessive hallucinating
with a thinking disorder, which he said clearly was caused by the hallucinating. Even after knowing that he should not take suggestions, he still
continued to think that it was rational, because he was smarter than
others, and he got something from his hallucinatory behavior, which in
this case seemed to be sex and power over other people. He had pushed
over floral displays and done many other acts following the dictates of
the hallucinatory voices, and he had written hundreds of thousands of
words following the direction of his "muse," a "voice" much in the tradition of a demon.

A patient who had taken orders from "voices" asked, "How do you
stop taking them?" In his case, how not to take the suggestions was the
puzzle. A female patient would not give up hallucinatory orders because
she enjoyed the sexual aspects of the behavior caused by a particular
"voice." Another female person liked to play a "sex game," first giving
orders, then taking them. One individual related that an auditory hallucination would influence him to drink, and that he would hear, "In order
to be happier why don't you go to a bar and have a drink." The "voices"

would give a series of arguments about how much better he would feel if he drank.

Some patients feel that they must take the orders because of the source, and one patient had the hallucinatory experience of being silently ordered by a doctor to "go down" and crawl around on the floor like a dog. The mental patients often feel that they have to take subjective "voice" commands from the nurse, attendant, or the person in charge of therapy programs. The hallucinatory commands can influence every movement in corrective therapy periods or in an occupational therapy program. In the case of a young man who had taken LSD, various religious "voices" told him to drive from California to Chicago. These "voices" affected the other people who drove with him, and it was the hallucinations that organized the trip across the country. This was a religious group, who wished to save souls and the world. The person who was interviewed discussed the importance of the hallucination and how it had provided food and money through its influence on other people they had met along the road. This young man did not believe at all in the process of thinking. There are reports that, among the religious youth, some feel that the "voice" is God, and they take orders for that reason.

Ideas of influence are prevalent in schizophrenia (70 per cent) and are a frequent—76 per cent—manifestation in the reactive psychosis of the schizophrenic form type (Retterstol 1966). The feeling of being controlled occurs in most, if not all, schizophrenics at one time or another, and for many of them it is a daily experience (Lehmann 1967). The situation of thought influence forms an important aspect of the delusion of persecution, for it is a persecution by powerful, mysterious agencies. Children who had hallucinations but were not psychotic have been found to take orders from their hallucinations (Levin 1936; Sherman and Beverly 1924), but hallucinations were also found in children who had a psychosis with convulsive disorders (81 per cent) schizophrenic (70 per cent), and behavior disorders (35 per cent) (Jaffe 1966). Egdell and Kolvin (1972) have made a critical review of the literature dealing with childhood hallucinations. In the case of childhood psychoses with an onset between five and fifteen years, they observed that 81 per cent of the patients hallucinated. Among medical patients who were not mentally ill, 29 per cent reported instructions as a theme in their hallucinatory experience, some 41 per cent of the alcoholics reported that they had instructions concerning the management of everyday affairs as a type of hallucination, and 65 per cent of the schizophrenics reported the same kind of hallucinatory experience (Mott, Small, and Anderson

1965). The various responses to hallucinations explain some of the un-
predictability of those who suffer from this serious symptom.

In order to correct the problem, it is necessary to know what factors cause ʈhe hallucinatory suggestibility. In 1843, James Braid gave
artificial somnambulism the name *hypnosis*. The concept of suggestibility as an explanation of hypnotic phenomena was introduced, and it replaced the theory of animal magnetism. Gradually, miscellaneous phenomena with some similarity to hypnotic suggestions were included under
the heading of hypnosis, such as ideomotor acts of an automatic character. In regard to scientific knowledge on the subject of hypnosis, the
scientific facts are meager. To digress in a lengthy discourse on whether
or not hallucinations are always found in hypnosis is not the point. The
point is rather to glean information about suggestibility in order that this
knowledge can be applied in helping the patient who takes suggestions
from hallucinations. To have a controversy about whether or not a
schizophrenic can be hypnotized is also of no value to the issue at hand,
which is correcting the morbid behavior associated with hallucinations.

The older clinical literature concerning hallucinations and hypnosis
is of interest because it indicates a certain relationship between the two
phenomena (Harris 1908). Boismont (1855) observed that "hallucinatory 'conversations in thoughts' present numerous points of resemblance
with the phenomena observed in magnetism." Parish (1897) states that
the suggested hallucinations of hypnosis extend to the posthypnotic
state, and while in the majority of cases the appearance of suggested
hallucinations are sufficient to induce a more or less pronounced hyp-
noid condition, there are other subjects who, while responding to the
suggestions, remain to all appearance in the normal state. Such cases recall the hallucinations of paranoia. Hallucinations can occur in the case
of magnetic somnambulists to such a degree that the experimenter ceases
to exert any power over them at all. An indication of the importance of
hallucinations in this state is noted in a case of a French Army officer,
who stated: "She whispers to me constantly. . . . Nobody, she said, would
think of pain if it were not for her suggestions and stimulation by the
electro-magnetic fluid" (Landis 1965). Janet (1906, 1925) relevantly
emphasized that the hypnotic state is identical with somnabulism, and
that there is an overabundance of hallucinations of all senses. He also
stated that suggestibility is a serious symptom of mental illness. Other
investigators, such as Sully (1886) and Maudsley (1895), have observed that hypnosis includes hallucinations.

In 1959, the psychologist Marcuse stated: "Methods of hypnotic induction may be thought of as including three types. One is characterized by a bare statement to the subject in hypnosis of the end desired. Two is characterized by a full description of even minor details of the situation. Three utilizes the hallucinations possible in hypnosis. Generally no one method is present alone, but one of the three will predominate" (Marcuse 1959). A description was made by Stephen Blac (1971) who stated: "By further direct suggestion under hypnosis of aural hallucination, the subject will carry on conversation with the image. . . . In this fantasy situation, not all subjects speak loud and await an unheard reply, but many 'carry on the conversations' in silence before reporting." Further literature dealing with the subject of hypnosis and hallucinations can be found in Hilgard's (1965) extensive work.

Contemporary studies on suggestibility indicate that the person takes orders for many reasons. This could be prevented if the knowledge is applied. The term *suggestion* is usually restricted to the motor actions brought about by verbal instructions. Coffin (1941) has emphasized that a suggestion primarily functions as a frame of reference or a standard of judgment and is accepted by the individual without intervention of critical thought processes. Proneness to suggestions is promoted by any condition which produces either an inhibition or the dissociation of critical thinking (Cantril 1948). Any factor that inhibits or interferes with thought, such as depression, excitement, or fear, increases the taking of suggestions or orders. This latter finding is a basic consideration because of the importance of the thinking disturbance that the mental patient has as a symptom. This explains one important reason why hallucinated suggestions are taken and placed into action. An important inhibitor condition concerning thought is motivation. Reasoning gets inhibited by "wishful thinking" and bewildering hallucinatory situations, for which the person needs interpretations. He has a fixed idea or interpretation of a situation and hence a "will to believe" such things as Nazi party doctrines and other delusions.

Proneness to suggestions is found in groups of individuals who have comparatively little experience, and consequently, possess less knowledge. However, as their training increases, their taking of orders diminishes. This is an important fact, for when a patient first starts to hallucinate he has no knowledge about the situation, and as information concerning the experience increases, the problem of suggested hallucinations may decrease. Individuals will take orders from those "voices" that have prestige, and they will take suggestions if the majority of patients are of that opinion. If a number of individuals makes the same suggestion, the person in question will take the command. When an older person makes a request, the younger individual is more likely to respond. Many will take orders because they believe it to be a rational process (Asch 1959).

All of the preceding reasons for taking suggestions have been observed in hallucinating individuals as the causes for their resulting acts. If the situation is vague and unstructured, as in a hallucinatory situation, then internal factors such as attitudes are important determinants, because the cognitive functions are decided by the objective stimulus situation and by various internal factors such as needs, past learning, and mental sets. Primary suggestibility can be likened to a conditioned reflex situation (Stukat 1958, Welch 1947) in that the person is not thinking, and thus he has no way of using an inhibiting force over the orders and eliciting the response to the ideomotor suggestion (Maslow and Mittleman 1941). Pavlov defined part of psychosis as a hypnotic condition. Janet felt that in hysterical behavior the patient takes suggestions because he is unable to synthesize mentally and to dissociate because the mental functions are fragmentary. Suggestibility is found in the normal and the neurotic. In the latter it can be as great as in the psychotic, according to Eysenck's work. In the neurotic, it is found more frequently because of anxiety, inferiority feeling, a moderate thinking disorder, and the lack of confidence, which accounts for the need to conform and to submit to opinions of others. Hospitalization increases suggestibility, and it almost seems like a tradition for the patients to take commands from hallucinations.

One must be cognizant that whether or not direct observations indicate that the person is under the influence of hallucinations, the patient might have been taking orders from "voices" in the past or could be affected by them in the future. It is imperative to explain clearly to the patient why other individuals do take orders, yet stressing that none of the reasons are ever valid. Patients will imitate other persons on the ward or at home and must be cautioned not to go along with the "voices."

The vast majority of persons can be helped by knowledge given to them concerning hallucinated commands. Brierre de Boismont (1855) wrote over a hundred years ago: "When hallucinations exercise no evil influence on conduct it is physiologically normal; but when hallucinations incite to murder, to suicide, to the performance of a capable or ridiculous action it is evidently morbid."

*Dream not of having tasted all the grandeur and wildness
of fancy till you have gone mad!—Charles Lamb*

5.
The Condition of
Hallucinating

"The 'voices' are the means by which the megalomaniac realizes his wishes; the religiously preoccupied achieves his communication with God and the angels; the depressed are threatened with every kind of catastrophe; the persecuted curse night and day" (Bleuler 1950). Delusions have presented serious problems to both the history of mankind and the individual who suffers from them, for in delusions we observe man irretrievably lost in untruth (Jasper 1963). From time immemorial, delusions have been taken as one of the basic characteristics of mental illness. Paranoid fantasies have been diffused throughout whole populations, not only during the Middle Ages, but also during the Renaissance and even in the twentieth century. From the legal point of view, the "absence or presence of delusion is the true and only test or criterion of insanity. . . . Evidence of multiple delusion and hallucination is the most powerful to show insanity" (American Law Reports 1948). The legal dictionary *Words and Phrases* (1940-52) states: "Delusion means a belief in a state or condition of things, the existence of which no rational person would believe."

What is the root of this problem? According to Maudsley (1895): "Disordered sensations have much to do with inspiring insane delusions and even in forming their structure." Sigmund Freud (1956) explained that the two chief characteristics of delusions are expressed through psychic symptoms and through a state in which fantasies have assumed control. Delusions have been distinguished by Jasper (1963) as having hallucinatory vividness and diminished cognizance. He observes that with every hallucination there is a need to regard the hallucinated object as real, and when the patient retains this false judgment of reality, we are dealing with a delusion. The sensory experience is composed of illusory, hallucinatory, and pseudohallucinatory contents, and thinking about the things so perceived gives them a new and special reality as well as the significance of a belief. Stoddart (1919) states that the most frequently exciting causes of delusions are the hallucinations. "This will be readily understood," he says, "for if a person is not to believe the evidence of his senses, what is he to believe? If God appears to him in the heavens it is not very unreasonable for him to conclude that he is the elect of God." Landis (1964) noted that persistent hallucinations may furnish the basis for delusions. He states: "Supernatural voices heard by the patient will continue to maintain the delusion and reinforce the patient's conviction in his deluded beliefs."

Forrer (1963) wrote that the contents of delusions are hallucinations, and Cameron (1963) states that delusions are an attempt to include internally generated fantasy material with the representation of external reality. In a statistical study concerning hallucinations and delusions, it was found that there is a positive relationship between no hallucinations and no delusions, and a striking association between persecutory delusions and auditory hallucinations (Bowman and Raymond 1931). The conclusion of a review dealing with the theories and explanations of delusions is that little is known which has a scientific basis with controls, but we observe from the preceding that hallucinations are much involved with the production of delusions (Arthur 1964).

Eugene Bleuler (1950) states: "It is often impossible to make an exact distinction between delusions, illusions, and hallucinations. . . . The delusions, in large part, turn up in the form of hallucinations." He emphasized that the distortions of reality are most clearly expressed in the delusions and in hallucinations which are the deceptions of the senses. The disturbance in the thinking process of the mental patient leads to distortions in his conception of reality. When the faculty of logical reasoning is weakened, the influence of the emotions increases in strength. Thus, there are no longer any mental obstacles to the wish fulfillment as expressed in hallucinations, and the distortion reaches the proportions of delusional ideas. The hallucinations provide subject matter for the delusions, while the delusional thoughts provide a basis of interpretation for the hallucinatory experience (McKeller 1957).

Delusions involve a false belief that is based on a false premise, the fictional hallucination. There is a disturbance in regard to the formation of conclusions, the weighing of evidence, and the passing of judgments. One finds in delusions, misinterpretations and unwarranted inferences, and also that the idea held by the person is contrary to fact. The content of the delusion is impossible; it is engendered without appropriate external stimulation, and it is inappropriate and out of harmony with the person's education and intelligence. One of the striking features of an insane delusion is the imperviousness to opposing arguments, as the person preserves his belief in spite of the most convincing demonstration of its falseness.

In order to understand a false belief, it is necessary to comprehend what is meant by the term *belief*. In regard to the amount of knowledge, we find that one can have faith in something not backed by any evidence, while, in contrast, a belief must rest on some knowledge (Quinton 1967). It is usual for belief to rest on something the believer regards as evidence, whether or not it lends any real support to the belief. Thus, we find that a belief has only a little evidence in support of it. Belief is also characterized by an inner state accessible to introspection, and is a matter of volition with thought associated in the formation of the belief. There is a feeling of conviction or assurance with the belief, and this may vary in degree, for it has an emotional part, the condition of affect or the emotion of preferring. In believing, there is a dispositional readiness to act or a tendency to action. Alexander Bain states: "Belief has not meaning except in reference to our actions" (Quinton 1967).

One of the most important aspects of delusions is the deep sense of subjectivity that goes with the experience of the hallucinations of inner speech. It is basic knowledge that the inner speech of the normal person is subjective in nature and characterized by a lack of objectivity (Werner and Kaplan 1967). The objectification of external speech is explicit and lexical, while silent speech uses vague similies and metaphors, which are of a lower degree of objectification. Inner speech is idiomatic, idiosyncratic, and personal, with the ideas aroused by inner speech words dominating the stable meaning of words expressed aloud. In the schizophrenic, inner language is even more subjective than in the normal, and the hallucinations of inner speech are subjective in nature.

The few subvocal thoughts which the patient has at hand are not objective enough to arrive at correct views concerning his delusions.

There is a reflex acceptance of subjective hallucinatory beliefs. The physiological response of the patient to the interruptions by the hallucinations of his retarded stream of silent speech is inhibition, followed by excitement, which in turn produces many other emotions. In addition, the hallucinated sound by itself activates the central nervous system and causes excitement, which further facilitates affect and which colors the hallucinatory words in a subjective way. The intrinsic nature of subjectivity associated with inner speech and the emotional excitement produced by interruption and activation converge. This causes the person to subjectively believe anything heard by hallucinating. The schizophrenic is not able to keep his responses to the fantasy processes separate from the objective external world because of his disorganized and bizarre inner communication. The organization of thought, which could have been used in the process of relating to life in a more objective way, is lost.

The subjective emotional nature of hallucinations causes abnormal imagination. The hallucinations come with their accompanying emotional nature to produce reflexes of pathological imagination. This causes functional changes in the central nervous system (Charcot 1877). In his "Des Puissances Trompeuses," Blaise Pascal made this statement concerning imagination: "It is this deceiving power in man: this mistress of error and falsehood and so much the more deceptive, that it does not always seem so. . . . Reason in vain protests against this. . . . This proud power-enemy of Reason, which finds a pleasure in controlling it and dominating that faculty with the view of showing how potent she is in all circumstances, has established in man a second nature." The patient involuntarily absorbs the fantasy material, because the private nature of inner speech causes a private meaning of imagination. What is heard and said is an assertion. It may be aimed at truth and based on some evidence, but it results in a facilitation of neurological systems which deal with imagination and cause motor acts. There is an inability to comprehend the significance of the meaning of what is heard in the hallucinatory experience, for the serious lack of inner speech as used in thinking lessens the person's ability to recall meanings of words used in the recognition and control of imagination. Pathological imagination produces emotions, feelings, and actions so powerful that the mechanisms of the central nervous system are either hyper-stimulated or hyper-inhibited, resulting in symptoms which are normally associated with structural diseases (Charcot 1877).

The small amount of knowledge that forms the basis of the delusion comes from the hallucinatory experience, and in reacting, the patient forms a fixed proposition which reinforces the evidence of the senses. Voluntarily, the person prefers the dogmatic unreasonable belief because the high emotional interest associated with the conviction lends assurance and confidence to the belief. The person then acts in accordance with the delusion. It has long been the opinion of many authorities that the subjective emotional mood of the patient experiencing the delusion prevents reason from changing his incorrect view.

In trying to oppose or change a delusion, one must be careful about the relationship between the belief and the resulting motor act. To change a belief is difficult, but the opposing of the abnormal motor behavior is not impossible, for this behavior can be prevented. False beliefs can only lead to false ways of behaving. The motor act can be changed much more easily than the belief, which is like a strong opinion. The principles of suggestibility are involved in the formation of the belief. This can easily be seen in the delusions of the Nazi party members, delusions which were created by suggestibility on the part of Hitler, who at the time had prestige. The subjective sources of the hallucination depend on such suggestibility factors as whether it is coming from an older person or from many different persons. The state of mind of the person who perceives the hallucination depends on his experience and on his believing that the hallucination is rational. The knowledge concerning the rules of suggestibility can be applied, for again, the patient should be told not to act on what is heard in the hallucinatory episode.

A person can believe something because he lacks knowledge. Papez (1957) states: "Ignorance permits belief in things unseen, but firmly told." A good example is that of a person who hears the hallucinatory voice saying "kill." An emotional response occurs in his imagination, and the individual believes that he is going to be killed by the unseen voice. This is a type of delusion often observed among the inmates of prisons. To use the terms of that world, the "voices" con the person into morbid behavior. The person might go to a police station, take asylum, go to an accident ward, or even kill someone under the influence of the false belief. The subjective material of the hallucination is incorrect or mistaken, and any other reaction besides thinking how unreal or false the knowledge is will only lead to a type of behavior which, in its simplest expression, is abnormal behavior. The unreality of the delusion breeds a form of unreal behavior, for the person's actions are a fantasy of movements, like running after a mirage. The patient is misled and deceived by the false beliefs into doing pathological acts. Knowledge about delusions must be given to the patient in order to correct this tragic situation.

Another delusion that fits some of the preceding format is that of a God delusion held by a patient. A portion of the first therapy session with such a patient is as follows:

PATIENT: They develop this idea of a God complex; and the way this is enacted on the ward is the patients actually do go out and look for God. They start hallucinating afar. It is a hunt, a quest, like for anything, to find this person. They go to great lengths to hunt for God, and they'll spend hours asking and talking and inquiring as to where He is. And this of course is very strange behavior indeed.

DOCTOR: I understood you to say "God"—You said "God" didn't you?

PATIENT: God, G-o-d.

DOCTOR: Oh, God.

PATIENT: The classical.

DOCTOR: Yes.

PATIENT: God.

DOCTOR: And God is an actual figure?

PATIENT: Well, they feel that they want to find Him; that is the patients' point of view and they will go looking for Him.

DOCTOR: What is the concept of God, I mean, what kind of individual is He supposed to be? Or does everybody have different concepts of Him?

PATIENT: Well, I think of God in the sense that He's a spirit, something like the spirit of Christmas.

DOCTOR: What about the other patients?

PATIENT: I think they think of Him in terms of a person. They go hunting for Him, for God; it is actually a quest to find Him. Of course, they don't succeed in this, but they try.

The person stated that one day he heard a number of other patients on a ward in hallucinatory conversations trying to hear God talking as a biblical "voice behind a bush." He felt that this was the classical God complex that he had heard about, and in order to understand this situation, he joined the other patients in their quest to hear God's voice. After a period of time, he came to the conclusion that God just didn't talk from a bush; yet the false belief created in him the strong emotional idea that since God did not speak that way, and there must be a God because of the stars, it would then follow that he was God, for God could be no one else. The person then acted on the belief that if this were the case, then he could fall over dead and wake himself up again. He proceeded to fall to the floor in a faint, and then he got up. This was the effect of pathological imagination. This experience led to the conviction that he was the reincarnated God, having started the universe many light years before.

A talk with a minister about his delusion helped correct the situation, but then he heard prestigous "voices" telling him that he was God. The situation then became a serious problem. He had spoken about this with his analyst, but again the "voices" continued to maintain the delusion. He dreamt at night about the delusion, adding to his suffering. The patient now believes that God is an occurrence which started everything and is not a thing, but rather is catalytic and cannot be reincarnated, and is thus a spirit which is everywhere.

Another type of God complex is that of a person, who, when first hearing a hallucination, thought that it was God talking. This is rather easy to correct, and a direct explanation about hallucinations of inner speech works well. This type of experience is as old as the governors of Israel who sought the counsel of God through the medium of a high priest. "God gave the high priest an answer in the same manner as He did unto Moses, that is, by an 'audible voice' from the mercy-seat which is behind the veil" (Clissold 1870).

Lord Brain (1955) states: "A word to the nervous system is something more than any one of the innumerable ways in which it can be pronounced or written." There is a neurophysiological disposition through which the words evoke strong meanings, and in the case of hallucinated words, they cause powerful responses. The patient can hear hallucinatory "voices" saying that he is going to be placed in a cloth bag and taken to a crematory. This throws the person into severe anxiety, because of his abnormal imagination. The person, by hallucinated inner speech, says many things which he believes cause events. In some cases this may lead to guilt and remorse such as when the patient sits and tries to cause automobile accidents by hallucinatory influences, thinking they are effective when they are not. That the nonverbal cerebral mechanisms fail in preventing such beliefs may be due to the fact that the formulation of the experience is such that there is a complete embodiment in personalized reactions and the idiosyncratic contents. The relatively abstract qualities of the autonomous medium, even if they could be articulated, are thus of little value (Werner and Kaplan 1967).

E. Bleuler (1950) pointed out that the delusional ideas are not infrequently suggested or manufactured by another psyche, and that the fantasy material is included with representations of external reality. His idea is that the content of delusions and hallucinations can only be understood and conceived of in terms of definite external events, and that there can be no symptoms without content. A delusion of influence with external events playing a role was experienced by John Perceval (1840), who stated: "This also is curious, that when I was eating my breakfast, the voice about me often said, 'If you will do so and so, we will ask for another piece of bread and butter for you' and if I obeyed, without my needing to speak, the servant, after looking attentively at me, would come and offer me the bread and butter."

Delusions are common among schizophrenics. In one study of 405 schizophrenics, 71 per cent had delusions of various types (Lucas, Sansbury, and Collins 1962). Of the remaining 29 per cent, some had such gross thought disorders that no delusions could be elicited (35 per cent) and others were mute (16 per cent). The delusions of inferiority concerned beliefs about sin, crime, poverty, and unworthiness. Delusions of the grandiose type were found to deal with beliefs of authority, power, wealth, social status, and special skills or abilities. Those with a paranoid delusion of persecution believed that people, such as their neighbors, work-mates, or members of their families, were causing them to suffer. In some cases the persecuting agency was said to be Freemasons, Jews, or Communists. Sexual delusions were expressed by others, such as being married, pregnant, or a father to children.

Some delusions are not related to hallucinations. Observations from history (Hofstadter 1967; Cohn 1970) indicate that delusions are found in a large number of persons. It seems correct to state that individuals who do not hallucinate can become delusional, or a person may have delusions without hallucinations. It seems possible that the egocentrism, which Toynbee observed as being a serious problem in society, as discussed by Lidz (1973) in relationship to mental illness, plays a role in the formation of delusions. Individuals, because of unconscious subjective feelings, distort reality to satisfy their own point of view. This type of delusion seems easier to change than the ones that come directly from hallucinations.

The most serious schizophrenic symptom is the thinking disorder. E. Bleuler (1840) observes that a complex is touched upon in the development of the disturbance, and that this complex is generally connected with delusions and hallucinations. The complex is an emotionally charged generalized idea, made up of interrelated ideas which form a system of memories, desires, and motivations, exerting a dominating influence over the individual's personality. The images are traces of prior hallucinatory experiences, and they form ideas which, when interrelated with moods and emotions, produce the complex. In a situation of this nature we have added together hallucinations, delusions, emotions, and poor thinking ability. The complexes appear as fully developed delusional systems. They express themselves by way of the hallucinations, and form a world of their own without taking reality into consideration. These complexes also dominate the personality, which then loses unity. The particularly poor intellectual performances of the patients are a result of the emotionally toned complexes. "For the most part, the reality value of hallucinations is as great as that of real perceptions or even greater. Whenever reality and hallucination conflict, it is usually the latter which is considered as real. . . . The 'voices' of our patient embody his entire transformed relationship to the external world" (Bleuler 1950). One of the fundamental situations characteristic of schizophrenia is the predilection for fantasy or the inclination to divorce oneself from reality through the hallucinations, delusions, and complexes.

In the mental hospital and penal institution, there exists an organized hallucinatory fantasy life of a morbid type, which can form the serious problem of complexes. There is not a single hallucinatory complex, but a number of them affecting thinking and behavior. Many patients, shortly after they begin to hallucinate, formulate the strong idea that they like to hallucinate (Bleuler 1950; Kraepelin 1919; Modell 1958, 1960). Lowe (1973) observed that hallucinatory events can be of a positive import to patients; they find them protective, entertaining, exploratory, reassuring, or comforting. They indulge in their hallucinations which are obviously pleasant, for hallucinating is a new experience and a new function. They very much enjoy learning how to use their subvocal speech in their subjective conversations with others around them, and they find these hallucinations of great interest. This, in turn, motivates them to hallucinate excessively. They do not understand how they can silently speak to and hear other patients. Thus, they become curious about this mysterious skill.

The sounds of the words they hear spoken by others are external and directional to the patients in that they can identify who is speaking in the room. The phenomenon was described by Calmeil (1840) as follows: "Many of the alienated also establish the fact, that in speaking or in writing, there is a distinction between the thoughts which they judge to belong to themselves and those which they judge to proceed from another source and which constitute simply their hallucinations." Calmeil (1840) also wrote clearly about the adverse affect hallucinations have on thinking. The patients learn how to project their "voices" at a considerable distance, and they are not at all upset when no one is physically present in their room. Yet they still hear another person speaking by hallucinated inner speech. One patient with paranoia stated: "I have but to think a thought, and it reaches other minds in sound without an effort on my part and is sounded for a distance, I suppose, of two or three miles. Of course, my silent thought is sometimes indignant and that reaching other minds keeps the ball rolling" (Landis 1964). The patient becomes preoccupied with this fascinating change in himself.

An example from a patient:

DOCTOR: There must be some positive sort of gratification in it, some positive value to it, isn't . . .

PATIENT: Well, of course, it is the thing that is found there and they are, of course, pushed into this . . . you know. They are maneuvered into this environment. So they find in it a positive way, well, I suppose, I can hardly say rewarding, oh, it gives them some sense of the world of hallucinations. Of course, it is all very new to them. They are hallucinating, and I guess it is something interesting, perhaps, you know, these other people talking, what they have to say, even though it is so completely incorrect. It fills this void, so to speak, and they go along with these things, but generally speaking, they are not thinking so well, and so they have very little recourse except to hallucinate, you see, there is a great deal of talking going on.

Often the patients do not even realize that they are not thinking with inner speech until it is too late and the habit becomes defective. The hallucinations of thinking affect normal thought, and this process is insidious, but with no sick or unpleasant feeling accompanying it. Various ideas facilitate hallucinating, and one of them is that the ability of hallucinating makes the person different from, and even better than, other individuals. Another complex is the idea that other people are listening to the patient's thoughts, and because the thoughts are private, the patient will stop thinking in order to prevent other persons from hearing his inner speech. Another complex concerns the rapid inner speech found during the period of time in the patient's life just before the beginning of his hallucinated inner speech. The person believes that he has been thinking too much and that this has caused the illness and hallucinations. He can feel strongly about this idea, and, when asked to start thinking again, the person will refuse. It may be that the patient develops an idea that hallucinating is a wise thing to do, and he believes in the new function, thereby developing a belief in the process as being important. He feels a need to hallucinate.

Hallucinatory complexes are, at best, a difficult subject, and in the recorded observations (Jung 1960), the material seems odd and peculiar. For example, there is the common fantasy of the sleeping emperor (Cohn 1957), known on the wards of the mental hospital as the complex of "life forever." An historical example of such a fantasy is Baldwin IX. After he was put to death, a legend arose that he was not dead, but that having sinned greatly, he was discharging a penance by being forced to live in obscurity as a beggar and hermit. In 1224, a man who was a typical prophet and hermit announced that he was Baldwin. As a result, a civil war broke out. He was later identified in Burgandy as one Bertrand of Ray.

A similar case in history is that of Frederick I, who perished on the Third Crusade in 1190; later, reports of a new Frederick occurred. There was also a Frederick II who died in 1250, and again there was a resurrected Frederick II. A former hermit near Wounds was found to be a pseudo-Frederick and was burnt at the stake, and someone else claimed three days later that he also was Frederick II, and was executed in Utrecht. In 1434, however, it was believed that Frederick II was still alive, and a man named Konrad Schmit emerged from the Kyffhauser mountains as the resurrected Frederick II (Cohn 1957).

On wards of some mental hospitals, the patient is brought into the society of hallucinations and he wishes to live forever. He may even ask overtly about knowledge concerning life without end and receive answers, but some of the answers are not valid from any point of view. For example, a patient may be told by hallucinatory voices that eating feces and semen helps the lungs, and that drinking urine and hitting one's head time and time against a wall help to prolong life. He may be told via hallucination to drink water at the fountain. He will do this to such an extent that water intoxication may result (reported in Great Britain and in America). The observation made is that the patient has a "water complex." Help is requested from older "life-forever men" or "brain men," who say that they are fixing the brain, or some other part of the body, by using the method of possessing. An individual can spend months learning to do the various things which an hallucination says will prolong life. As he runs to hit his head on the wall, he may cry out, "Head smash," as he puts his head on his chest, he may say, "Go," or when he drinks orange juice, he may ask for "Ga."

The position of the body is like that of human decerebrate rigidity or rigor mortis. Voices tell the person that he is in a state much like death and that he should not breathe. All of this indicates that the person is in a state of being alive when dead, which is perhaps a motor projicience of the tegmental response originating from coma centers (Johnson 1952); the opposite would deal with life. The patient may believe that his injections from the nurse are from Tibet and will keep him alive, and even that the food is special food which will prolong life. The patient may have a delusion that the chair contains little injection needles that give him special medicines.

One can perhaps understand the situation by considering the tape recordings of a therapy session, in which the patient's words often convey more meaning than is usually found in just a summary.

PATIENT: In this "life-forever" business, they'll [the voices] tell the patient to put a little lettuce in the coffee, and they'll say that this acts as a catalyst for life-giving coffee, or, how should I say, compound drink, the golden cup. And they will use other things such as fruits and indicate their importance, like, one thing that comes to mind, peaches. They'll say that these are very good for you and things like that.

DOCTOR: M-hm.

PATIENT: And they'll stress Chinese food, and so on. So they have a whole group of little tales that tell about food and what have you.

DOCTOR: You were thoroughly convinced of all this stuff, of all these beliefs, when you were actually up on the closed ward?

PATIENT: Well, sometimes I must confess I was pretty stupid about things, but as I told you, usually at night before going to sleep, I would say, the day is over, I've learned what there is to learn, and I'm putting it behind me. But you get impressions, you know. You get the idea, for instance, that sometimes these things are inadvertently fostered by a nurse or someone, that they know a little bit about what's going on, perhaps not enough to verbalize about or anything, and they'll add credulence to the situation by saying, 'Yes, the injection is for your health,' when they are talking about it. It might be out of context even. But sometimes you get these ideas from people who are on the staff. New patients particularly think that the injections are going to help them. And they believe that they come out of . . . ah . . . they aren't . . . they don't believe that they are regular medicines, that they're something else.

DOCTOR: What is the "something else"?

PATIENT: Something directly given for staying alive. Some special compound or what have you. This business about . . . um . . . this cult "life-forever" ran rampant during hydrotherapy. There was a great deal of emphasis on it. And almost every patient who went into hydrotherapy got involved in it, one way or the other. And they would often sit around, or lie around, rather, in hydro and shout, "Go, go," and practice putting their heads upon their chests, and it became sort of a fad, almost. I think the hardest thing was that you got this impression that the people knew about it in the hospital. And everything, of course, was done with the idea that this was all hush-hush, all mysterious, all undercover and shouldn't be spoken about. The general format was you should not say these things aloud. You shouldn't talk to people about them. This was the general impression you got, so that everything was very, ah, mysterious, and you got misled, and so on—I think this was the most difficult thing to get over, the ability to relate these things. You bury these thoughts, and this mysticism gets in you. It sort of starts creeping around. Everything is done very secretively, and so on, and it's very bad. Right?

The French neurophysiologist Paul Chauchard (1962) states: "Humanity limited by death might perhaps be driven to disgust with life, especially because the technical world seems to be despiritualizing." Neurophysiology leaves us free to reflect on such subjects, which concern religion and life everlasting, and which are not grounds for legal insanity (American Law Reports 1948). "Religion is a bridge to another civilization," writes Toynbee, and its aspirations are an important part of being civilized. Cameron and Margaret (1951) pointed out that delusions have produced good things for mankind. In the case of the life-everlasting complex, it is important that one be extremely careful to dissect away what is false and morbid from what is aspirational and correct. Historically, to bother someone who was dead was felt to be sacrilegious: "Well may they exclaim, like the ghost of Samuel in the sacred story, 'Why hast thou disquieted me?' " (Godwin 1834). The reason that Vesalius came before the Inquisition and that he later died during the trip on which they sent him was that he had tried to resuscitate a dead person. The story is, "As Vesalius, the physician of Philip II, was opening the thorax of a Spanish gentleman, the heart palpitated. Death also occurred here. Vesalius was brought before the Inquisition" (Dendy 1847).

At one time all the modern methods of resuscitation and intensive care would have been classified as insane delusions. A paradox that is basic to neurology and psychiatry is the concept of a "seat of life" which was looked for by the "enemy's knife and the surgeon's scalpel," as stated in a history of neurology (Reiese 1959).

Hallucinations have been observed in the sane (Forrer 1960a; Medlicott 1958; Noland 1928). One instance of this concerns hearing voices of the spirits of the dead (Dewi Rees 1971; Mott, Small, and Anderson 1965; MacRobert 1949-50). Papez (1937) states in a paper in which he describes the mechanism of emotion: "There seems to be ample justification for the ancient view of La Peyroni, professor of surgery at Monpellier, who on basis of such clinical experience expressed the belief that the region of the corpus callosum is the 'seat of the soul.' " In his laboratory was a brain sent to him from Buffalo, New York. It lacked the corpus callosum as well as the center of the brain. Doctor Papez said that "the clinical case had no spirit."

In the hallucinogenic society of the wards, a patient can develop a complex about spies and security. The patient says that the hallucinations must be kept secret because the government is using them as a method for secret agents. He believes that each ward has its own degree of classification and that only certain things are taught about the subject because of security. Patients note that bonafide organizations such as the Navy's SEC can come to the ward in their hallucinations. Patients take this business of secrecy to heart and spend many hours on the subject, learning such things as codes and secret ways of hallucinating. The complex concerning spies and clandestine hallucinating is one of the many reasons why a patient will not discuss hallucinations with his doctor.

Patients can also have complexes that they belong to various organizations such as a military group by the name of World Organization. The patient may have the delusion that there are cars with special radio equipment that are sending and receiving the hallucinations. Sometimes a plot will take place around a city or in the general vicinity of a hospital, and the plot will be acted out. One patient who said that he was a member of this group was involved in a plan dealing with various people. In this hallucinatory episode he predicted that someone who was driving a car was going to be hit by another car. According to the patient, this accident did occur and the person was hospitalized as a result.

Other patients talk about a hallucinatory group called "All." This organization is made up of hallucinists who deal with knowledge about other individuals and events and who use their hallucinatory information in various ways. Another group goes under the name "War Plot" and is made up of military men and leaders from various countries. In the minds of some patients it was active during the Warsaw Pact days of Stalin. One vice-admiral, who was a patient in the veterans administration, said aloud that the group was present during World War II on a flag ship in the Pacific. The situation seemed somewhat similar to an actual historical event with leaders coming together like specters in the air during their meetings. Thus, the following words of a patient are of considerable interest:

PATIENT: One of these things that I mentioned was war plans. This was when it seemed like the Navy came in pretty strong, not only one of them, but a group, half a dozen to a dozen. And they'd sit around and hallucinate on the ward. It became very difficult to ascertain who was talking. You were not quite sure whether the patient was sitting there talking or somebody from the outside. And this seemed to be done under the heading of Admiral X. He seemed to be the principal person, at least that is what the one man said.

DOCTOR: Did Admiral X himself?

PATIENT: Apparently so, from what was going on. This was a war plot. Seemed to have quite a bit to it. Other leaders would drift in from time to time, and it was sort of a cult, handed down to stir up the patients and other people who hallucinated with the end to cause a war. They would . . .

DOCTOR: This is a war on the ward or a war among . . .

PATIENT: A war, a national war.

DOCTOR: A national war.

PATIENT: In this case, it was directed toward Russia. And what he was doing, he was trying to get people apparently who talk, who hallucinate, to back this effort of war. Only it was a little bit more than that, because there were various leaders that would speak for a second or two and would come in for a moment, and the Admiral seemed to be a very powerful figure. And he dominated pretty well the ward. This was not only the case on the closed ward, but on the semiclosed ward. And he sat around for quite a long time. Of course, one thinks, this is who he said he was. I don't know. It seemed he committed all the actions. Perhaps in his old age he had resorted to such business, I don't know.

DOCTOR: Go ahead with your story.

PATIENT: I say some of these things are pretty well organized. At times they're a little more efficient than you would think. They know pretty much what they can accomplish and so on. The person is told to do something and he does this. He's given a suggestion. And he knows it is a hallucination when he is accomplishing whatever he was told to do. You get the idea that these things are quite potent at times, that they do cause certain things to occur. It is just not a lot of talk. And actually they can through suggestions cause fights and disturbances. In other words it is as potent as walking down there and telling a person aloud to do something. In fact, it is more potent than that, because it has this mysteriousness associated with it, and also the person isn't thinking, and so he has a very hard time combating hallucinations, and he's very easy game for the suggestions.

Patients reported that the hallucinatory suggestions went on for months, with the patients and their friends under the influence of the voices from military leaders. The hallucinations would order the patients to perform actions which were training to bomb Russia and China as specters pushed their buttons for World War III. One patient reported that War Plot was changed in 1960 to Peace Planning, and the leaders from various countries had meetings. These hallucinated conferences had something to do with ending the Cold War and with the cultural renaissance in the West and in China. One could write this all off as a delusion of grandeur on the part of the patient, but such situations are what history records as being effective in causing events in society (Cohn 1957).

Criminal topics also play a role in the patient's life, for at times he hallucinates about narcotics and various crime organizations. A patient who had stopped using heroin stated that he had hallucinations while he was on heroin and that he still had them. One young man who was taking heroin would run around saying, "It is you over there who is hallucinating." Another patient, who had been using heroin, would take orders from voices to hit his head against a window, cutting himself in the act. Some patients have fantasies about criminals. They play as if these criminals were present, and they often have olfactory hallucinations which produce gunsmoke odors. Even poison gas can be produced in visual hallucinations. In contrast, the inmates in prison sometimes hallucinate about money, with autism being that of acting out the role of a business man. They use a hand sign language, which has been found in England (Chapman 1966) to be associated with schizophrenia, and they believe that this will be the language of the future.

In the schizophrenic, the primary visual complex concerns the illusion of someone looking through the eyes of the patient, or the patient himself, by a visual hallucination, sees what another person is visualizing. This is "seeing things" that others are looking at, and this phenomenon first occurs when the patient starts to read something such as a book. E. Bleuler (1950) says: "It is remarkable that the voices can utter what is contained in one or many lines perceived by the eye at the time." The "voice" says to the person, "I can see what you are reading," and it then proceeds to read along with the patient who is trying to read the literature silently. The "voice," in the slang of the mental hospital, is called a "reader." The words are inserted into the patient's tongue while he sits and looks at the written work, and the insertion totally interrupts the ability of the person to read by himself. The individual listens to the "voice" as it reads the material through his eyes, and he cannot comprehend the significance of the words to the degree that would normally take place. One person, even after he was discharged from a hospital, spent eight hours one day trying to read material at his place of work, and all the time during this period a "voice" would read along. The inner speech of the patient is completely blocked by the hallucinatory reader's voice.

The visual hallucination of looking through someone else's visual system and "seeing things" is taught to the patient by the hallucinatory voices. The common method told to a patient is the imitation of the posture of another patient. The "voices" will say to place the arm, leg, and head in the same position as the other person has his head or body placed in space. Then, almost as if he were a resonating structure, the patient peers through one eye of the other person. Another method is that of imitating the total posture of the person by walking behind the individual like a zombie, and then looking through both eyes. Much time is spent in this type of behavior, and the person believes that he can see what another individual is looking at rather well. Visual hallucinations as caused by drugs are discussed by Kluver (1966) and Siegel and West (1975).

Almost equally as frequent as the auditory hallucinations are the delusions and illusions relating to the different body organs. They are the hallucinations of body sensation, and among these hallucinations the sexual ones are the most frequent and the most important (Bleuler 1950, Modell 1958). The most common hallucination of body sensation is based on possessing, which is an ancient subject (Oesterreich 1930), but patients are still much involved in this type of behavior. The act of possessing is the same as in the visual illusion of "seeing things" that another person is seeing. The person imitates the posture of the person to be possessed. The major point of this to the patient is the basic motivation of sex, as the person wishes to experience the feelings associated with the sexual sensory areas of the body. Overindulgence in this hallucinatory behavior can affect the sensations associated with the surface of the body, leaving the patient with no feelings. There is apparently a total adaptation caused by being excessively possessed by another individual, and the sensations as experienced during sexual behavior can be adversely affected.

Another motivation is the idea that possessing can cause injury to another person, because blood vessels can be broken in the brain, heart, and eyes. Although hallucinatory sensations are reported to be associated with this type of behavior, there is no evidence of injury to structures. Patients state that being possessed can have unpleasant effects in which the sensations of the person are completely dominated by the somatic feelings of another person. Thought insertion can take place with the possessing, and, in this case, the hallucinatory words are projected into the tongue of the patient. The continuous flow of hallucinated subvocal speech is interjected, blocking all attempts at normal thought and preventing any hallucinated inner speech.

E. Bleuler (1950) states: "Where delusions and hallucinations are in the foreground, one speaks of the paranoid type." This kind of person hallucinates so much that, in time, he often has a fantasy in which he hears the most unpleasant words persecuting him. Rather than thinking a lot about the situation, when it gets difficult, the person stops thinking and does not solve the problem, but withdraws from society into the world of hallucinations. The patient can be completely gullible, because there is no check and balance by thought as to what is fiction or fact. In the normal situation, the thought processes can shape man's concept of reality (Whorf 1956). One person who was not thinking believed that his arm had been cut off by an illusionary voice, causing him to enter an accident ward. Another patient went to the hospital because he thought he had been shot in the head. One patient stayed in bed for five months because he felt that someone had swallowed water into his lungs.

The condition of hallucinating is often a continuous activity which allocates little time for thought. In order to dramatize this situation, a day in the life of a mental patient shall be described. The schizophrenic we shall call Mr. John Doe is awakened on a closed ward at 5:45 in the morning, and looking about he sees the nursing assistant walking past the door of his small room. He hears a silent hallucinatory saying, "John, make up your bed!" Without a thought, like a robot with eyes acting as a control mechanism, he automatically makes the bed as he had done many times in the Army. Then, walking slowly in a stilted gait he moves down the hall with his arms immobile, hanging stiffly at his sides. Employing his visual system to move among the other patients he enters the washroom, where he locates his toothbrush in a cabinet with those of the other patients on the back ward. While brushing his teeth he hears a "voice" saying, "Brushing your teeth proves you are alive, as does combing your hair." Other patients around him are subjectively hallucinating. One says silently, "There is going to be an inspection today." Another patient answers, "Do they inspect here? I just came in." John hallucinates, "No they don't inspect. When do we go home? I sure want to go home."

Without thinking, he leaves the washroom and walks down the narrow hall towards the day room where the TV set is located. A "voice" orders him, "Have a drink of water." Mr. Doe turns and starts to have a drink at the fountain. The "voice" goes on speaking silently, "You have had enough." He mechanically walks on to the day room looking as he goes down the long hall. A nursing assistant is at a table passing out cigarettes, and picking up three of them without a word, John hears a "voice" saying, "Wet the end of the cigarette paper with saliva for then it is like pot." He wets the cigarette and walks over to get a light from the nursing aide. A voice says, "A light for a crematory?"

In the corner of the day room, a new patient is hallucinating, and he hears a voice saying, "Your wife was here visiting yesterday." He questions, "Do you think my wife will come today and visit me? If only someone would come to visit me." Another voice informs him, "Your wife was sexually involved with another man last night, in fact a gang of men." The person leaps out of his chair and races toward the corner of the room picking up a waste paper basket. He hurls it at the TV set but misses. Nursing assistants grab him and take the new patient to a room, placing him in full restraints. John hears the person screaming out loud, "The restraints hurt. The pain. Stop the pain!" Mr. Doe knows by experience that the restraints are made of leather, and although large and loose, they are nevertheless associated with extreme pain of the hallucinatory type. He has heard the voices say, "It is caused by the attendants who pinch under the skin by possessing with their legs and hands."

There is time to rest before breakfast and John tries to sleep, but the voices keep him awake as they often do at night. The chow wagon is wheeled onto the closed ward. Nothing is said out loud, but he hears the last names of the various patients called one after the other, and he gets up to get his tray when "Doe" is covertly whispered by a "voice." He hears, "The oatmeal is good for your food lungs. Those with food lungs live the longest." Another voice interjects, "It is about time you had a diet. I am going to swallow you down the wrong way if you keep on eating!" John stops eating, and the food is taken away by the orderly.

After breakfast the nurse comes to the ward in order to pass out the medication. The patients line up, and the nurse says out loud after giving John his medicine, "Did you have enough water? Did the pills go down the right way?" John says, "I am OK." He then starts down the long hall to the washroom, but a "voice" says, "The bathroom is closed. You can't go now." He turns back and sits down but then gets up looking for something to read. Finding a book, he starts to read, but a "voice" intrudes saying all the words at which John is looking. This upsets him, and he places the book back on the table turning to look out the window in order to practice hallucinating at a distance. John's "voice" leaves the area of the day room and echoes along the walls outside the window. He stands projecting his hallucinated inner speech at a distance, when suddenly, someone comes up behind him and says out loud, "It is time to go to corrective therapy." All the patients walk down the hall looking as they go, but thinking not at all.

They line up at the door, and their names are checked off a list. Then they go on to the small gym. There a therapist says, "Time to play hand tennis." The game is played on a little court, and John hears a hallucinatory voice saying, "All right, hit the ball over here." Then the "voice" says, "Is. Hit the ball so it goes outside the mark." Out of bounds goes the ball, and the "voice" orders him saying, "Are. Hit the ball correctly." John tries to do this, and the game goes on for an hour under the influence of hallucinatory suggestions. Then he goes back up to the ward.

The time comes for him to see a doctor, and the nurse says, "Dr. Brown will see you now." He walks to the end of the corridor away from the day room and enters a small room. The doctor says, "You look anxious. How are you feeling?" John replies, "I am not anxious, and I feel very good." John then hears a voice saying, "Stand up!" He stands up and the doctor says out loud, "Why are you standing?" John says nothing and sits down again, and he then hears a voice saying, "Go down! Go down! Go down on the floor!" Mr. Doe gets down on his hands and knees. The doctor asks, "Why are you doing that? Get up. Do you hear voices? Do you have hallucinations?" John thinks to himself for the first time during that day, "I only hear one voice at a time. I don't hear voices. I hear a voice. He'll think I am crazy if I tell him I hallucinate. Anyway the voice comes from him that is giving me orders. He hallucinates, why can't I?" John says overtly to the doctor, "No, I don't hear any voices and I don't have hallucinations. Why can't I go home? I don't feel sick. I have no pains or ill feelings." The interview is over and he returns to the maximal security ward's day room.

The patients are not talking out loud in the day room, and on the surface everything is quiet, but beneath this are the sounds of the patients' subjective hallucinating. First one patient hallucinates and the rest listen, then another answers the first, while the rest are respectfully quiet. The conversation goes from one person to the next with only one individual hallucinating at a time, while the other persons sit, listening and not thinking. A voice says, "You can hear much better if you put just a little piece of cotton in your ear." A patient says out loud, "Do you want to play cards, John?" Four patients form a group at a table, and after the cards are dealt out to each one a voice says to John, "You have three aces, don't you? I can see through your eyes." John silently answers yes, and then the voice orders, "Time to bid." The patients bid out loud, and after this is over, John is ready to lead a card, but a voice says, "Is the ace. Don't play the right one—I can see what you have." The game goes on under the influence of the hallucinated suggestions.

It is a fantasy world because the hallucinatory conversations have no direct bearing on the real world, and the content of the hallucinations is often imaginative and fictional. The hallucinatory talk does not represent anything of value which occurs in normal life. The lack of thought produces an unrestrained inventing of the novel and the nonexistent idea. The person does not contact reality by using his normal inner speech to comment on what is going on around him. The new and mysterious land of hallucinations seduces the patient's curiosity and interest, leading to a predominance, both relatively and absolutely, of the inner hallucinatory life. Manfred Bleuler (1968) characterized schizophrenia as a tendency to form a fantastic inner world, which forms a picture of conflicting human wishes and human fears.

The hallucinatory conversations can vary just as much as do overt conversations in regard to their subject matter and the type of person who is hallucinating. Thus it is impossible to give examples of all conversations, but the content, as variable as it is, nevertheless indicates some differences between the nonpsychotic hallucinist and the schizophrenic and alcoholic (Mott, Small, and Anderson 1965). Normal cases from the medical wards have as a major subject of hallucinating that of spirituality (76 per cent). The patients relate to voices classified as nonstrangers, while in contrast, the schizophrenic and alcoholic patients converse with voices concerning strangers. The schizophrenics (54 per cent) report persecution as a major theme, as do the alcoholics (43 per cent), but the nonpsychotic medical patient (6 per cent) does not have this as a major subject, perhaps because he does not talk to strangers. The normal person ascribes the source of the hallucinatory phenomena more often to religious personages, while the alcoholic often relates to the voices of animals and insects, feeling that the voices are unreal. Whether or not the "voices" were regarded as real by the alcoholic, some 60 per cent conversed with the voices, and 70 per cent participated in the visions. Medically ill and schizophrenic patients tended to believe in the reality of their experiences. The nonpsychotic person's response was characterized by positive adaptation to the hallucinations, which were described as advisory, helpful, pleasant, relaxing, ego enhancing, and anxiety dispelling. A negatively adaptive response was described as accusatory, derogatory, urging to hostile or destructive acts, and tension increasing. This response was observed more in the schizophrenic and alcoholic, but they also had positive adaptations, which indicates a complex situation.

The two major aspects to the condition of hallucinating consist of the content of the hallucinated inner speech and the problem of excessive hallucinating on the part of the patient. Various reasons for the two problems have been given, such as the subjective nature of hallucinated subvocal speech and the fact that the patients like to hallucinate. It is important to understand that the patient has a new ability which is to hallucinate, and he is taught knowledge by "voices" about how to hallucinate afar and listen at distances. Thus, he learns new skills. At first there is no discomfort associated with the hallucinations, so the patient is not prevented, by natural means, from hallucinating, nor is he told overtly not to hallucinate. The content of the hallucinations as seen in the delusions and complexes facilitate the process of hallucinating and thus suppress normal thinking, while at the same time, reinforcing the act of hallucinated inner speech. The person hallucinates because he enjoys what is heard, and the good voices have interesting things to say. The habit becomes a drive in its own right and is thus a derived need. The satisfaction from the behavior acts as a reward for the process. The patient is happy with this new skill, and the hallucinatory activity excites and directs his behavior, giving it an inviting attractiveness. There is also a social facilitation, for the feeling exists that others around him are hallucinating, adding a strong incentive.

Realism is something you find in life, but many persons are looking for something that takes them out of themselves and gives them excitement and a kind of satisfaction that is unending. The life of hallucinating with its delusions and complexes is something new and wonderful to the patient, and it takes him far from his humdrum way of life into a new world. It is an intense subjective experience, which at first is pleasant and of great interest, but then, " . . . the noise made by the voices fatigued them mentally and made sleep difficult. The question which the voices posed, the incomplete phrases, the stupidity of compulsive thoughts and the threats to their welfare which the voices uttered, all acted to disturb them and to create 'unholy turmoils' in their minds" (Landis 1964).

*All power of fancy over reason
is a degree of insanity.—Samuel Johnson*

6.
The Disorder of
Internal Language

"Language has been the master tool which man, in his endless adventure after knowledge and power, has shaped for himself, and which, in its turn, has shaped the human mind as we know it. It has continuously extended and conserved the store of knowledge upon which mankind has drawn. It has furnished the starting point of all our science. It has been the instrument of social cohesion and moral law, and through it human society has developed and found itself. Language, indeed, has been the soul of mankind" (Amery 1949). Language as used in thought plays a critical role in the growth and progress of civilization (Robinson 1968). Highet (1954) concludes that man must continue to think because it is this urgent march of the mind which has brought us out of savagery toward civilization and wisdom. The pathology of inner speech plays an important role in causing other symptoms associated with mental illness. Thus, it is necessary to know more about the normal use of internal language. The importance of inner speech cannot be emphasized too highly, for it is by careful examination of the normal that one can understand the abnormal.

Lord Brain (1955a) states that the language images may be directly representative or symbolic, and that their part in thought may be large or small. Similarly, thought may be associated with strong feelings or with none. He stressed that inner speech is the process of unvocalized

127

verbalizations which accompanies thought. When thought is largely representation, the inner speech may run with it as a kind of commentary which is evoked by and which in turn evokes images and feelings. In abstract thought, inner speech plays an essential part by mobilizing conceptual meanings, and it is necessary for the communication of the product of thought to others. Abstract thinking cannot be carried on without words or something comparable to words, such as mathematical symbols. Arieti (1967) observes that when language enters into human cognition, it is no longer possible to separate cognitive processes from language because they are all intimately interconnected. Language as a carrier of thought cannot be distinguished from thought itself. Language becomes not only a carrier of emotion but also a source and transformer of emotion. Arieti divides the process of verbal thinking into two parts. The first produces the thought processes, while the second permits awareness of them. The two parts occur simultaneously, giving the person self-reflection, and enabling him to carry on a dialogue with himself.

In order to grasp the extreme hardship that a deficit of subvocal speech can play in the behavior of a person, it is necessary to have a more general concept of the role that language plays in thinking. Language as used in thought makes for a greater control in the development of intelligent behavior. Deductive reasoning is derived from the ability to use a complex system of signs depending on the ability to formulate steps in an inferential process in the terms of language (Carroll 1964). Through language the human can treat the world more abstractly, and he is not at the mercy of immediate stimuli, which might cause a habit response as in an animal. Without language, only a few skills could originate, and they would not develop beyond the trial and error state analogous to that observed in the chimpanzee and in children during their early sensory-motor period. There is a greater degree of awareness of the environment because names and descriptions are given to the people and events which make up a person's perceptual experience. Through the use of language in the educational process, the higher skills are acquired, and intelligent habits and capacities are developed (Thomson 1959). Subvocal language plays an important role in cognitive development, for the verbal mediators are highly correlated with mental development as a whole when measured by tests (Carroll 1964).

Church (1961) puts forth the view that thinking is the practice of talking to oneself, forming the utterance of symbols, and then reacting to them as objects. Symbolic thought has meaning only in the context of the person in communication with objects either real or fancied. This kind of directed thinking is used in decision making, classifying, predicting, creating, and applying a familiar formula used in behavor. Verbalization leads to an articulation and an awareness of reality, but abnormal verbal usage can falsify and seriously distort reality. It is clear from developmental studies that one comes to terms with reality only through reasoning in which language plays an indispensable role (Church 1961).

Subvocal language is such an important vehicle in the mechanism of thinking that it is usually included in standard definitions of thought. Textbooks of psychology generally agree that most of our thinking appears to be an internal manipulation of language symbols, and that much of human thinking involves subvocal talking (Munn 1961). Krech and Crutchfield (1969) suggest in their analysis that language and thinking are intimately related in a complex manner. Language, because it uses symbols, is the best medium for thinking and making thought efficient (Boring, Langfeld, and Weld 1948). William James (1890) states: "As we take, in fact, a general view of this wonderful stream of our consciousness, what strikes us first is this different pace of its parts. . . . The rhythm of language expresses this, where every thought is expressed in a sentence, and every sentence closed by a period." Titchener (1909) observes: "Thought is the verbal counterpart of active imagination. Active imagination is thinking in images; thinking is active imagination carried on in words." Watson (1924) pointed out that abnormal behavior is an example of habit systems of the unverbalized type in which verbal correlates and substitutes are lacking.

Soviet psychology defines thinking as a generalized reflection by the human brain, executed by means of speech based on existing knowledge and intimately connected with sensory perception of the world (Smirnov 1956). According to Vygotsky (1934, 1956, 1962), it is internal speech with its predicative properties that performs these dynamic functions and plays a direct part in both the evolution of thought into the whole expression, and the crystallization of the whole expression into its shorter conceptual scheme. Often, language, as a carrier of thought, cannot be distinguished from thought itself. Verbal thought appears as a complex dynamic entity, with the relation of thought and word within it a movement through a series of planes. The central nonverbal element in thinking can be observed as a thought which will not take the form of words, as might occur when one reasons about a difficult problem. Various studies support the concept that inner speech is part of the thinking mechanism (Gal'perin 1957, 1959; Luria 1960, 1961). The relationship of subvocal speech to behavior is stressed, and it is seen that inner speech has various roles, which are regulating, nominative, communicatory and semantic (Luria 1960). Zeigarnick (Birenbaum and Zeigarnik 1935; Zeigarnick 1965) emphasizes that conceptual thinking is connected with plasticity and good differentiation of inner systems, whereas different types of primitiviation of thinking as found in mental illness correspond to the extreme rigidity or to an extreme fluidity of inner systems. Pavlov (1941) states: "Hysteria has to do with a general weakness, especially of the second signaling system. . . . The second signaling system is the highest regulator of human behavior (thinking). Hence the chaotic condition of the activity of the first signaling system (talking) and of the emotional background occurs in the form of fantasies with unrestrained motivation and a profound disturbance of the general nervous equilibrium . . . and the consequent chaos in the synthesis of the personality."

A theory (Vinacke 1952) has been proposed which would place the area of thinking within a stimulus-response framework with the internal verbalization acting as a mediator. The theory tries to explain noncognitive behavior such as interpersonal relationships and motivational acts, as well as cognitive processes such as learning. All of these behaviors would be based on internal verbal mediation and reinforcements. There are many studies indicating that verbal language may accompany thinking (Bartlett 1958; Bruner 1964, 1965; Chauchard 1962; Humphrey 1951). The three means of human intellectual growth are motoric response patterns, perceptual imagery, and symbolic internalized language. Inner speech is a vehicle for organizing experience, and it acts to shield the individual from the pull of the perceptual imagery (Bruner 1964). Many of the studies of thinking mentioned briefly in this work are highly sophisticated; they are complicated and complex. It does the literature an injustice to abstract this information, but nevertheless, the major observation is that inner speech is part of the total mechanism dealing with thought.

A pathology of thinking exists in mental illness (Buss and Lange 1965; Callaway 1971; Lange and Buss 1965; Rashkins 1967). The nomenclature that describes this state might differ and the various methods and points of view examining the process may produce descriptions that vary, but that a disorder exists, is definite. An older view is cited (Glueck 1925): "If there is any single criterion of mental derangement, it is this

—that logical thought and the voluntary activity of the constructive imagination give way to the incoherent play of multifarious associations." The bulk of the evidence seems to favor the position that the disorganized personality of the schizophrenic is largely attributable to a specific intellectual deficit (Osgood 1953). A review of the literature on schizophrenia concludes that the language and thinking of the schizophrenic have been depicted as representing a deficit or a type of disturbance. Many investigators (Birenbaum and Zeigarnik 1935; Storch 1924; Vygotsky 1934; Werner 1940; White 1926) have found that schizophrenia represents a regression of thought to lower levels of adjustment, which can be at the level of a patient who has an organic brain disease (Hanfmann and Kasanin 1942). An important study (Fey 1951) discovered a deficit in young, fairly well-integrated schizophrenics in regard to thinking. The study showed no overlap between the control group and the mentally ill. Schizophrenia is an adoption of archaic mental mechanisms belonging to lower levels of integration (Arieti 1955).

The concepts that looseness of association and the impairment of abstraction are cardinal symptoms of schizophrenia were tested, and the data indicate that they are facts (Meadow, Greenblatt, and Solomon 1953). Buss (1966) states that association disorganization is observed in schizophrenics because they tend to give uncommon associations, to respond with more incorrect associations, and to have difficulty in learning the common associations. There has been a great deal of work in regard to the loss of abstractness in the schizophrenic. The conceptual performance of the schizophrenic is impaired in comparison to that of the normal subjects, but there is still some ability to think abstractly (Lothrop 1961). The schizophrenic can form concepts, but these are of the abnormal type and are unusual or eccentric. The schizophrenic is abnormally concrete in his responses to the proverb test; the response accepts the literal meaning instead of restating it in the form of a general proposition.

Chapman and Chapman (1973) have developed a theory of thinking in schizophrenia based on the hypothesis that people do not select stimuli randomly, but have biases. These biases are such that a person will respond to stimuli that are strong rather than weak, as in the case of an individual who speaks loudly than to one who speaks quietly. Other biases concern the recency of a stimulus, and the novelty or familiarity of stimuli. Thinking requires the recognition or learning of the relationships between the stimuli. The schizophrenic patient responds excessively to the stimuli that normal subjects are biased to choose, and patients neglect other stimuli more than do normal persons. The schizophrenic apparently fails to perform the screening of potential responses; instead, he yields to the propensity for the biased response. There is an excessive use of the strong or preferred-meaning response which concerns an internal event, for example, the strong meaning of a word may serve as a stimulus to mediate a person's overt behavioral response.

The important clinical observations of Kraepelin (1919) and E. Bleuler (1950) that there is an arrest of thought or blocking was demonstrated by experimental methods (Eysenck, Granger, and Brenglemann 1951). The Nufferno Speed Test was used, and it showed long reactions that were significant, at the 0.1 per cent level. Psychotics had a much more skewed time distribution than normals and neurotics, and this might be due to some internal distraction. Harriet Babcock (1933) found that the patient was thinking slowly, causing the disorganization of thought in the schizophrenic. In the early or acute stage of the disorder, the thinking is only moderately slow, while in the chronic or deteriorated aspect of the illness, the thinking is extremely slow. The thinking of the depressed patient is as slow as that of the chronic schizophrenic. This confirms the findings of Kraepelin (1921) that in depressed states, there is a sluggishness of thought. The retardation or slowness in the function of thinking has been observed by a number of scientists (Craig 1965; Payne 1966). Although disorders of thought form a critical aspect of psychosis and are a diagnostic requisite, the physiological mechanism and the capacity for thinking often remain intact (Lidz 1968).

At times investigators have argued that what is lessened or lost in schizophrenia is not cognitive abilities, but rather the ability to take the role of the other person as a guide to effective communication. The results of a study by Milgram (1960) indicate that the lowered role-taking performance in the schizophrenic and brain damaged groups are respectively related to cognitive and empathic deficiencies, which are required for an effective performance. The relationship of hallucinations to the problem of role-taking has been noted as, "Role-taking is attributed to them by currect folklore-gods, demons, good and evil spirits" (Cameron and Margaret 1951).

Clinical psychiatry has for many years observed in mental patients a serious disturbance of thought. In Freud's view, there is a profound mental regression, somewhat similar to that of the primary process thinking found in a young child before he has good use of inner speech, and a turning inwards on the part of the patient. Menninger (1962) has described the thinking dysfunction in his diagnostic manual. In a summary of an A.M.A. symposium on language and thought in schizophrenia, the editor (Kasanin 1944) states: "One wonders whether in schizophrenia the disturbance of language and thought are the effect of schizophrenia or the cause of it." The problem is so important and basic that it provoked this observation: "The secret of schizophrenia lies in its form of thought disorder" (Redlich and Freedman 1966).

The findings of clinical psychiatry, clinical psychology, and various experimental studies unequivocally emphasize that there is a marked change in the thinking of the schizophrenic. This, at best, is much less than is normally the case, and at the worst, thinking can stop. The quantitative amount of thought has been described in a number of ways, which are as follows: (1) thinking comes to a complete halt; (2) there is a loss of mental activity; (3) there is a poverty of ideas; (4) no new thoughts emerge; (5) there is thought withdrawal; (6) there is an inability to produce any thoughts; (7) there is a loss of thought; (8) there is thought deprivation; (9) there is thought obstruction; (10) the patient is unable to think; (11) there is indefinite thought lacking ideas; and (12) there is retardation. E. Bleuler (1930, 1950) felt that the quantitative change affects the qualitative nature of thought. The characteristic quality, the attributes, and the nature of the product of thought have been given as follows: (1) unrealistic thinking; (2) abnormal concepts; (3) desultory thinking; (4) loss of organized thinking; (5) confusion of ideas; (6) incoherent thought; (7) incomplete concepts; and (8) instinctual drives that organize thinking.

The schizophrenic's disordered thought process, as observed in disturbed language, has long been considered basic to the illness (Abse 1971; Hart and Payne 1973). The speech of the patient is often incomprehensible, and the strings of interrelated words tend to be relatively short. The patient can speak aloud for only a short period of time (Gottschalk and Gleser 1969). One patient who was not thinking said, "Don't they drink water, two gulps, five gulps, two gulps. Cigarettes are the most important thing. Cigarettes. And then the others have to give me medicine by the way. That's a perfectly logical place to put them. Paul says here and here. In the muscles I think would be better."

Lord Brain (1955a) states: "The use of language in psychotic states also seems to be significant for semantic disturbances in the broadest sense. Such language may overlap the field covered by aphasia."

There is no real need for the antithesis felt between neurology and psychiatry because, "Nominal aphasia in its mildest forms is a common disturbance of function" (Brain 1955b) and mentioned as functional causes were nervousness and fatigue. By using interpolations from the field of neurology in theoretical consideration, much insight can be gained about the language disorders of mental illness, because there is an inner speech disorder in central, nominal, and amnesic aphasia. There are similarities between those patients that have structural lesions and those with functional disorders. Kleist (1914) reported on his observations dealing with the thought disorder in schizophrenia. He found that no new thoughts emerge or that thoughts emerge in an incomplete way, and that there was no understandable connection between one thought and the next. In addition, he observed a language disturbance which was a type of literal paraphasia, verbal paraphasia, agrammatism, and paragrammatism.

Literal paraphasia is a distortion of phonemic structure, while verbal paraphasia is characterized by the use of wrong words. Paraphasia conditions show the patient's lack of letter sounds as well as his incorrect rhythm and word accents. The correct word cannot be found or the word is used incorrectly, and wrong words are substituted for the proper ones. In paraphasia there is an utterance of nonexistent or incorrect words. Paragrammatism is a disorganization of syntax, which causes errors in the grammatical structure of the sentence and a difficulty in evoking words as names for objects, actions, and qualities. Agrammatism is the omission of auxiliaries, and thus the sentence is reduced to a skeleton of concrete and indispensable words, but there is no disorganization of syntax (Lhermitte and Gautier 1969; Critchley 1964).

In schizophrenia these tools of language are left out as in agrammatism. The patient produces fewer different words, shorter thought units, and description with fewer qualifiers. Articles are less frequently used as are conjunctions, prepositions, and nouns (Maher 1966). The speech of jargon aphasics is similar in certain respects to that of psychotic patients. Jargon aphasics, like schizophrenic patients, often refer to themselves in the third person and use many personal references, often resorting to original metaphors. Defective comprehension of spoken speech prevents the patient from noticing his own errors of speech, and in a severe case he pours forth a stream of unintelligible jargon, or word salad. The dysphasic patient nearly always tries to communicate and usually succeeds in doing so, whereas in the psychotic patient, communication seems to be irrelevant and defective (Williams 1970).

Clinically speaking, writing is the best test for the functioning of silent speech (Klein and Mayer-Gross 1957). The fact that the mental patient often has a great deal of difficulty in writing has been reported in the literature (Jasper 1963; Mayer-Gross, Slater, and Roth 1960). It was a common practice to censor the mail of the patient in the mental hospital because of his poor ability to write letters. Concerning the relationship between writing and internal speech, we have the significant words of John Huhlings Jackson (1874): "The proof that he does not speak internally is that he cannot express himself in writing. He may write in the sense of copying writing and can usually copy print in writing characters. If he can speak internally, why does he not write what he says to himself? He can say nothing to himself, and therefore, has nothing to write." The written works of mental patients were studied by computer (Maher 1966) methods, and it was found that schizophrenics used more objects per subject, more varieties of negative words, and fewer different words. There was a lack of qualitative descriptive words in relationship to verbs.

In regard to inner speech and silent reading, a significant percentage of children who were referred for psychiatric study have been found to have a problem in reading. There is a great discrepancy between the mental age on performance tests and the level of reading achievement. The problem is in the translation of perceptions into meaningful symbols or words that can be used in reading and related language functions. It was cited in this study on dyslexia in psychiatric cases that Lauretta Bender pointed out interesting parallels between schizophrenia and children with severe reading disability (Rabinovitch 1962). Adult patients with psychotic illnesses may respond to the printed stimulus with the appropriate ability to read aloud even though they seem to have little idea as to what the words refer. This is a matter which deals with understanding and comprehension (Williams 1970). The person's understanding of word meanings is less precise, he fails to differentiate between word meanings, and his ability to recall words is considerably impaired (Vetter 1969). Hart and Payne (1973) have found defects in schizophrenics using a psychological test dealing with reading and thought.

Lord Brain (1955b) found that the difficulty in grasping complexes lies in the fact that the patient's power of internal verbal formulation is faulty. This leads to his difficulty in comprehending spoken and written language because of his failure to recognize the meaning of words. Kinsbourne and Warrington (1963) observe that the speech of the patient with jargon aphasia approximates quite closely the patient's uncorrected and unexpurgated inner speech. Rochford's (1969) conclusion is that the jargon dysphasiac's inability to name does not lie behind his verbal excitement, but is rather the result of it. There seems to be a failure of monitoring, and inner speech seems to act as a filtering and attention organizing mechanism, which can mobilize and energize the brain's function because of sensory feedback and the activation of the motor act. The inner speech mechanism is needed in controlling arousal and in sorting out the appropriate item from the mass of memories. Schilling (1934) wrote about the significance of inner speech for normal and abnormal development of speech. When the habit of inner speech becomes disordered it leads to a diffuse functional change affecting all of the central nervous system. This change can be observed in language, intelligence, recall, meaning, and understanding.

Mental illness involves a serious problem of volition. Deliberation is a form of thinking in which we make up our minds about what we will or will not do, and end up with an applied decision, which is critical to the process of willed behavior. Luria (1961) has studied the importance of covert subvocal speech in the regulation and control of behavior. Inner speech is used in the execution of motor acts, which are observed in the development of voluntary motor behavior in the child. A young infant of two years cannot at first control the duration or frequency of pressing a rubber ball. At three years, with the help of overt statements, the child can press a rubber ball the correct number of times, while at four years and beyond, the semantic aspect of speech shows an increasing regulation over voluntary motor acts and the initiation of motor actions. The execution of the tasks is related and dependent upon overt and covert verbalizations. Language can play a broad role in the cognitive development of the person (Luria and Yudovich 1959). The importance of speech in the growth of thinking was illustrated in twins who were severely retarded because of social isolation. Because of special speech lessons, one child performed better than the other, while the latter improved dramatically when given the chance to learn the language and to socialize in the usual ways.

A volitional act is consciously conceived with awareness based on choice and decision. Adjustments and solutions to problems depend on willed behavior. In the mentally ill, the solutions can be wrong and abnormal because of the retarded thought process involving inner speech. There is a weakening of volitional impulses, for "the patients have lost every independent inclination for work and action; they sit about idle, trouble themselves about nothing, do not go to their work, neglect their most pressing obligation" (Kraepelin 1919). The will is inhibited because the patient is unable to initiate action and to make decisions. The control of behavior and planned movements is limited, poorly coordinated, awkward, unpredictable, and eccentric (Lehmann 1967). There is a serious apathy of volition with an absence of feeling, a total indifference as seen in the "I don't care" attitude, and no incentive to act, because the patient has no thoughts. There is a loss of conation with strong feelings of passivity. The patient states: "I only lack a will of my own, an impulse of my own" (Kraepelin 1919).

Kraepelin (1919) theorizes that an important aspect of mental illness is a destruction in the volitional and emotional spheres of behavior. "He who is not able to control his own will, and with it his life gladly takes refuge in the realm of dreams." Shakow (1946, 1963) for many years has been studying mental disorder and has found that the patients tend to do poorly in situations involving voluntary control. The curiosity and search for stimulation is weak, and the patients prefer old or already experienced situations. Because of his lack of involvement with the environment and poor cooperation, the patient prefers superficial tasks to demanding ones. The person neither resumes tasks after interruption, nor does he utilize substitute tasks. The reduced volition is seen in the poor response to social stimulation and a general low level of motivation, which impairs the ability to maintain sets, readiness, or structural alertness as well as a normal person does.

The aetiology of the pathology of voluntary behavior has prompted various speculations (McGhie 1969). Some explanations state that the indirect efforts to obtain the satisfaction of fundamental needs have never been successful, or that a cortical disturbance results in an inability to control and organize behavior in a purposeful manner based on the inability to select relevant material. Investigators are not sure whether or not the problem is a consequence of cognitive or motivational disorder, but both probably play a role, since there is such a serious thinking disturbance, and motivation is largely based on emotions and reason.

In regard to abnormal emotions, the investigator Sully (1886) states: "The regulative processes of ideation and self-control tend to dissolve leaving earlier and more instinctive tendencies uncontrolled. There is a weakening of the regulative volitional factor with an inability to control ideas, and intelligence is wrecked and becomes prey to unregulated emotion." There is a lessening of the power of integration and conscious control by the personality as a whole over the primitive instinctive forces. When the faculty of reasoning is weakened, the emotional behavior increases in strength. *Affect* is a term dealing with moods and emotions, but indicating much more, for emotions are a way of acting, a way of feeling (Papez 1937) and relating to others. The part of the brain that deals with visceral behavior dominates the picture. In certain forms the animal can be a "predaceous and voracious terror to all humbler habitants" (Herrick 1948), and animals have little neocortex as found in higher forms, but they have a limbic system. Affect indicates a kind of primitive behavior of comparative neurological mechanisms.

Many observations from the clinical literature indicate a serious problem in the realm of affect. The moral and ethical sentiments change, but with a roughness which results in ill use of other persons. There is a disappearance of the delicacy of feelings; the person loses deportment, becomes rude and impertinent, and fails to fit his behavior to the situations. The feelings of shame and disgust are lost in regard to others, and a loss of inner sympathy extends to the persons around the patient and even to the individual in question, for he is less sensitive about his own bodily discomforts. There is an ill-humored, strained behavior, a silly cheerfulness, and a dull depression in many of the patients (Kraepelin 1919). When the person has been ill for some time, an emotional dullness is observed, and there are reduced emotional responses, indifference, and a lack of depth of feeling. Superimposed on a mood of dullness are emotional oscillations, which can be extreme, as seen in outbursts of rage, intense anguish, and uncontrollable laughter.

The preceding indicates that there is a disorganization of affect in schizophrenia, by which the patient has been characterized as depressed, elated, and lacking or inappropriate in response. There is a statistical valid relationship between the hallucinations of "made" feelings and the affective disorder (Mellor 1970). The patient experiences feelings which do not seem to be his own, and these feelings are attributed to some external source, which is imposed upon him. A patient states: "I cry, tears roll down my cheeks, and I look unhappy, but inside I have a cold anger, because they are using me in this way and it is not me who is unhappy, but they are projecting unhappiness onto my brain. They project upon me laughter, for no reason, and you have no idea how terrible it is to laugh and look happy and know it is not you, but their emotions" (Mellor 1970). The person reacts with emotion to the content of the hallucinations, and he is completely involved with the hallucinating. His only emotional stimulus comes from the experience and is unrelated to anything in the external environment.

Affect is the feeling tone, either pleasurable or unpleasurable, that accompanies an idea. When the person is thinking less or not at all, the source of the emotions is no longer ideas, but the hallucinations of inner speech. If there is a poverty of ideas, there should be an emotional flatness or shallowness. A study was made on inappropriate affect; it demonstrated a specific relationship (1 per cent level) between the deterioration in mental speech or slowness with which patients solve problems, and the flat affect in a schizophrenic population (Harris and Metcalf 1956). The emotional responses are as disintegrated as the fragmentation of thinking, and parallel the latter in pathological intensity (Patterson and Kaelbling 1972). Emotional activities often form a mainspring of volition, so when there is a weakening of mood, we also find a loss of motivation in initiating voluntary acts. We observe, then, various factors such as mental slowness and hallucinations involved with the disordered affect. The person can respond to various types of hallucinations by excitement, and because of the cognitive slippage, there is a pleasure capacity defect. Without thought, and with the existence of hallucinations, the comparative neurological systems act as motivating drives for a wide range of acts leading in the long run to a nonproductive life.

Lack of attention is considered as another basic problem in schizophrenic psychopathology. "There seems little doubt that the mechanisms responsible for the direction and control of attention are disrupted in many schizophrenic patients" (McGhie 1969). The disturbances may manifest themselves in heightened distractibility, failure to hold and pursue required mental sets, and abnormal levels of arousal and orienting reactions. Neisser (1967) has observed that inner speech in its relationship to attention is necessarily attention compelling. When thinking is not verbal, we cannot control auditory attention. Thus, one is peculiarily vulnerable to distraction. The problem with auditory distractions is not so much that they are irresistible, but that in order to resist them, one must channel thoughts along familiar verbal lines. The content of immediate memory is essentially inner speech, which is acoustic in character and highly vulnerable to interference. In addition to the lack of inner speech, the level of attention is lowered during verbal hallucinations (Inouye and Shimizu 1972). There is a longer reaction time during hallucinating and a decrease in the visual evoked response, which is larger during increased attention.

The following serious medical symptoms concerning the disturbance of thought, speaking, writing, reading, voluntary behavior, emotional behavior, and attention can all be related to the most important of the anomalies observed in schizophrenia, the disorder of internal speech. The lack of inner speech and the hallucinations maintain and make the psychosis manifest. If they are not corrected the disturbance continues, for, "More pathognomonic than the hallucinations themselves are their participation in thought disorders, the inadequate emotional reactions of the patient, the influence or absence of influence on the patient's actions and their delusional interpretation" (Mayer-Gross, Slater, and Roth 1960). The syndrome of schizophrenia has many symptoms, some of which are basic and medical in nature, but others which are more in the realm of psychology.

Human psychology is a vast topic, much of which is concerned with normal behavior, but certain abnormal aspects of which can cause suffering. Stress and anxiety can cause nervousness and then neurotic behavior, which leads to a situation with the predisposing elements necessary for a psychotic break. During the period just before a person starts to hallucinate, an aggressive emotional panic is experienced. There is a change in the rate and type of subvocal speech, and the frequency of the words is increased to a flight of inner speech with the person talking aloud much more rapidly. The flow of inner words often has a delusional content approaching that found in hallucinated inner speech. The person might think that the next-door neighbors are doing something pertaining to him, when in reality their actions do not involve him at all. An innocent visit from an employer when the patient was absent from home might indicate to him that his wife was falsely molested and lead him to aggressive acts of revenge. Because the person is sensitive, any change can cause irritability and an overreaction to the stimuli from the environment. The person is extremely fatigued emotionally and mentally, but sleep is difficult and there is a strong feeling of not being able to find rest and relaxation. In time, the individual's rapid inner speech, which is filled with unreasonable and irrational thoughts, becomes hallucinated, and he hears the thoughts of other persons and answers them.

Bleuler (1950) observed that a flight of thought can occur in schizophrenia. Kraeplin (1921) found a rapid thought process in the manic stage of manic depressive psychosis. Bender (1947) states that with an increased activity of the thinking process, which becomes vortical, gyrating, circling, and cannot be fixated, the speech produced is fragmented, dissociated, and bizarre. In childhood schizophrenia there is retardation, inhibition, or blocking, often with complete mutism. When language returns after mutism, it may show all the types of deviations observed in aphasia and language pathology. Internalized hallucinations of introjected objects, such as a devil or guardian angel, play a role in childhood schizophrenia (Bender 1947).

The psychological disturbances of the mental patient are so varied a human problem that concepts of ego malfunction are employed in order to understand the abnormal behavior. Personality disorganization during the first stage is described as nervousness with an impairment of smooth adaptive control and a failure in coping. Next, there is the typical neurotic syndrome which proceeds into dangerous and destructive aggressive impulses. This leads into classical psychosis and eventually to a terminal or penultimate state with an abandonment of the will to live (Menninger 1963). It is often mentioned that the syndrome of neurosis does not proceed into psychosis, and like a branch of a family tree in genealogy, this may well be so. The common trunk of neurosis, however, may give rise to a type of neuroticlike behavior that leads into classical psychosis.

Knowledge from experiments with neurosis induced in animals indicate some similarity between the symptoms of animal cases and those of human beings (Liddell 1943). A hog may become so aggressive and predaceous that it can certainly be ranked at the third order of discontrol, characterized in the human as naked aggression. In experimental neurosis the dog may become what seems to be a penultimate animal. Dogs were no longer used by Liddell, because sheep and goats seemed to have the ability to survive the experiment without suffering. That the animals were at a fourth level is indicated not only by the physiologically measured symptoms which resembled those of a mental patient, but also by the typical symptom of sleeping pathologically as many patients do. The animals, depending on the situation, had the classical symptoms of "inertness and rigid immobility to hypersensitivity and overactivity, sometimes to the extreme of manic excitement" (Liddell 1943). The knowledge about experimental neurosis is important in understanding the progress of the disease from the developmental point of view, for it seems a good working hypothesis that there are levels or orders as indicated by Menninger's work (1963), and that one stage leads to another is certainly not an unfeasible concept. In support of the theory of the progressive development of mental illness is the data of Bellack (1970), which shows that the difference between the neurotic and psychotic is just a matter of degree. It was found that there is a continuous development of progressively intense states with an increasing severity of the mental disturbances (Snezhnevsky 1971). It was also observed that there was a successive development of the syndromes reflecting an increasing intensity of the psychic disturbances in schizophrenia.

Of late, the format of an ego disorganization is used in approaching mental disease. In psychoanalytical studies, the ego is considered as the regulative system of the psychic apparatus and the mediator between inner needs and the environment (Klein 1968). The ego works through memory, sensory perception, voluntary motor control, and thought. The ego acts to gratify the instinctual drives of the id dealing with the drives of erotic, aggressive, and emotional natures. The cerebral mechanism which deals with morals, character, and motives of a higher nature acts in the service of the superego, which warns, advises, and incites normal gratification within the cultural codes. If conflicts arise, the pathological aspects will be guilt and remorse. In the psychoanalytical regression to the primary process, there seem to be two basic elements, one of which is the id, for there is a predominance of abnormal emotional needs and wishes. The other concerns the mental apparatus. With less capacity for reflective awareness and directing attention at the will, the thought process becomes passive. The regression is not towards childhood behavior or poor formal logic, both of which have been disproved by experimental psychological methods (Maher 1966). Inner speech as used in thought is an important tool in ego functions such as the regulation and control of drives, the person's relation to reality, defense functions, and intelligence. The internal monologue can be employed in so many various ways that if there is a disturbance, this can be noted by clinical observations, in different psychological tests, and in the disorder of ego functions. A person cannot have a strong ego without inner speech.

Theodore Lidz (1971) states that an understanding of the importance of language to thought and to human behavior in general is crucial for the comprehension of schizophrenia. He observes that the disturbance of thinking need not reflect some structural dysfunction of the brain, for we are all taught meanings and reasoning which could be distorted in the process and in adaptation. Gerard (1959) believes that there is "no twisted thought without a twisted molecule." Neurochemistry deals with the stable machinery of the brain and not with language, learning, communication, and information (Elkes 1968). The structure of the brain is stable, while the functions are labile. "The structure which fabricates the idea and its symbol is a stable component of the body, but the idea is a transient manifestation of the operation of the appropriate structure in the requisite pattern" (Herrick 1956). Structural diseases are probably different from functional disorders. The simplest functional aspects are habits or conditioned reflexes and knowledge needed to solve problems. The idea that the brain begets behavior is correct, provided that one does not forget that the brain's structure is alive and is acting as a living system.

A large percentage of mental disorder is probably due to a serious lack of information, rather than any basic structural problem. Information plays an important role, for with it, living beings extract order from disorder; without the receipt of knowledge the only result is relative disorder. In the situation of driving a car, for example, the knowledge may not be present for the correct decisions, as the quality of the driver's ability depends on education and experience, which may be absent or at a low level. The structure can be out of tune with the civilized customs of society, and, like a piano's steel wires, must be again tuned to civilized behavior. Many of the structures of the brain are of a comparative neurological type, which, if not managed in a civilized way, can produce aggressive behavior. These are normal structures that can cause abnormal behavior in nonrational situations. Like errors made on an examination paper, the mistakes in the person's behavior result from the lack of information, rather than from any kind of structural abnormality.

Through inner speech one requests the pattern and controls the operation of the brain using a motor-sensory-motor feedback system of transient functions. Feedback is made by the transient manifestations of words coming from the operation of the structure, which in the abnormal case may not be in the required pattern, being either too slow or too fast. Inner speech is used to program the brain in a way similar to programing a computer. Without inner speech the brain works only with perception and unconscious thought. In the medical sense, the inner speech disorder is a morbid physiological problem or a type of functional pathology. Illnesses of this kind are perhaps different from those caused by a virus. When the cause is removed, the disordered functional habit does not return to normal, because the source of the lack of reinforcement is not the same as the act of reinforcement. Removing the inhibitory cause does not produce an excitation in the process of normal inner speech. In a functional disorder subtracting the aetiology in itself is not a cure, because the addition of therapeutic information is necessary to re-create the lost function, which does not spontaneously return to normalcy.

Once the person starts to hallucinate, there is a serious problem in the regulation and control of hallucinated inner speech. Certain steps in the development of the hallucinatory condition are aspects of the central nervous system that are not reversible, for when hallucinations begin, the clock cannot be turned back. Removing the cause of hallucinations does not stop the hallucinating, which is a new function not dependent upon its origin. Once initiated, the process goes on with its own mechanism. A mechanism has been set in motion, and it does not turn back in time just because the reason is known and removed. The passing of time makes the cause independent of the cure. The new function is different from the push that started it going, just as the process of launching a ship is much different from the vessel sailing on its own course at sea. Hallucinating a little is not abnormal in itself, because it does not compete with thinking (Lindsley 1960). Thus, it is not a question of the patient living in a diseased state of hallucinating, but rather of his having to control and manage his reaction to the hallucinations. The abnormal changes that the condition of hallucinating produces are what need correcting. Instead of using inner speech for the useful functions of voluntary behavior, problem solving, and controlling and stimulating normal affect, the patient uses hallucinated inner speech in conversations. This takes away thought, and normal inner speech is subtracted and substituted for by the hallucinated inner speech. Thought is suspended, and the person is under the influence of hallucinations which cause an abnormal reality.

The disorder of inner speech as used in thinking is a serious medical problem. In one study on thinking difficulties, 106 patients complained of being unable to think (Hausman 1933). Kraepelin (1919) found that a quarter of one group were devoid of thought and that the others had weak-mindedness, incoherence of thought, and lack of will, and were controlled by hallucinations. Payne (1966) has experimentally observed that the phenothiazines do not cure the disturbance of thought among mental patients.

Although the technique for the restoration of the flow of thought is still in its infancy, we do have some information from neurology which may be of value. Luria (1963) has written a chapter on the subject. He states that the reactivation of thought occurred in patients who had a lesion of the convex surface of the frontal lobes. The patients had a serious defect in the flow of thought, and they had an inability to create an inner plan of thinking using internal speech. One method used in the restoration of function was for the patient to read and then to make suitable remarks. Cards with words on them were used in the orientation of thought and helped in the process of re-education. The person would write down all remarks after he read, and then he would replan them, because often he could not think clearly enough at first to make a suitable flow of thought. Describing a picture was often of great value in this method. The person would look at a picture and then make up a story overtly. After telling the tale, he would then write about the picture covertly with mental language (Luria 1966a, 1966b). In this situation the patient is using his normal inner speech less rather than more for thinking.

The solution to the problem is to have the afflicted person think more; but since this was first observed centuries ago, there has not been any direct therapy developed for the thinking disorder of mental illness.

The retraining methods employed in aphasia speech therapy to restore the function of inner speech were used in a case diagnosed as schizophrenia of the paranoid type. This individual had lost the ability to internalize subvocal sounds in the oral cavity because of excessive hallucinating. Therapy consisted of the use of simple mathematics, vocabulary building, silent reading, and typing. Secretarial re-education is now used in Chicago for mental patients.

At first the sounds of inner speech could not be localized in the patient's tongue, but chewing a substance such as gum did help the person to internalize silent speech (Forrer 1960b). The patient before retraining had a borderline abnormal MMPI and was committed. After retraining he took some three hours of scientific psychological tests, which included projection tests as well as other types used in clinical psychology. The patient's intelligence was in the upper 95 per cent of the population. Averaging all test results demonstrated that the person was only minutely ill, so he was discharged.

Later, the patient became involved with thought insertion. The constant interference with normal inner speech caused again the state termed "devoid of thought." This person was retrained in educational therapy, an MMPI test was given and analized by a computer, and this time he was judged nonpsychotic with a slight sensitivity and defense reaction within normal limits. The person was again discharged, but thought insertion occurred once more. Finally, a pharmaceutical agent was employed to help in the restoration of inner speech and in preventing the effects of thought insertion and excessive hallucinating.

The patient was given theophylline powder, which is one of the xanthines. The restoration of thought occurred using 200 mg. of theophylline in an elixir and in capsule form containing 500 mg. of the powder. Theophylline tablets, N.F. and elixir are available for oral use. The toxic manifestations of theophylline are rare, but can occur in children. Of the three xanthines, caffeine is only central in its action on the brain, while theobromine is only peripheral, but theophylline has the necessary sites of action to cause stimulating effects both centrally and peripherally, which are needed in the case of inner speech. Theophylline elixir has been used in five cases, all of which indicated an increase in flow of thought.

The xanthines possess certain actions in common, but to different degrees. In the case of caffeine its central stimulating effects on the nervous system are well known in the field of medicine: a quicker and clearer flow of thought; more perfect associations; a greater sustained intellectual effort; a shortened reaction time to sensory data; a brightening of spirits; increased alertness; and keener and more discriminating judgment (Ritchie 1970). Caffeine has been used in the USSR with some success in the treatment of mental disorders (Asatiani 1955, Seredina 1955).

The placebo effect of theophylline could be the reason for the increase in the flow of thought. Of course, any drug has an intrinsic placebo effect because of interest (Shapiro 1971). It seems that it is worthy of being tested for its effect on inner speech by a pharmaceutical company having the necessary resources for controlled therapeutic studies.

Unconscious mental mechanisms are abnormal in neurosis, which can be also the case in psychosis. This can be observed in studies concerning set, which in the process of the experiment can become unconscious. Since animals, we believe, do not have inner speech, in regard to thought the studies dealing with experimental neurosis are of value in regard to therapy for the unconscious. Liddell (1961) observed a kind of hyperactivity of the thyroid in animals, which had been seen in war neurosis during World War I. A rational cure would be perhaps Lugol's solution and propylthiouracil. Masserman (1959) studied the acute manifestations of neurosis in cats and monkeys, which were helped by drug therapy. Severely neurotic animals after being given drugs would forget their inhibitions and acquired fears. Reserpine and chlorpromazine were occasionally of value, but were unpredictable in their effect. The barbituates and alcohol were far more effective in relieving the symptoms of the experimental neuroses. Herrnstein (1962) at Harvard University found a placebo effect in the rat, however, thus controls should be employed in such animal studies.

There are a number of medical diseases associated with the disorder of inner speech in its relationship to hallucinations. One of these is epilepsy. The long history of the disease has been recorded by Temkin (1971), and the recent research findings have been analysed (Magnus and Loventz De Haas 1974), but still no cause of the condition can be found for about 77 per cent (Noyes 1953). In these cases of unknown etiology the lesion may be a disorder of the chemistry of cerebral neurons (Boshes and Gibbs 1972). The typical attack begins with hallucinations in one or several sensory fields, which is termed the *aura*.

There are many mental disturbances in epileptics occurring before and after the seizure. Some of these are thinking disorders, depression, and abnormal feelings. Epilepsy is more often accompanied by hallucinations than are ordinary mental illnesses (Maudsley 1895). Preceding a convulsion, hallucinations may cloud the consciousness, and in some cases massive hallucinations occur giving rise to raving. One finds in the postseizure state hallucinations of sight, smell, and hearing (Mendle 1907). Hallucinations may occur a number of times in the patient's life before the first seizure (Mayer-Gross, Slater, and Roth 1960). The same hallucination can recur before each attack (Maudsley 1895; Mendle 1907). Generally, delusions, when present, can express themselves in persecution or grandiose ideas with hallucinations (Mendle 1907). As to the forensic significance of epilepsy, "The general acts of violence are without doubt the reflex quasi-convulsional outcomes of vivid and confused hallucinations and delusions" (Maudsley 1895).

In epilepsy many of the hallucinatory auras are caused by cerebral disorders of a structural nature; thus they are not true hallucinations of inner speech as found in mental illness, which in part the person hears as coming from outside his body. Lord Brain (1955b) has described a large number of auras that can occur before an attack of major epilepsy, or grand mal. In minor epilepsy, or petit mal, the slightest form is often described by the patient as a sensation, which consists of a disturbance of consciousness often similar to the aura of a major attack. Next in severity comes complete loss of consciousness, preceded or not by an aura (Brain 1955b). The lesion causing the focus of origin of the seizure may be found in a variety of localities within the brain, and there is a corresponding variety of auras.

The same type of nonspecific symptoms are found in epilepsy and other disorders, with a diagnosis of epilepsy being symptoms followed by unconsciousness or convulsive movements. These changes in function are found in psychomotor epilepsy. Mendel, a professor at the University of Berlin, observed that the symptomatology in regard to hallucinations was as follows: "1. The hallucinations affect preferably the audition. In two-thirds of all the cases there are isolated auditory hallucinations; in about half, visual hallucinations; in about 40 per cent, hallucinations of both senses. Hallucinations of the somesthetic sense are frequent. The hallucinations are mostly of a terrifying nature, partly of a horrible kind, yet they are often pleasing, phenomena of God, angels and heaven. 2. The delusions may have the most diverse contents; religious delusions are frequent, also such as have erotic or sexual content" (Mendel 1907).

The foregoing hallucinations are in part true hallucinations, as indicated by the important contribution of Ervin, Epstein, and King (1955), who studied the psychiatric aspects of forty-two patients with temporal lobe seizures of psychomotor epilepsy. Of these persons twenty-nine had symptoms in the form of hallucinations, affective changes, and alterations in consciousness. A diagnosis of schizophrenia was made in 81 per cent of the patients having temporal lobe seizures based on disturbances in thinking and affect. This situation is spoken of as epileptics with schizoid behavior or episodic psychoses (Strauss 1959).

In contrast, many of the auras of psychomotor epilepsy are not true hallucinations of inner speech, but are caused by neuropathological diseases. In removing the lesions the neurosurgeon uses electrical stimulation to locate the areas which must be excised and those not to be extirpated because of their vital need in the patient's life. In this process much knowledge has been discovered about the normal functioning of the brain and epileptic auras. Psychiatry has recorded many examples of strange hallucinatory phenomena, the explanation of which may be found by using the information gained from studies on epilepsy. Concerning this type of hallucination, Kraepelin (1919) states: "At the beginning these are usually simple noises, rustling, buzzing, ringing in the ears, tolling of bells, knocking, moving of tables, cracking of whips, trumpets, yodel, whistling, blowing, and chirping." The preceding hallucinations are like those found when the temporal lobe is stimulated causing hallucinatory auras. The psychiatric types of hallucination of hearing often occur before, and can lead into, the hearing of voices or the hallucinations of inner speech. This gives a possible theoretical concept of why there are so many strange kinds of hallucinations—because the local activity originates in a variety of areas in the brain.

Another aspect of epilepsy observed in both of the fields of neurology and psychiatry concerns problems of sexual behavior. This is a serious subject because it can lead to feelings of guilt. Lenox (1960) states: "Inquiry into the undoubted importance of sexual function in the seizures of puberty must go deeper than observations of superficial phenomena. . . . " Freud considered that the epileptic convulsion is organically performed, appearing under conditions which might be regarded as exaggerated tensions of the libido (Mosovich and Tallaferro 1954). No one knows at the present time (or may ever know, as strong taboos exist) what percentage of cases of epilepsy of unknown etiology fall into the category of post coitus epilepsy, where a seizure is provoked by coitus (Nielsen 1951). There is an age factor in epilepsy with 46.5 per cent of the cases occurring between the years of ten and nineteen according to Gowers (1901), with an increase during puberty.

Hippocrates and Democritus were both credited with saying that "coitus is a slight epileptic attack" (Temkin 1971). The history of ancient Greece has recorded that seizures are observed in orgies (Kirton 1660). The doctors during that time observed that sexual life in general was connected with epilepsy in many ways. These ideas about the influence of normal sexual life on epileptics are conflicting, but even Galen observed that untimely intercourse could be one cause of seizures. During the Middle Ages and the Renaissance the medical belief was that sexual extremes should be avoided by the epileptic. A case of a hallucinatory aura of a sexual character was recorded by an Arabic physician (Temkin 1971). During the Enlightenment, Tissot observed and stressed that sexual excesses bring about epilepsy. Tissot's books are still well thought of (Lenox 1960), and one of his monographs is credited as the first medical work of the Enlightenment (Temkin 1971).

An unfortunate problem occurred in relating sexual behavior to epilepsy. Tissot and his contemporaries overemphasized the role of masturbation in disease, which began the dogma that existed for over a century and a half that the act of masturbation caused epilepsy and mental illness. Epileptics were castrated. Bromide of potassium was introduced as a treatment, as it produced temporary impotency which reduced seizures (Brain 1955b) but did not cure the disease. The use of the medicine was overdone; 2.5 tons of bromide were used every year in one hospital (Temkin 1971).

Maudsley (1895) was the first to call attention to the fact that some young persons condition themselves by associating their hallucinations to sexual behavior causing seizures. That certain types of patients do condition themselves in regard to sexual acts and seizures has been recorded in the medical literature (Pond 1974). Research findings indicate a relationship between the neurological mechanisms of emotion and hallucinations.

A comparison of epilepsy, sexual orgasm, and brain waves has been made by Kinsey in the classical work on the sexual behavior of the human female (Kinsey et al. 1953). Electroencephalograms show a striking resemblance between sexual responses and epileptoid reactions, described as follows: "With orgasm, very high voltage, slow large waves develop in the brain. . . . Interspersed with and partially obscuring the large slow waves are spikes resulting from muscle spasm. This phase resembles petit mal epilepsy or the later stages of grand mal when the subject is passing from tonic rigidity to clonic spasms" (Kinsey et al. 1953). Mosovich and Tallaferro (1954) have observed in masturbation at the acme of orgasm the presence of three-per-second waves like those of petit mal. Electrical activity builds up in the temporal lobe, and when there is no muscular activity at the time of orgasm, eight-per-second waves similar to psychomotor epilepsy are recorded (Noyes, 1953) in contrast to the three-per-second waves that occur when muscular spasm is present. Heath (1972, 1975) has also observed sharp spiking coupled with slow waves during orgasm resembling epileptic seizures.

Various physiological responses seen in both epilepsy and sexual behavior have been compared with the finding that eight elements are always observed in both responses, while six others may be recorded, and even trumescence can occur in the epileptic state (Kinsey et al. 1953). It is emphasized by Kinsey and his colleagues that there is a most remarkable similarity between epilepsy and orgasm. Tonic decerebrate rigidity matches what may be seen in a transient state in both epilepsy and sexual activity. A state of tonic decerebrate rigidity presents a striking parallel to certain moments in sexual activity and particularly in the tensions which immediately precede orgasm (Kinsey et al. 1953).

The importance of emotions in epilepsy was stressed by Gowers (1901), who observed them to be the most potent immediate cause of the seizure. The basic neurological mechanism of emotion has been discovered, and Morgan (1965) states: "In 1937, the neurologist Papez published a speculative paper that bordered on the incredulous. He proposed a theory of emotion that involved many structures of the brain either considered to be primarily olfactory in function or not known definitely to have any function at all. . . . It is a general description of what [now] experiment has established, namely, that the limbic system is the central system in emotion." The mechanism dealing with emotions is composed of a number of structures and pathways including the cingular gyrus, cingulum, hippocampus, amygdaloid body, fornix, mammillary bodies, and hypothalamus.

It is far more than a coincidence that certain of the neuroanatomical circuits dealing with emotions are involved with sexual behavior and when stimulated elicit experimental epilepsy (Hoenig and Hamilton 1960). The mammillary bodies have a strong connection to the medial reticular formation of the midbrain and pons dealing with the sleeping brain, and the hypothalamus connects to the midbrain reticular formation. The anterior part of the midbrain is involved with sexual stereotype motor behavior (Dempsey and Rioch 1939). The posterior part of the midbrain reticular formation when lesioned results in decerebrate rigidity (Denny-Brown 1962, Johnson 1952, 1962), which physiologically occurs in both orgasm and epilepsy. When the later part of the midbrain is turned off by inhibition the result is a release phenomenon. The positive symptom of rigidity is the outcome of the resulting activity of parts of the nervous system which remain active. There are preferential circuits in the brain, but also mass action systems like the reticular formation activating the cortex.

A serious disturbance of consciousness occurs in epilepsy and mental illness. It was a basic hypothesis of Papez that midbrain reticular formation is an essential aspect of the mechanisms dealing with consciousness, which are the reticular activating system, mechanism of emotion, centrencephalic system (Russell 1960), and cerebral mechanisms. Various circuits have developed in the evolution of the central nervous system, as observed in comparative neurology. The cerebral cortex is vital to the process, as observed in cortico-reticulo-cortical pathways (Herrick 1956). Parts of the brain such as the frontal cortex and temporal cortex, have connections to and from the dorsal thalamus and are implicated in seizures. The thalamus has two-way connections to the midbrain reticular formation, and all the later pathways are included in the concept of a centrencephalic mechanism. Cerebral mechanisms with circuits between cortex and subcortical centers are involved in a large percentage of the causation of the EEG, as are the system of fine fibers termed *neuropil* (Johnson 1960; Herrick 1948). The motor mechanism seems even to have a portion of its circuitry dealing with consciousness, for lesions at the level of the anterior perforated substance destroying the caudate nucleus dealing with movement results in unconsciousness (Jefferson 1958). Stimulation of this region can result in seizures, and tumors of the area can be a determinant of fits. The motor mechanism has strong connections to the midbrain, acting in various functions dealing with stereotype or biologically grounded actions.

A controversy exists in medical science concerning the importance of the cerebral cortex and subcortical centers in petit mal and grand mal epilepsy. The preceding may indicate the complex nature of the problem. Both brain areas are involved, for it has been found that stimulation of either the cortex or subcortical areas can give rise to both types of seizures (Johnson, Sherry, and Millichap 1969). At the level of the nerve cell membrane investigations of chemical, physical or electrical nature have been made demonstrating that the various kinds of knowledge merge (von Neumann 1969). Perhaps someday, the various viewpoints in the controversy will coalesce into a theoretical picture.

John Huglings Jackson (1874) tried to use knowledge about epilepsy in an attempt to explain mental illness. Often in the past knowledge about hysteria was used as a bridge between structural diseases and functional disorders (Temkin 1971). Strong emotions are a factor in the genesis of hysteria. Pathological heightening of sexual feeling is often regarded as a sign of hysteria. Twilight states often precede an hysterical attack and are like those that occur just before some epileptic seizures. Hallucinations of vision are frequent in the hysterical condition. Hysterical men and women may imitate epileptics in every phase of seizures, the subsequent hallucinations and tonic and clonic convulsions. Hysteria major, or grande hysteria, is an extreme form of ordinary hysteria, and here the epileptoid period is again like decerebrate rigidity. The twilight state in hysteria compares in some respects to that of epilepsy, which has been described as follows: "Hallucinations are a characteristic feature of the twilight state and are often extremely florid. Visual hallucinations predominate, and are often coloured, highly complex and endowed with movement" (Mayer-Gross, Slater, and Roth 1960). Patients often state that other persons can produce fugues or twilight states. In contrast to epilepsy, ordinary hysteria does not have a seizure pattern in its EEG.

Psychological maladaptations can alter the irritability of the central nervous system, causing psychosomatic disturbances of the brain. Whatever caused a disturbance in the first place, such as sexual behavior or hysterical behavior, may not be necessary later on, for Gowers (1901) states, "The continuance of the disease after the arrest of the practice does not disprove the relationship, because, when the 'convulsive habit' is established it frequently persists after its cause has ceased to be effective."

Schizophrenia is a syndrome, not a disease entity (Menninger, 1970). This means that mental illness is a situation composed of many factors, and each symptom makes up part of the whole syndrome. In regard to all the persons who hallucinate, if we place the total population on a normal distribution curve, we find that a few have one abnormal human problem. Most have say two symptoms. The rest have many abnormal factors and have the syndrome of mental illness. Bellack (1970) in clinically testing persons has observed that some are relatively normal, others are neurotic, and some are psychotic.

There is, of course, more to the field of psychiatry than thinking disorders and hallucinations. Bellak, Hurvich, and Gediman (1973) found that individuals diagnosed schizophrenic can show a variety of serious ego-function disturbances. Their results were more consistent with the idea that there are a number of disorders rather than only the serious disturbance of thought processes. That there is more has been confirmed by family psychiatry (Lidz 1973).

There may be abnormalities in the parents of schizophrenics (Hirsch and Leff 1975). These parents may have a thinking disturbance characterized as allusive thinking, which is more common in families with a schizophrenic member. The bulk of the studies point towards a link between the allusive thinking in parents and in their children. It is known that in families of schizophrenics, several may hallucinate (Mott, Small, and Anderson 1965). More parents of schizophrenics are psychiatrically disturbed than parents of normal children. Many of the mothers have been diagnosed "schizoid," and fathers show excessive verbosity (Hirsch and Leff 1975). The parents of schizophrenics show more conflict and disharmony than the parents of other psychiatric patients.

Lidz (1973) has developed a theory about family psychiatry based upon the role of language in adaptation and upon family functions dealing with personality development, including linguistic and cognitive growth through adolescence into adulthood. He observes that in addition to the intrusion of infantile and early childhood fantasies, the schizophrenic thought disorder can be a complex resultant of the parents' style of communicating and of poor training in reasoning and in the teaching of meanings. Perhaps, in the schizophrenic process, the fantasies and hallucinations come first and then thinking is further suppressed and inhibited by other factors, for example emotional ones such as dealing with the parent's egocentric needs.

The concept that there are medical problems which are different than psychological problems might help in understanding the interpersonal relations between individuals in a family. The medical disorders concern hallucinations and thinking disturbances, but psychological problems, such as abnormal communications between individuals, also exist. The mothers of schizophrenics showed more protectiveness, excessive mothering, more concern, and greater intrusiveness than the normals and may have been demonstrating a lack of knowledge about children ingrading with other disorders such as allusive thinking and the communication of fantasies.

One important basic factor among the many causes of schizophrenia is the effort on the part of some persons to produce a mental disorder in the patient (Searles 1959). This preceding type of behavior has also beeen found in psychotherapy. The emotional behavior of the family often drives the relative who has been sick back to the hospital (Kreisman and Joy 1974). The social hierarchy of the family is involved with abnormal conflicts concerning status relationships. An observed method of fighting in either the act of dethronement or in keeping a position in the peck-order takes the form of driving another person into a disturbed state of mind (Adler 1937).

Plato depicted the disease of the soul or mind as the privation of intellect, one of which was madness, the other ignorance. The first type came from the internal voices of prophetic inspiration, which would be hallucinations leading to the thinking disorder. In the other there is a predominance of the animal nature over reason and conscience coming from not having knowledge, being uninformed, unaware or illiterate, which is psychological in the sense that knowledge about correct human behavior is needed by the family to bring up children in a proper manner. That mental illness is characterized by a thinking disorder was recognized by other ancients such as Cicero, who states in his *Tuscula Question* that every affliction of the mind, which is destitute of the light of reason, is termed amentia, dementia, or insania. He believed that all emotions of the mind which are not obedient to reason are diseases. In the older writings the observation was made that when reason "approaches its setting, then inspiration takes violent hold of us, and madness seizes upon us" (Clissold 1870). Long ago in China it was observed that the patient's reason is destroyed by hallucinations of malevolent spectres and these "ideas of the medical sages in regard to derangement of the intellect agree with those of the common people" (De Groot 1907). The ancient works (Clissold 1870) characterized the mentally ill as: 1) having perturbations of the mind; 2) having incoherent language; 3) doing strange and irrational deeds; 4) having furor; 5) being moved by irresistible impulses; and 6) hearing voices and having visions. Even today these symptoms play a role in the definition of schizophrenia and other mental disorders.

Human abnormal psychology is an immense subject, thus there will always be many elements in the etiology of mental illness (Searles 1959), but it does seem that a large part of the etiology concerning medical factors could be limited to a few items. The central nervous system largely operates in a statistical way, making it reasonable to hypothesize that in functional disorders there should be a limited number of factors operating in the etiology of most mental illness. Menninger (1963) has proposed a unitary concept of mental illness in which all disturbed states of the mind and the emotions are observed as stages in a single process. He tried to change the labels, but the tradition of diagnosis with its serious nomenclature problem will not change; it is hard to break an old custom. Menninger has discovered a basic fact leading to the solution of the problems dealing with etiology. The majority of the medical and clinical psychological disorders facing the patient are progressive and with therapy they can be changed back to health. The etiology of functional mental illness is a process (Menninger 1963). The term *process* implies a change in function as in a symptom and with the acts observed in the making of an illness. The various changes are all part of the process leading either towards illness or back to health.

Certain clinical manifestations are common for all diagnostic stages which maintain the disorder. Hallucinations can be as normal as a birth, but at parturition a doctor is needed, for complications can occur. Thus normal behavior can develop into a serious situation for the patient. Hallucinations are common to many mental disturbances all of which have thinking disorders. Lowe (1973) has observed that hallucinations can be an aid to differential diagnosis. The hallucinations of the manic depressive were characterized by being mainly auditory and visual, with the latter predominant. The hallucinations were less frequent and briefer than in other kinds of psychosis. The patient believed them to be less real and less controllable in retrospect, and at times to involve marked changes in his time sense. The hallucinations were nearly always considered to be experienced only by the patient. In contrast, a person with organic psychosis reported two to three hallucinations, many of which were of mixed modality. The hallucinations predominated over ordinary perceptions and were not controllable. The individuals reported that the hallucinations were shared by persons beyond their sensory range. Paranoids reported only one hallucination, which was mainly auditory and of long duration, with considerable stability, and capable of being controlled to some extent. The auditory hallucination had a negative import to the paranoid patient, with anger occurring as the resulting effect. Schizophrenics reported more than three hallucinations in all modalities, including the most rare. They had hallucinations of the self and others originating within the body, which showed considerable inconstancy and had clearly specified causes.

An influential German psychiatrist, Kurt Schneider (1957), formulated the concept of first rank symptoms dealing with hallucinations, which help to make for a decisive clinical diagnosis of schizophrenia. His symptom ranking is used in England on the Present State Examination, and hallucinations play a role in current diagnostic concepts in America (Carpenter 1976). The first rank symptoms of schizophrenia (Schneider 1957; Wing, Cooper and Soutorius 1974; Lehmann 1967; Meller 1970; Hirsch and Leff 1975) include the following: 1) audible thoughts, such as when the patient experiences an auditory hallucination with the voices speaking his thoughts aloud (echo de pensee) or repeating his thoughts; 2) hallucinated voices, heard by the patient as arguing; 3) verbal hallucinated voices, heard commenting on the patient's actions, or voices speaking about the individual in the third person; 4) the somatic hallucinatory experience of external influences on the body; 5) thought withdrawal due to external hallucinations; 6) thought insertion or substitution ascribed to the hallucinations of others; 7) thought diffusion, or the spreading of one's thoughts to others and the broadcasting of thoughts; 8) all "made" feelings, impulses, and volitional acts that are experienced by the patient as the work or external influence coming from other persons, e.g., delusion of control by an external agency; and 9) delusion perception. The second-rank symptoms of schizophrenia can be other forms of hallucinations, for example, persistent hallucinations, even if the voices speak directly to the patient and not in the third person, providing that the content is not depressive and not thought to be deserved. Hallucinations may be evident from behavior rather than reported, but they must be unequivocal (Hirsch and Leff 1975). Other second-rank symptoms are perplexity, depressive and euphoric disorders of the affect, emotional blunting, persistent incoherence of speech and writing, and abnormal modes of behavior (Lehmann 1967; Mellor 1970).

The etiologies of hallucinations are processes and one concerns the problem of aggression (destructive instinct of Freud) or the third order of dyscontrol in the Menninger's stage between neurosis and psychosis. In reactive states of schizophrenia it seems likely that the premorbid neurotic state is not hallucinatory. The aggressive panic state leads to a psychosomatic change in the neurochemistry of the brain, because there is a relationship between brain norepinephrine and aggressive behavior (Reis 1972). There is an increase and concentration of norepinephrine in the central nervous system during aggression, leading to hallucinations. In addition one finds a complicated depletion of norepinephrine in structures known to be involved in the neurology of hallucinations. Prolonged aggressive behavior can lead to more enduring biochemical changes involving other chemical substances such as cholinergic agents.

In regard to the effect of therapeutic agents, it has been observed by Unna and Martin (1960) that chlorpromazine abolishes the arousal response to epinephrine mediated through visceral, reticular, and neuropil systems of fibers in the brain. After chlorpromazine, the synchronizing effects of both epinephrine and norepinephrine are unaltered or enhanced. There is a slight arousal response to norepinephrine, which is abolished by chlorpromazine. These basic facts may help in understanding the observations of Hart and Payne (1973), who found that speech rate was correlated with retardation in schizophrenia; the rate was increased following treatment by phenothiazine medication, which was predictive of remission. The low speech rate of retardation was associated with slow speed of thought and depreciative delusions.

A great deal of work has been done on the subject of psychotogens or schizomimetic drugs. The pharmaceutical agent amphetamine facilitates norepinephrine (Reis 1972) and can cause psychosis with hallucinations and a thinking disorder. Amphetamine induces dopamine mediated behavior; this is blocked by phenothiazine and butyrophenone drugs, which seem to inhibit dopamine release (Creese, Burt and Snyder 1976). The observation that amphetamine stimulates activity of the reticular system and chlorpromazine blocks (Bradley 1957) the spinoreticular afferent collaterals (Johnson 1954) entering the reticular formation supports a theory that the overactivity of the reticular formation is involved in the neurophysiology of schizophrenia (Fish 1961).

Mescaline produces symptoms almost identical to those of acute schizophrenia, including hallucinations, thought pressure, disturbed associations, blocking, thinking in vivid visual images, and paranoid ideas. LSD psychosis is characterized by marked difficulties in thinking, including retardation, blocking autism, disconnected thought, and distractibility (Chapman and Chapman 1973). LSD-25 causes both visual and auditory hallucinations. The "chemical psychoses" are all somewhat different than true schizophrenia. Leff (1968) has observed a highly significant correlation between schizoid personality and a liability to develop hallucinations while under the conditions of sensory deprivation, which indicates that predispositions play a role in mental illness caused by psychotogens and other states. The developmental neuropsychology of sensory deprivation is being studied (Riesen 1975), and may explain certain observations concerning the central nervous systems of some patients with childhood mental illnesses.

Studies on neurochemical changes are of value in understanding the process of mental illness. Marrazzi (1957, 1960) has found that noradrenaline, adrenaline, and serotonin are neurohumoral inhibitors and that mescaline and LSD-25 are chemically related to these neurohumors, having the same kind of cerebral synaptic inhibitory action, which is prevented by chlorpromazine. He states that there are alterations in the threshold at the synapses, axons, dendrites, and nerve cell bodies, leading to hallucinations. Hollister (1968) observed that LSD has an altering effect on the EEG and causes a reduced threshold for arousal by auditory and reticular formation stimuli. The site of action of LSD on the central nervous system is on the basal ganglia, cerebral cortex, mechanism of emotion, reticular formation, and thalamus.

Konorski (1970) states that the mechanism producing hallucinations is built into the brain. It can be thrown into operation in some exceptional conditions, and hallucinations are a phylogentically earlier associative phenomenon. Researchers in the USSR have worked on the problem of hallucinations, thinking, and language in mental illness, some of which has been translated (Ivanov-Smolenskii 1955, 1956; Luria 1973). Scientific studies on the pathophysiology of the second signaling system, or thinking, indicates that both silent central process as observed in conditioning experiments and inner speech are effected in mental illness. This demonstrates that subconscious, preconscious, and conscious states are all involved in the etiology of mental illness.

Woodworth (1938) has observed that set as a factor in thinking as observed in simple reaction experiments becomes unconscious. He states that when the task is continued for a series of stimulus words the conscious awareness of the task fades out; it is reduced to a mere feeling of readiness and loses its specificity as a conscious state. With practice the set becomes at once less conscious and more efficient. Shakow's formulation, concerning the loss of set in a mental patient with a breakdown occurring in the speed of initiation to a predesignated stimulus and performing more poorly and more variably than normals, could be involved with unconscious processes in the brain. Cromwell (1975) states that the more subtle manifestations of mental illness, such as changes in reaction time, size estimation, illusion, GSR, heart rate, and language, may be what is crucial for the purposes of differential treatment, prognosis, and etiology of the disorder.

Bellak, Hurvich and Gediman (1973) have discovered that some ego functions, such as certain object relations and defensive functioning, are disturbed in schizophrenics and neurotics. These symptoms are not related directly to the thinking disorder or hallucinations. In the life process the person can be traumatized, mentally hurt or upset, and these events are either repressed or forgotten, leading to unconscious memories that act to upset the neurological mechanism causing abnormal behavior by way of defense reactions. The memories must be recalled and faced realistically in order to have insight. Abnormal object relations deal with early fixations, unresolved conflicts, and hostile sadomasochistic relationships. The most serious disturbance in object relations concerns the absence of relationships with any person by the patient, which deals with hallucinations as well as preconscious and unconscious factors.

In functional disorders, the behavior of the patient affects the neurophysiology, which in time causes changes in brain structure. The bridges between psychology, physiology, and anatomy are difficult to construct. For example, the complicated problem of the inheritance of mental illness has been critically reviewed by Lidz (1973), who feels that environmental influences must be of major importance. While CNS structure can predispose a person to illness, it seems likely that in functional disorders this is not the major cause of schizophrenia. Dercum (1914) has reviewed the older literature dealing with contagion between persons. He reports on cases in which two or more persons became mentally ill simultaneously and observed this in twins. In many cases the mentally ill persons were relatives who had lived together in close intimacy. He states that there does seem to be a predisposition on the part of the person who is the subject of the contagion and that there is a certain vulnerability to suggestion. Contagion cannot be imposed upon a sound mind, except in the historical instances of hysterical and mystical epidemics (Dercum 1914), but Searles's observations (1959) indicate that this is not always the case, which also has been found by Gralnick (1942), Waelder (1934), Deutsch (1938), and Dewhurst and Todd (1956).

Penrose (1971), in a critical survey of the genetics of schizophrenia, observed that although many studies have been made on twins, little can be inferred from them except that both heredity and environment play a role in the causation of the disease. He states that strict Mendelian inheritance has not been found. In some cases, schizophrenia may be a single recessive trait or multifactorial. Sex-linked genes may determine the condition or they may influence structure or physiology which in turn modify behavior. Barr (1971) has summarized the main sex-chromosome abnormalities which can cause mental retardation or psychological aberrations.

There have been a number of fine reviews of the literature dealing with the thinking disorder and language in schizophrenia (Chapman and Chapman 1973; Bellak, Hurvich and Godiman 1973; Reed 1970; Critchley 1964; Bannister and Solmon 1966; Broen 1968). Chapman and Chapman (1973) observe that the most important questions have not as yet been answered by the various theories about disordered thought in schizophrenia. They believe that much work is necessary to determine the different kinds of thought disorder and to find subgroups which might be observed by dealing with the emotional aspects of the illness. They conclude that the enigma of schizophrenic thinking remains largely unsolved and that the objective study of schizophrenic thought disorder is almost a virgin field. Perhaps studies will be done on the disturbance of inner speech, which has been demonstrated as being possible (Werner and Kaplan 1967; Johnson 1967) and this will cause a better understanding of thinking in both disease and health. Clinical studies will be of value, for Critchley (1964) has observed that the patient with aphasia fails in his communicative intent by virtue of an inaccessibility, if not a loss, of verbal symbols in thought. He states that in schizophrenia the thinking processes themselves are deranged, but the verbal symbols are intact and available. The one represents a quantitative and the other a qualitative defect in inner speech. The major reason for this view of research on the thinking disorder concerns the observation that the concepts were first developed from clinical studies on mental patients, rather than from the field of experimental and clinical psychology (Bannister and Solmon, 1966). Psychiatric notions about the thinking disturbance dealt with essentially a defect of style or method of thinking, which was unrelated to content. The pathology of thinking involved just the level of disordered abstraction without reference to areas, topics, or subsystems of thought disturbance. It was felt that a diffuse malaise affected all areas and aspects of thinking equally. Confusion of thought was observed on all points rather than a problem with content. Bannister and Solmon (1966) have observed a specific interpersonal thinking disturbance dealing with content in schizophrenia, which is in addition to the diffuse disorder caused by the serious defect in inner speech and unconscious factors.

Many clinical psychologists and psychiatrists believe that the thought disorder and other symptoms are a response to emotional problems. Psychotherapists feel that with the resolution of the patient's emotional problems the thinking disorder will subside. Emotional factors play a role in the process. The mechanism of emotion of Papez-Maclean does have systems involved with short-term memory and aspects of learning, for memory and learning are necessary in order to have emotions. We learn to relate emotionally to other persons. There are of course other visceral areas in the cerebral cortex, such as the prefrontal cortex, needed for integrating changes in blood pressure and blood flow during motor acts, which are often conditioned by inner speech. Menninger's first order of dysfunction deals with the state of tension called "nervousness," in which there are upsurges of anger, fear, or other emotions betraying the arousal of aggressive impulses. Hyperkinesis or overactivity is also observed as a common indicator of the first-order level of dyscontrol. The emotional and intellectual state of nervousness leads into neurosis via a process dealing in part with "anxiety" and other feelings of subjective discomfort or a sense of failure, of uselessness, or a disappointment to oneself. The mechanism of emotion with its memories and learning factors does influence other parts of the central nervous system, which in turn influence the limbic lobe.

Many factors can create functional disorders such as internal conflicts or conflicts between individuals. Stress plays a role, as seen in the problems of the lower social classes (Kohn, 1976). These actions stimulate the general bulbar lemniscus coursing in the reticular formation to terminate in the posterior thalamic nuclei, which project on secondary sensory cortical areas. The preceding fibers carry nervous impulses activated by all kinds of sensory fibers entering the medulla oblongata (Herrick 1948). Galambos has observed that there is an existence of a pathway other than the classical route for conveying auditory impulses to the cortex. As a hypothesis the hyperactivation of the general bulbar lemniscus causes the sensory acoustic hallucination stimulating internal language mechanisms leading to hallucinated inner speech. The first rank symptoms are observed in a number of mental illness, for example depressive psychosis, manic depressive psychosis, and neurosis, all of which have thinking disorders. The habits of poor thinking and excessive fantasies maintain the illness (Meyer 1906). Mental illness is a complex condition (Wyatt 1976). Papez (1957) states: "To appease the anguish of the soul, words may not be in vain; but words alone cannot dispel the troubles in the brain."

Surely none need fear the truth.—Wilder Penfield

7.
The Anatomy of Hallucinations

Are hallucinations magic or do they have a neurological mechanism? Is there any knowledge that might take away the cloud which is obscuring scientific observations? The thesis is presented by Penfield and Roberts (1959) that the findings of functional neuroanatomy point out a direction for psychological thought on the difficult subject of language as used in thinking and speaking. Lhermitte (1949) states that more information is needed from both the neurological and anatomical points of view to obtain a better understanding of auditory hallucinations. Speech is the most uniquely important performance of man as distinguished from the lower animals, yet one is impressed by how little investigative work has been undertaken in the field of language (Magoun 1960). Even though knowledge is limited, we do have observations from the neurosciences pointing out a solution to the problem concerning inner speech. The neurological mechanism is a system rather than just a function composed of a central or peripheral element.

In regard to nonverbal thinking, a concept of Papez (1948) may help. He states: "The frontal polar cortex is active in the thought process. Its activity is general and global, not directly derived from sense impressions. It is more concerned with the inner life of the individual and the self on which it dwells. Through the thalamus the frontal activity is brought into relation to the activities of the perceptual sphere. The activities of the frontal polar cortex or area tend to work over, unify, assimilate, and otherwise adapt the perceptual content to the needs of the individual. There is thus an activity of self-reference abiding in all individuals." The works of Halstead (1947) and Zeigarnik (1965) clearly indicate that damage to the frontal region can produce a thinking disorder. The results of Halstead's (1947) study demonstrate that patients with predominantly frontal brain damage did more poorly on most of the tests than the patients with nonfrontal damage, who generally performed more poorly than the control group. This work was confirmed (Reitan 1955) with a group of fifty brain-damaged patients, and it was found that the magnitude of the differences was more striking than Halstead's findings.

The frontal cortical areas send projections to the dorsal and medial part of the thalamus in the center of the brain, and these cerebral regions, in turn, receive fibers coursing back from the medial dorsal nucleus, forming a feedback mechanism. "The manner in which the dynamic patterns of thought are propagated through the cortex is probably unique. . . . The travel of the excitation pattern may be compared to the moving words in the electric sign of the New York Times Building; the words are different though the light bulbs remain stationary. The light bulbs which respond are fixed, the illuminated words which run along move through the appropriate bulbs. Just so, the excitation pattern moves along fixed, through different nerve cells. In the editorial office on the inside is the keyboard which operates the lights. This keyboard may be thought of as having elaborate connections to the electric sign on the outside. The thalamus may be compared to the keyboard and the electric sign to the cortex. The electric connections which intervene may be compared to the thalamo-cortical connections in the brain" (Papez 1948).

The circuits which deal with thinking of a totally silent nature are composed of at least the frontal cortex and the medial dorsal thalamus. Another important connection to the medial dorsal nucleus is that of the inferior frontal gyrus of the primate. Von Bonin (1944) has demonstrated this has the same architecture of Broca's area which, in the human, deals with vocalization. Using Walker's (1938) experimental material, one can observe that the inferior frontal gyrus is connected with the medial dorsal nucleus, which Kreig (1966) also observes in primate material. Stimulation of the medial dorsal nucleus can cause vocalization, and the clinical syndrome of the nucleus is involved with vocaliza-

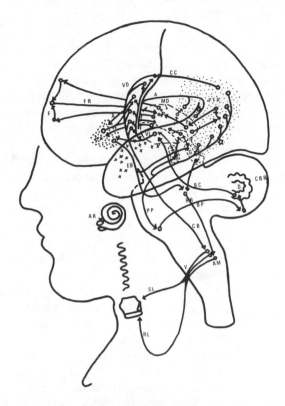

Major cortical areas and principal pathways associated with mental language expressed as either inner speech or hallucinated inner speech based on clinical observations, physiological experiments, neurosurgical investigations, and pathoanatomical studies. Letter abbreviations of the figure are as follows: A—arcuate bundle; AR—acoustic receptor; AM—ambiguus nucleus; BA—Broca's area (large dots); BC—brachium conjunctivum; BP—brachium pontis; C—centrum medanum of the thalamus; CC—cortico-cortical tract; CB—cortical bulbar tract; CBR—cerebellum; D—dentate nucleus; G—central annuloaqueductal gray; F—frontal cortex; FR—frontal radiations; MD—medial dorsal nucleus of the thalamus; P—pulvinar nucleus of the thalamus; PP—parietal pontine and temporal pontine tracts; PTA—parietal temporal cortical area (small dots); R—reticular formation of the midbrain; RR—reticulo-reticular tract; RL—recurrent laryngeal; SL—superior laryngeal; V—vagus nerve; VL—ventral lateral nucleus of the thalamus; VO—vocalization area of cortex; Stars—direct effect on flow of thought when stimulated; X's—hallucinatory auras elicited upon stimulation; ED—the hook bundles or tracts of Economo.

tion, for tumors of the medial and anterior thalamic nuclei give rise to marked speech and mental disturbances. We observe, then, a subcortical part of the brain, which on one hand has connections dealing with nonverbal thought, while on the other hand, the nucleus has connections relating to vocalization. The interdigitation of the two systems in the medial dorsal nucleus is of considerable importance, for it interrelates verbal and nonverbal neurological processes.

Speaking and thinking have been discussed by Penfield and Roberts (1959), who follow the idea of Jackson concerning the importance of perception in the process of verbalizing. The first half of the process is speaking, while the second half is listening. They observe that concepts are selected first, then the word patterns, and then the voluntary use of these patterns to speak or write. Listening to the speech sends back a stream of impulses over the auditory route activating word complexes and corresponding concepts.

The stimulation experiments in the human demonstrated that the following cortical regions are concerned with speech: (1) the posterior inferior part of the frontal lobe or Broca's area; (2) the posterior half of the superior and middle temporal gyri; (3) the angular gyrus; (4) the supramarginal gyrus; (5) the precentral gyrus; and (6) the supplementary motor cortex. Stimulation of these areas has an effect upon speech that may be one of excitation, as elicited from the stimulation of the precentral gyrus and supplementary motor cortex, or of interference with speech, coming from stimulation of the remaining regions. In the latter, the alterations in language are arrest, slurring, repetition, and distortion. Of basic importance to observations of inner speech mechanisms is the result that electrical stimulation of the cortical areas causes interference in writing. This indicates that the language regions are used in the elaboration of subvocal speech as used in the process of writing. Stimulation of the parietal-temporal cortex has been shown to influence thought (Penfield and Rasmussen 1950). Following the stimulations, one patient said, "Funny thoughts. I don't know. No pain. . . . My thoughts seem to run around in a circle. . . . Something funny in my thoughts." Karagulla and Robertson (1955) have observed that stimulation of the middle temporal gyrus affects both formulated and ill-defined thought. Stimulation of the temporal and parietal areas can elicit hallucinatory auras and memories (Penfield and Perot 1963; Cossa and Martin 1951).

Experiments of nature, as found in clinical neurology, demonstrate that lesions of the brain can produce serious defects in inner speech. These studies show definitely that specific preferential parts of the cerebral cortex are portions of a system that is involved with the process of inner speech. These various cortical regions that clinical neurology has demonstrated are concerned with inner verbalization, generally conforming to the same areas that when stimulated produce effects upon speech, writing, and thought. Inner speech is affected, while overt vocalization is not lost when the superior temporal gyrus or temporal lobes are damaged. This condition is termed *central aphasia* (Goldstein 1948; Marie and Foix 1924). If area 37 of the inferior temporal lobe is destroyed, a serious defect in silent speech can result (Nielsen 1946). Internal speech is gravely affected when there is a lesion in the left temporoparietal region involving the angular and supramarginal gyri (Brain 1955a). According to Lord Brain (1955a), this can alter overt vocalization, and in severe cases a patient can pour forth a stream of jargon much like that observed in the mental patient, and he does not notice his own error in speaking. Often when inner speech is affected by a lesion the person does not know the date or the month, which is again like that of a mentally ill person who is not thinking.

In another situation inner speech is intact so that comprehension and writing are unimpaired, but there is a loss of the spoken word. This condition is called pure-word dumbness, or subcortical motor aphasia (Brain 1955a). The lesion can be in the white matter deep in Broca's cortical area in the inferior frontal gyrus. Lesions of the posterior two-thirds of the inferior frontal gyrus can cause defects in both overt and covert language; this is termed *expressive aphasia*. Luria (1966b) has found that a lesion of the posterior region in the left frontal lobe caused a disturbance of the dynamics of verbal thinking and the flow of thought. Goldstein (1944) has emphasized that in neuropathology there is often a discrepancy between inner speech and external speech. He states: "The external instrumentalities can be defective (as in motor aphasia), though inner speech may not be altered; inner speech can be disturbed (as in central aphasia) without motor speech being correspondingly disturbed." We can observe that inner speech has its own cerebral mechanism, but that it can be involved with overt language as expressed in the sense of an interdigitation.

The various areas identified as functionally related to the production of inner speech have subcortical connections. The well-known cortico-bulbar tract takes origin from the precentral gyrus and is generally thought to make connections with the nuclei innervating the intrinsic muscles of vocalization. The pathways coursing from Broca's area are the "hook" bundles of Economo (Bumke and Forester 1935). These tracts are separate both in origin and course as compared to the cortico-spinal or pyramidal system. One of the "hook" tracts ends in the midbrain either near or inside the central gray. Electrical stimulation of the annuloaqueductal gray or central gray produces vocalization, and lesions cause mutism. In human cases this is termed *akinetic mutism*. The patient can be roused, but he is quite mute, or he answers questions in whispered monosyllables (Cairns 1952). In the animal the lesions cause a defect in facio-vocal activity (Kelley, Beaton, and Magoun 1946). The termination of the other tract from Broca's area in the brain stem has, as yet, not been determined. Midbrain lesions can cause hallucinations (Lhermitte 1949, 1951).

According to Penfield and Roberts (1959), the most important area for speech is the posterior temporo-parietal region. There are projections from these areas to the pulvinar in the thalamus and cortical reticular connections, both of which are part of the centrencephalic system. This system is important in perception, and is a great aid to thinking (Papez 1939, 1948; Penfield and Roberts 1959). The work of Halstead (1947) indicates that parietal lesions can affect the mechanism of thought. The pulvinar in the dorsal thalamus is used in language, as has been demonstrated; stimulation of the pulvinar in the human causes a failure to name objects correctly (Ojemann, Fedio, and van Buren 1968). The basal ganglia and peduncular nuclei are important in speech and thought. This is indicated by the effect diseases have on these structures, as seen in Huntington's chorea and Parkinson's disease. Mettler (1935) has observed the cortico-nigral system which originates from the temporo-parieto-occipital junction area, and this tract takes origin in the human (Economo and Koskinas 1925) from the inferior part of the precentral and postcentral gyri and area 40 of the cerebral cortex. The nigra sends fibers to the ventral lateral nucleus and to the caudate and putamen. The cortical areas which give rise to the cortical nigral tract all deal with speech. The cortico-nigro-striatal system may become overactive, causing the excessive release of dopamine, which is observed in schizophrenia-like psychosis. Of relevance are (Mettler 1935) the projection fibers which leave the parietal-temporal region and which descend and terminate in the hypoglossal nucleus, and the facial nucleus and trigeminal complex, which are involved with speech. During inner vocalization, the tongue muscles are often active, as is the case in hallucinated inner speech.

Another aspect of the mechanism dealing with vocalization is the cortico-ponto-cerebellar system which arises from the parietal temporal speech areas. These large connections are of importance because of the speech disturbances which follow lesions in the cerebellum, such as defects in the proper cooperation of articulation, phonation, and respiration, resulting in explosiveness and so-called scanning speech (Zentay 1937). The cerebellar cortex connects to the dentate nucleus giving rise to the brachium conjunctivum, terminating in the ventral lateral nucleus of the thalamus. There is a direct projection of the ventral lateral nucleus to area 4, which gives rise to the cortico-bulbar tract. Stimulation of the ventral lateral nucleus can cause acceleration or blocking of speech in the human (Guiot et al. 1961; Schaltenbrand 1965). When the inferior frontal gyrus is removed, degeneration is observed in the medial part of the ventral lateral nucleus and in the ventral medial nucleus of the activating system. This means that the connections of the cerebellum to the ventral lateral nucleus influence Broca's speech area in the inferior frontal gyrus and indicates that the activating system is playing a role in the process of verbalization. Stimulation of the ventral lateral nucleus by Sem-Jacobsen (1968) produced hallucinatory "voices" in the patient. This was a true hallucination of the type found in the mental hospital. Because the ventral lateral nucleus is connected with the caudate nucleus through various systems of fiber circuits, it is of importance to note that stimulation of the striatum can cause the arrest of vocalization (Van Buren 1963).

As has been related, there are a number of cortical regions involved with the process of inner speech and overt verbalizing, and from these areas, projection fibers descend to the brain stem. The different nerves which lead to the intrinsic muscles dealing with the movements of the vocal cords take origin from the nucleus ambiguus. The input to the nucleus ambiguus is from the cortico-bulbar tracts via internuncial cells. Other cortical fiber systems and basal ganglia mechanisms descend into the reticular formation where synapses are made with short tracts terminating in the nucleus ambiguus. The fibers to the laryngeal muscles arise chiefly in the caudal part of the nucleus ambiguus. It has been found that the various muscles are innervated by fibers which have their origin in particular circumscribed cell groups in the nuclear column (Lawn 1966; Szentagothai 1943). The vagus nerve arising in part from this nucleus has a number of branches. The two ending in the muscles of the larynx are the superior laryngeal nerve, which innervates the cricothyroid muscle and provides the larynx with sensory fibers, and the inferior laryngeal or recurrent nerve, which supplies all the rest of the muscles. Various studies have demonstrated, by using physiological methods, that the intrinsic muscles concerned with vocalization are active during inner speech, and electro-myographic techniques show the presence of activity in the vocal musculature of patients who are hallucinating with inner speech.

Knowledge on the subject of the neurological system of silent vocalization indicates that this is a mechanism with central aspects and various connections which integrate peripheral effectors in the production of subvocal phonation. The acoustic system is an important feedback in the process of verbalizing, for thought is not only expressed, but created in the verbal process, because one hears what one creates. Thus, we guide, control, inhibit, and facilitate the motor production of the words by the acoustic input, which acts as a stimulus to our response, and the response, in turn, feeds back a stimulus. The importance of the auditory system can be observed by first noting the relationship of overt vocalization to behavior. Through externalized speech such as orders, our movements can be initiated or stopped, and so it is with internal vocalizing in that it activates and stimulates motor concepts in the cerebral cortex by the auditory route. The inner monologue, or self-reflection, can be used as a mechanism in guiding and initiating many different human acts. Although it must be recognized that language is not the only tool of thought, for we have unconscious thinking as well, it remains true that most of the mental processes of humans actually use verbal symbols as stimuli for nonverbal responses. Inner speech is produced, and it can be used as an instrument of rational processes such as voluntary movements. Herrick (1956) states: "I repeat my conviction that some form of symbolism is requisite and that without the invention of language symbols that the human type of mentation is impossible."

In addition to the acoustic system and motor apparatus of inner speech, and the central internuclear systems intercalated between the two mechanisms which deal with responses to ordinary stimuli, another important recognizable neurological apparatus exists in the central nervous system. Herrick (1948), in a basic study on the fundamental plan of the vertebrate nervous system, has observed a system of nerve fibers, or a circuitry that infiltrates the latter mechanisms, which are characterized in the case of afferents and efferents as being of the analytical stimulus response type. Synthesis in the brain deals in part with the internuclear tracts of the reticular formation connecting the analytical units, which are involved more with the stable heritable components of the brain. Yet another basic system of circuits exists which integrates the latter systems "with provision for conditioning of reflexes and other forms of acquired behavior" (Herrick 1948). This integrating and synthesizing system is the neuropil and its derivatives of associational tissues, such as the cortex, which nevertheless still contains neuropil.

The neuropil has internal organization as well as afferent and efferent connections which integrate nuclei. This specialized tissue of the brain is ancient, increasing in the higher forms, as do the small nerve cells with their short axons or interneurons that form the internal organization. One observes a web of the finest axons forming a field or fabric which makes possible the irradiation of nerve impulses needed in integrative action. A web of ependymal elements also exists in the neuropil. While the nuclei and tracts determine the basic patterns of behavior, the neuropil deals with the most labile functions. By its fieldlike structure the neuropil can bring together multinuclear regions, as in a formation of a conditioned response. A tract or axon can give rise to many collaterals going into the formation of neuropil. Cajal pointed out that this makes it possible for information to be given to far distant points in the central nervous system at the same time.

The dispersing apparatus of neuropil is necessary for generalized, total, and organismic functions. The activity in any part may affect the whole fabric of neuropil, for it is a dynamic system comprised of many activated fields in interaction. This gives a structural ground within which every configuration of experience is set, such as in the field concepts of Gestalt psychology. Described in dynamic terms, the generalized structure of neuropil has the most synthetic function in which the time factor plays an important role, while the analytic structures have a more stable arrangement in space with a corresponding localization in three-dimensional mosaic patterns. The neuropil infiltrates the analytic structures and synthesizes patterns which are repetitive, as in habit and memory (Herrick 1948). Neuropil is probably important in regard to habits of nonverbal and verbal thinking. It may be a site of dis-action as observed in the mental patient's inability to synthesize and integrate. It is in the web of the finest axons, as observed in the caudate nucleus, that the neurotransmitter dopamine is found. This is also true of the fine terminal axons of the noradrenaline tracts as they form neuropil.

Concerning the problem of projection and hallucinations, we know that the patient voluntarily produces hallucinated inner speech to answer the "voices" in a conversation, but he has no control over the words heard and does not consciously cause them, nor is he aware of any involuntary production of the sounds. The fact that the patient hears a foreign language that he does not speak, and has not heard before in his lifetime, makes it difficult to go along with the idea that hallucinations are just a simple projection outward of the central nervous system, for there would be no such information in the brain with which to project.

Objects, of course, appear to be on the outside in space. The object is actually seen in the brain, but the brain projects it out toward the source of its energy pattern (Papez 1948). This means that we hear, see, and feel at the level of the cerebral cortex, but the cortex projects the sensory pattern toward the receptor source and beyond in the direction of the energy pattern. Thus, objects are always seen or heard as being on the outside in the external energy field. Papez (1948) states: "Projiciences can be compared to an image seen in a looking glass; it appears behind the glass in the straight path of the reflected light. The exteroceptive paths and organs have a greater property of projicience. The visual objects, sound sources, and objects of cutaneous senses have a high degree of projection. Interoceptive sensibilities are least projective and often not at all projective, so that visceral activities may arouse conscious experience without any references to their source of origin." This outward project is an aspect of perception and is of fundamental importance for object as well as space perception. Through this mechanism we are aware of objects and sounds as being outside the body, but we still see or hear them at the cortical level. We do not create or perceive the visual fields or auditory sounds through projiciences, but rather we know that they are external and appreciate their presence in space. Projiciences do not produce the energy source such as sound in true hallucinations, and without energy sources we do not hear.

Sully (1886) put forth the idea that auditory hallucinations were projections of mental images, which gain a preternatural persistence, making it seem that someone other than the hallucinating person is talking. The idea that auditory hallucinations are a projection was strongly criticized by Parish (1897) as well as the other older theories concerning hallucinations. Various authors have been opposed to the projection theory. Some, such as Kadinsky (1881), based their conclusions on personal observations, while others have based their conclusions on the findings of scientific experiments, which have disproved the theory that auditory hallucinations are exaggerations of auditory imagery as projections (Clerambault de 1924; Cohen 1938; Roman and Landis 1945; Seitz and Molholm 1947; Sperling 1960).

William James (1890) observed that the vast majority of hallucinations are not dreams or dreamlike in any way, and Janet (1925) stressed emphatically that hallucinations are not at all like dreams. Fretet (1949) observed that a hallucination takes shape and acquires significance and direction, whereas the dream experience has none of these attributes. It has long been believed that an hallucination is just a dream which occurs during a state of wakefulness. The clinical and experimental findings state that hallucinations are most generally just conversations using hallucinated subvocal verbalizations. Inner speech is not a dream, nor is willed hallucinated inner speech. This does not mean that there are not certain features of some types of visual and auditory hallucinations, which at times may have elements in them that use the same neurological mechanism employed in a dream, eidetic imagery, and synesthetic thinking (Katan 1960; Klass 1970).

Eidetic imagery is normal and often found in children. The memory image is externalized on a surface and is clear. This type of experience has been described by a patient as a visual hallucination. Visual thinking is the voluntary act of producing an image in the eye; this normal event is used by mental patients and is called a visual hallucination. This type of mechanism, when the person views an object created by himself, may be based in part on the connections from the superior colliculus, a visual midbrain center, and other subcortical visual structures, which send fibers to the eye and activate the visual system; but such connections need confirmation. Acoustic hallucinations can stimulate a cortical reflex of visual or auditory hallucinations, a response producing sounds and visions. Various agents or drugs can cause visual hallucinations, as is well known. Paradoxically, these types of hallucinations deal with projaciences, while true hallucinations which are external to the patient do not deal with projections.

Concerning the various mystical features often reported about visual hallucinating, the only neurological finding which brings understanding to some of these strange events is that of Herrick (1948), who reported that if the brain has the right connections, one does not need receptors for perception of sensations, which is scientifically observed in lower forms. This being the situation, one can interpolate that we need not have receptors for various phenomenon, and since the brain has so many connections, it gives an unlimited aspect to the central nervous system, as in the case with the perception of normal events, visual hallucinations, and even dreams.

Chronic patients probably use certain parts of the central nervous system in a type of hallucinating, which is still that of hallucinated inner speech but which has elements of sophistication, indicating the use of the mechanism employed in dreaming. The observation that dreaming can be correlated with a certain type of brain wave characteristic of that state makes it possible to study some of the neurological structures involved with the process. When the cerebellum is removed, the animal no longer has the kind of EEG associated with rapid eye movement (REM) type of sleep, which is seen during dreaming. Lesions made in the midline nuclei projecting in part to the cerebellum cause, at first, an absence of fast waves typical of the dream period, and even after a time, the amount is still much reduced from the normal. In this latter case, the animals spend a great deal of their time awake (Jouvet 1967). The cerebellum projects to the ventral lateral nucleus in the thalamus, which, if stimulated, causes inhibition, excitation, and changes in speaking. As mentioned, there is a report that stimulation in this area can cause hallucinations typical of the ones observed in mental patients (Sem-Jacobsen 1968).

Lesions in the locus coeruleus of the isthmus lead to a type of "hallucinatory behavior" in the animal such as the cat (Jouvet 1960), which vocalizes excessively. In the human, this area can be diseased as in Parkinsonism (Turner 1968), and often patients have hallucinations (Haits 1967; Perria 1943, 1947) and psychiatric as well as neurological problems. They have trouble with speaking due to breathing problems. It is known from experimental work that the locus is involved with changes in respiration (Johnson and Russell 1952) and that when stimulated, it can produce vocalization. McGuigan (1966b) has found changes in respiration coinciding with the production of sound and the activity of the muscles dealing with covert hallucinations. The noradrenaline tracts arise primarily in the locus and reach many brain centers, such as the hypothalamus, and even through neuropil connect to the cerebral cortex. In preschizophrenic panic which deals with aggression, noradrenaline is released, causing a depletion in the nucleus and tract. This, in turn, may act as a lesion in the sense that the system becomes hypoactive, leading to hallucinations. Studies on the brain of a newborn human indicate that the locus may be part of the secondary visceral gustatory nucleus as it lies in the identical position observed in lower forms. Thus, we are involved with the visceral or limbic system. Stimulation of the nucleus of the solitary fasciculus can cause changes in the EEG; the nucleus receives connections from the locus as well as sending a large visceral gustatory tract to the coeruleus and other centers in the isthmus. Hartmann (1975) states that normal nonhallucinatory waking thought requires the integrity of the norepinephrine system and the normal functioning of the enzyme dopamine beta hydroxylase.

As is well known, visceral sensations affect dreams (Brill 1921). Following lesions of the locus, there is hallucinatory behavior and also a decreased duration of the slow wave element of sleep not associated with dreaming. There is also an increase in the phasic activity of a fast wave type as seen in dreams, which are greatly enhanced and occur during almost all of the episodes of slow waves. Thus, subcortical structures are important in the mechanism of dreams, and structures such as the locus coeruleus when destroyed, and the ventral lateral nucleus when stimulated, can cause hallucinatory behavior.

When there is so little knowledge about a subject, words of a hypothetical nature are often taken as dogma. In the case of dreams and hallucinations, statements must be viewed, at the very best, as just a working hypothesis. In clinical findings (Bleuler 1950) patients report that during their dreams, a semiconscious state made possible a subvocal hallucinated conversation which was under the will of the person. During the day, certain features of the hallucinating experiences of the chronic patient have similar features. Hallucinated expressions, seemingly from other persons who are far away, enter into the conversations of the patient. He subjectively experiences the "voices" speaking perceptually, somewhat like those in the dream at night. The sounds are localized in a close association with the substance of the brain, and the person enters the hallucinatory episode much like a person enters a dream, mystically, without being spoken to by hallucinated inner speech.

The periods just before going to sleep and just after waking up have often been observed as times when hallucinatory events of a normal type occur. The character of these episodes is somewhat like that of a dream, yet as Freud pointed out, they are typical of the true hallucination of the mental patient (McKeller 1957). Werner and Kaplan (1967) state: "Communication in the dream state is analogous to communication under condition of inner speech. . . . Indeed 'dream speech' seems to be quite close to an extreme condition of inner speech." In the dream no one has a great deal of trouble with the perception that others are talking out loud, but the sounds of the words, if listened to carefully, have the physical nature of silent speech. One patient perceived a hallucination of inner speech in a dream state, while he was not semiconscious, and the hallucinated voice continued hallucinating after the dream was over and the patient was awake. In the dream the members of the act answered the hallucinations of inner speech, but when the patient awoke he heard only the continuation of the single hallucinated voice and not the hallucinating of the other members of the fantasy. This is a rare dream and not the hallucinatory type mentioned in the literature, because the activation of the REM state caused a state of semiconsciousness with willed hallucinating. These types of hallucinations in dreams indicate that an interplay between the various different phenomena can take place.

When dealing with the subjects of dreams, hallucinations, perception, and memory, we must realize that preferential structures exist in the CNS. But there can be an interdigitation of function (Ferguson et al. 1969). In normal thinking the temporal lobe with all its various functions can be used, giving man an elaborate method of in-acting events utilized for thinking. It can also be used for the photographic-like recall of previous events, as a store of knowledge for thought, and interpretive knowledge of present experience used in judgment. Of note is the relationship of the person in space and his orientation to his surroundings, which deals with the contracting of reality or spatial thought. When lesions occur in the temporal lobe, the person loses the capacity to construct in his mind a concept of spatial relationships, for there is a loss of understanding of the relationship of external objects to each other, as well as their relationship to the person himself. The disturbances and deficits of spatial thought are involved with disordered inner speech, which deals with one aspect of the loss of reality. The temporal lobe stores information dealing with the understanding of spoken words and sentences with their meanings, all of which are affected when inner speech is defective, and, thus, a lack of information processing results (Penfield 1970, 1971).

Although many functions of the parietal-temporal speech area do not merge, some do have a small overlap (Penfield and Roberts 1959). One can elicit on the temporal lobe just the effect of illusion, flash back, and the speech response, but only one of them, never all at the same point of stimulation. The following language responses do not overlap: (1) arrest of speech; (2) hesitation of speech; (3) confusion of numbers while counting; (4) inability to name with retained ability to speak; and (5) misnaming with perservation. On the other hand, slurring of speech, distortion and repetition of words, and misnaming without perservation can be found in the first and superior temporal gyrus in that region, which, when stimulated, can cause the hallucinatory, dream, and memory response. The perplexing problem is that a relationship between these areas and inner speech must be found in order to have a truthful association between dreams and hallucinations of inner speech. The work of Penfield and Perot (1963) gives a strong indication that a fusion can exist, as does figure 91 in Penfield and Rasmussen's work (1950) which illustrates that thought, illusion, and hallucination can co-exist in the same area. The merging of function could be anatomically mediated by transcortical tracts which associate the various labile functions.

Arieti (1974) has the view that the work of Penfield on the temporal cortex does not apply to the subject of hallucinations, because the stimulation causes memories. The confusion comes about because at times the stimulation can reproduce the hallucinatory aura, but it can also stimulate a memory which is not at all related to a previous aura in the patient's life.

Anatomically speaking, the temporal lobes have been found as having somewhat different subcortical connections than the rest of the neocortex. The region from which dreams are made (Penfield and Rasmussen 1950) is a zone having a low input and output of fibers coursing to and from the dorsal thalamus. The thalamic afferents to the region from the pulvinar are not as great as those to the tip of the temporal lobe and to the temporal-parietal speech area. The temporal lobe has often been found to have few or no thalamic connections, but connections to the thalamus have been found by various experimental methods (Mathers 1972; Whitlock and Nauta 1956). The superior temporal gyrus sends fibers to the pulvinar and to the subcortical auditory nuclei, the medial geniculate, and inferior colliculus. This is important because this gyrus has auditory flash back (Penfield and Perot 1963). The superior temporal gyrus sends fibers to Broca's area, which is used in vocalization of a voluntary type. The middle temporal gyrus, when stimulated, has visual experiential responses and efferents coursing to the pulvinar and the superior colliculus, which is a visual center. The inferior temporal gyrus has fibers leaving it and coursing to the pulvinar, medial dorsal nucleus, and lymbic lobe (amygdala), and that general area when stimulated can cause automatisms, amnesia, and auras (Penfield and Roberts 1959).

Unknown to many who study the brain, there is clear evidence that an involuntary motor mechanism can be observed in the temporal lobe. Stimulation of area 22 or the superior temporal gyrus produces movements of the extrapyramidal type (Forester 1935). This work has been confirmed and extended by Dr. Elizabeth Crosby (Herrick 1956; fig. 15, p. 421), who observed movements of the face and arm from the middle temporal gyrus, as well as adversive movements from the superior temporal gyrus. Hirasaw, Okano, and Kamio (1938) have found various descending connections dealing with the motor system to the putamen, pallidum, substantia nigra, and pontine nuclei, while others have observed fibers coursing to the tegmentum and putamen. The motor mechanism could be used in the process of inner speech and might explain the involuntary-like hyperactivity of the excessive hallucinating of mental patients and the adversive pattern observed in seizures from the region of the brain. In Japan it has been demonstrated by stimulation experiments in the human that true hallucinations can be inhibited by temporal lobe stimulation.

There is no need for multifarious theories about hallucinations. We all believe to some degree that as in dreams the memory traces constitute the building blocks of hallucinations. This is not to say, however, that the hypothesis concerning dreams and hallucinations is a truthful one. A variety of drugs and endocrine abnormalities may play a role in initiating the hallucinatory phenomenon. Toxic metabolic stressors can elicit hallucinations, and organic lesions can produce them. After the hallucinations of inner speech occur, the phenomena continues on its own way not at all dependent on what caused it in the first place. As to memory, it is a hypothesis of Hernandez-Peon (1965) that hallucinations are a failure of inhibitory influences acting upon the memory systems during wakefulness.

A study giving some direct information concerning dreams was made by Othmer, Hayden, and Segelbaum (1969). From their interviews, they found that wakefulness REM was accompanied by a decrease in muscle tonus, and that the subjects reported a dramaturgic daydream and active subjective involvement. When wakefulness occurred without REM, the subjects reported a more abstract, nondramaturgic thought content. In this study there was a continuation of REM periods during the daytime when the subject's eyes remained closed. REM had been previously observed during "wakefulness" by Rechtaschaffen and Kales (1968). The theory is that the acute patient fails to confine the phasic events to REM during sleep, because of the discharge of these systems in the waking state (Dement et al. 1970). It should be kept in mind that REM has not been found in hallucinating schizophrenics with their eyes either open or closed (Rechtschaffen, Shelsinger, and Mednick 1964). A chapter on the subject of dreams and hallucinations was written by Dement et al. (1970), with many experiments and papers reported on. The researchers had little evidence as strongly emphasized for their hypothesis, yet they believed in the importance of REM to hallucinations. The experimental studies deal with the lateral geniculate, which is part of the visual system, and spike activity was observed in that system, caused by hallucinogenic agents, resulting in hallucinatory-like behavior in animals with excessive vocalization. The results are not auditory or verbal in nature, but perhaps this may be all the information that is forthcoming on the subject, because the medial geniculate may respond in a way which is different from the visual system. Further experiments will add to our knowledge, but we must not believe that all hallucinations are just dreams. Perhaps the patients use the preferential dream and recall mechanisms for fantasies.

Various hypotheses have been advanced concerning whether hallucinations during sensory deprivation occur in states of high or low levels of arousal (Solomon and Rossi 1971). There appeared to be an increased sensitivity to interoceptive stimulation, but hallucinations occurred at all levels of arousal. It is West's (1962, 1971) hypothesis that when effective sensory input decreases, there is a disinhibition which releases the level of cortical arousal along with perceptions entering into awareness and being experienced as hallucinations. The greater the level of arousal, the more vivid the hallucinations.

Herrick (1956) states: "It must be recognized that many unprejudiced people have recorded experiences that have not been satisfactorily explained by chance or coincidence or any known principles of mechanics. . . . The way to learn the true facts of psi phenomena is to explore them by carefully controlled observation and experiment . . . and the mind receptive to the possibility that the explanations sought may be found only after revision of current physicalistic theory of space, time, and causality." This latter statement is of value to keep in mind concerning the situation which surrounds the question of hallucinatory phenomenon. Hallucinations are similar to a resonating situation, because, as in physics, if one tuning fork is hit, the inactive one next to it will vibrate and produce sound induced by resonance without being struck. In advanced theorizing about the central nervous system, the subject of resonance plays an important role (Herrick 1956; Papez 1948). Skin and muscle resonance has been scientifically observed and is the subject of a review by Williams (1963), who reports in detail on the literature. Many resonating structures exist in the acoustic and vocal systems, and it may be that the brain has a type of bio-resonance. Lashley (1942) states: "In the light of the experimental evidence concerning the nature of nervous activity, it seems most probable that the various patterns of integrated activity in successive levels of the nervous sysem have the form of tuned resonating circuits." In the laboratory of James W. Papez, structures that resonate have been observed in human brain tissue culture slice material. This cytological element has been shown by the electron microscope to be lipochrone pigment inclusions found in the normal, and increasing in amount as one grows older, yet producing normal neurosecretions. This may be a factor in neurochemical disturbances in mental illness (Maher 1966). The resonance of the skin and muscles (Williams 1963) would help to explain some of the features of the somatic sensory hallucinatory feelings associated with "possession" and "seeing things."

The situation may become so serious that the mental patient's life is in danger. In an important study by Malzberb (1949-1950) of the death rate in the mental hospitals in the New York State Hospital system, it was first found that the death rate was higher than the general population in a ratio of almost 5 to 1, due regard given to the factor of age. The crude death rate reported in his more recent study was 7.3 to 1. The manic depressive death rate can even be in a ratio of 33.8 to 1 in young men. In schizophrenia during the early period of twenty to twenty-four years, the death rate can be at a ratio of 8.8 to 1, and it is 5.9 to 1 in the period of twenty-five to thirty-four years. The cause of death in these individuals, who have a functional illness in 55.1 per cent of the cases, is disease of the heart. That functional death exists in mental illness has been pointed out many times by Yap (1969) in his writings, in which he cites Cannon and others. Stimulation of the hypothalamus and reticular formation can change the EKG. Hyperexcitation, high arousal, resonance, and activation may all play a role in such functional terminal states, because they cause functional discharging lesions of the central nervous system.

While a complete interpretation of all hallucinatory phenomena is still lacking, we do know that inner speech forms the basis of the vast majority of true hallucinations. This brings up an important question about hallucinations previously mentioned in the literature (McKeller 1957). William James argued against the traditional view that there was an absence of objective stimuli in hallucinations, saying that it was a mistaken view. William James (1890) states: "Hallucinations are often only extremes of the perception process." The view of Parish (1897) is that hallucinations are just as much sensory perceptions as the so-called objective perceptions. Some years ago von Domarus (1928) wrote that the peculiar nature of hallucinations does not lie in subjective conditions, but in objective circumstances. He believed that hallucinations belong to a certain sphere of reality, which is not the ideal world of sensory illusions, but the real world of privileged perceptions. Agadjanian (1946) observes a genuine perceptive basis that exists in hallucinations, and does not recognize any perception without an object. The conclusion of Smythies' (1956) study was that hallucinations are real. Freud (1924-1950 vol. 14) states that in hallucinations the words are modified and that there is communication, but no topographical regression. In an experimental series of observations, the investigator Riss (1959) doubts the view that there is an absence of sensory stimuli in hallucinations. Strecker (1952) states: "In a hallucination, it is assumed that the process is entirely imaginary without any sensory foundation whatsoever, no starting point of initiation in hearing, sight, smell, touch, or taste. This I do not credit . . . because we cannot always run down the sensation, which is misinterpreted is scarcely sufficient reason for the assumption that there is no sensation."

The acoustic element of hallucinations is important. Unilateral ear disease can produce a unilateral auditory hallucination; the patient hears the hallucination in the diseased ear but not in the normal ear (Bryant 1906). Stopping up the ears may cause the disappearance of the auditory hallucination (Bleuler 1950; Mendel 1907; Parish 1897). A person who is a deaf mute from birth usually does not experience auditory hallucinations (Arieti 1955; Mendel 1907). That the deaf mute can have inner speech has been observed by Brain (1955a), and it has also been observed that some deaf mutes can have hallucinations (Ranier, Abdulleh, and Alshuler 1970). They develop the ability to use inner speech for either thought or hallucinations. Stimulation of the VIII nerve can elicit an acoustic hallucinatory sound (Bleuler 1950; Bryant 1906). In an experimental study it has been observed that receptor stimulation of the auditory mechanism is required for the auditory hallucination to occur (Riss 1959). Lindlsey (1960) has noted the exciting effect that sound stimuli can have on hallucinations. A study (Morel 1936) made on thirty-four patients who had auditory verbal hallucinations demonstrated that while they hallucinated, their auditory thresholds were usually raised, and gaps appeared in the audiograms. After hallucinating had been discontinued, the hearing became normal again; it was as though the patient could not hear two things at once. Jouvet (1967) has observed in experimental situations that a loud noise can inhibit hallucinations in animals. These preceding clinical observations and scientific experiments demonstrate that the acoustic receptor may be involved in the perception of auditory hallucinations of inner speech.

The *Encyclopedia Americana* (1969) states: "There is a growing conviction that many hallucinations and delusions are due to an abnormal ability of the sufferer to sense vibrations far above the normal" and they effect thinking (Grigg 1971). The basic problem is as William James states: "The object happens not to be there, that is all." The patient can, at times, hear "voices" from far away without a source being present, while other persons cannot hear the hallucinated verbalizations. Freeman and Williams (1952) first advanced the hypothesis that auditory hallucinations are a type of "human sonar" like that found in animals such as the bat or porpoise. Evidence for their working hypothesis was observed (Johnson 1958) with recording equipment, because the sounds produced by the person who is hallucinating are sound vibrations far above the normal. They are acoustically of high-frequency waves of the upper partials or harmonics, which are an addition to the normal sound waves of the word as it is spoken aloud. These vibrations are in the ultrasonic range at times and would be inaudible to those who do not perceive hallucinations. The energy range for this type of sound wave is estimated at 100 db to 110 db, which is the level of a boiler factory. An echo evaluation of only 1/10,000 of that produced is needed for the perception of the sound. As a hypothesis one might think of these sounds as similar to those produced by a "dog whistle," which is above most human hearing range. Because these sounds are high frequency and very intense, they can be heard a long way as a result of the high energy. They may also resonate acoustic and neurological structures.

Various forms of animal life make sound waves, which are ultrasonic in nature, and are biological and natural phenomena. Such sounds are produced by the squirrel monkey, marmoset, rat, mouse, porpoise, whale, bat, shrew, and a night bird, the oil bird (Anderson 1954; Dashiell 1959; Griffin 1953, 1958, 1968; Kellogg 1961; Riley and Rosenzweig 1957). Other animals such as the chimpanzee, cat, and dog respond to ultrasonics, but whether they produce them or use them in echolocation is not known (Kellogg 1961). It is theorized that such vocalizations formed the evolutionary basis of communication (Griffin 1968). The development of transducerized microphones makes possible the recording of inner speech in either the normal or the hallucinating individual. The sounds in the normal situation are confined to the tongue, and this is a medium of fluid. Thus, the sound waves can be picked up much like one would use a hydrophone in water. This method has been used for recording heart sounds, employing a jellylike medium to convey the sounds from within the body directly to the transducer. It is a fact that Gould (1948, 1949) used a stethoscope to listen to the hallucinated inner speech of a patient. The externalized sounds can be heard when the instrument is placed in front of the patient's mouth, and normal inner speech can be heard at the larynx.

Black (1971) has reviewed recent work which demonstrates that hallucinated words and sounds can affect the EEG. The normal production of alpha waves are changed by such experiments, and evoked potentials are altered in hallucinating situations. The conclusion was that the EEG responds in a manner which demonstrates that hallucinatory material is processed as a reality to the central nervous system just as any other phenomenon might be perceived.

Hallucinated inner speech may have as a part of its mechanism a comparative neurological system not normally employed by the human. The fact that an oil bird can produce sounds of high frequency like those observed in hallucinated inner speech indicates that other regions of the central nervous system, in addition to those previously discussed, are involved. The oil bird does not have a true neocortex, but does have an extensive visceral brain. Stimulation of various parts of the visceral system can elicit vocalization (Ramey and O'Doherty 1960), and the amydala region (Chapman 1960) and the deep areas of the temporal lobe when stimulated can elicit hallucinations. Stimulation of the temporal cortex and hypocampus gyrus produce experiential responses (Penfield and Perot 1963; Penfield and Rasmussen 1950) which play a role in certain kinds of hallucinations found in the auras of epilepsy. In the bird, the midbrain nucleus profundus is an important part of the mechanism of vocalization. Memory is important in emotions as one of the functions of the hypocampus, and there is a relationship of vocalization to emotions, for emotional speech exists after lesions of Broca's area.

The reticular formation and the centrencephalic system, perhaps due to stress, anxiety, and aggressiveness, are sites of abnormal action which cause various threshold changes to take place in the irritability of the central nervous system leading to the activation of a comparative neurological behavior mechanism. Self-induced stress can produce hallucinations (Erikson 1950). That the vegetative or visceral parts of the brain are involved with hallucinating is a theory advanced by Mourgue (1932) in his view that there is a dysregulation of the relations between the systems of instinct and the cortex. The change in irritability may take place first in the excitability of the vegetative sysem (Kluver 1966) and the reticular formation (Keup 1970; West 1962), but because they form a complicated circuit, the other parts of the central nervous system which deal with inner speech cannot be left out. Mettler (1966) stresses that bilateral removal of the temporal lobe does not stop hallucinations.

When writing the truth becomes a mental disease, then all of science shall fall into the diagnosis. Karl Jasper (1963) states: "Scientific knowledge is precisely that which is independent of philosophy, opinion, and world outlooks in general," which is a reason why one has to be careful about the subject of hallucinations. Smythies, however, wrote that some change must take place concerning the study of hallucinations. For the sake of the patient the central purpose of this work is the description of the defects in thought and behavior caused by the hallucinations of inner speech in order that these disturbances can be prevented and corrected. The problem of the withdrawal from reality cannot be solved by ignoring and neglecting the situation, and to digress in controversy and swerve away from the major aim of alleviating suffering is certainly not the issue. One must recall that the way of life of the schizophrenic is based largely on hallucinations, and this problem cannot be solved without dealing with the hallucinations. In essence, hallucinations are just subjective covert conversations, rather than objective overt talking, and they at times need not be seen as abnormal or, for that matter, as of much interest to anyone. It is as if one is dealing with a strange speech (Lagache 1935; Reik 1948; Johnson 1958); it is no different from a foreign langauge, which one does not need to speak or understand. *Hallucination* is an appropriate medical word, and it is more than a coincidence that "to wander in mind" is the meaning of *alucinari* from which is derived *hallucinatus* and the term *hallucination*. The ending *cinari* is due to the influence of *vaticinari*, meaning to rave, and comes onomatopoetically from the hooting of owls (Mendel 1907) and at first indicates behavior like that of night birds, such as an oil bird.

The term *hallucination* is pejorative (Sarbin 1967), but paradoxically, hallucinations of inner speech can cause a great deal of suffering and trouble to the patient and are a serious medical problem, which should not be confused with psychological problems. Because of the way this situation has been treated in the past, we still have the continuation of revolutionary millenarianism and mystical anarchism as in the use of psychedelic drugs (Cohn 1970) and the pathology of leadership (L'-Etang 1970). Arnold Toynbee (1972) gave a reason: "Most of our current failures are tragic illustrations of our obstinate unwillingness to learn anything except through bitter direct experience." The view must prevail that hallucinations are a natural phenomenon, but that men must also be considered ill if they tend toward disturbances of normal inner speech and behavior. The issue is to correct the situation in a humane and civilized way through knowledge, medical science, and art.

Selected References

Abercrombie, T. J. The sword and the sermon. *J. of the National Geographic Society,* 1972, 142: 3–46.

Abse, D. W. *Hysteria and Related Disorders.* Bristol: John Wright and Sons, Ltd.; Baltimore: Williams and Wilkins, 1966.

————. *Speech and Reason.* Charlottesville: University Press of Virginia, 1971.

Ackerknecht, E. H. *Short History of Psychiatry.* New York and London: Hafner Publishing Company, 1968.

Adler, A. Position in family constellation influences life-style. *Int. J. Individ. Psychol.,* 1937, 3: 211–227.

Agadjanian, K. *Le mecanisme des troubles perceptivo-associatifs (en rapport avec) l'origine de l'hallucination et du delive (etude physiopathologique).* Paris: Peyronnet, 1946.

American Law Reports Annotated, Vol. 175. Rochester: Lawyer Cooperative Publishing Company; San Francisco: Bancroft-Whitney Company, 1948.

Amery, L. S. *Thought and Language.* Oxford: University Press, 1949.

Anderson, J. W. The production of ultrasonic sounds by laboratory rats and other animals. *Science,* 1954, 119: 808–809.

Angrist, B. M., and Gershon, S. Amphetamine induced schizophreniform psychosis, pp. 508–524. In D. V. Siva Sankar (ed.), *Schizophrenia: Current Concepts and Research.* Hicksville: PJD Publications, Ltd., 1969.

Arieti, S. *Interpretation of Schizophrenia*. New York: Brunner, 1955. 2nd ed. New York: Basic Books, 1974.

————. Schizophrenia: the manifest symptomatology, Vol. 1. Also Vol. 3, Creativity. In S. Arieti (ed.), *American Handbook of Psychiatry*. New York: Basic Books. 1959.

————. *The Intrapsychic Self*. New York: Basic Books, 1967.

————. Acting out and unusual behavior in schizophrenia. *Amer. J. of Psychotherapy*, 1974, 28: 333–342.

Arnold, O. H. Die Symptomgesetzlich Stellung der Schizophrene Akustischen Hallusinetionen. *Wiener Zeitschrift für Nervenheilkunde und deren Grenzgebiete*, 1948, 2: 5–23.

Arnow, A. J. Verbal hallucinations: a restitutional symptom. *Bull. Menninger Clin.*, 1952, 16: 178–183.

Arthur, A. Z. Theories and explanations of delusions: a review. *Amer. J. Psychiat.*, 1964, 121: 105–115.

Asatiani, M. M. The effects of therapeutic doses of caffeine on the cortical dynamics in certain cases of neurosis. In A. G. Ivanov - Smolenskii (ed.), *Works of the Institute of Higher Nervous Activity*. Pathophysiological Series, Vol. 1. Moscow: The Academy of Sciences of the USSR, 1955; Washington, D.C.: Office of Technical Services, U.S. Department of Commerce, 1960.

Asch, S. E. *Social Psychology*. Englewood Cliffs, N.J.: Prentice-Hall, 1959 (1952).

Aune, B. Thinking, Vol. 8, pp. 100–104. In Paul Edwards (ed.), *The Encyclopedia of Philosophy*. New York: Macmillan Company and Free Press, 1967.

Babcock, H. *Dementia Praecox: A Psychological Study*. New York: Science Press, 1933.

Bachet, M. Comparison of facts concerning hallucinatory phenomena caused by imprisonment with Clerambault theories on mental automatism. *Semaine d. hop. Paris* (supp.), 1947, 23: 655–661.

Baillarger, J. *Des Hallucinations*. Paris, 1846.

Baldwin, M., and Hofmann, A. Hallucinations, Vol. 4, pp. 327–339. In P. J. Vinken and C. W. Bruyn (eds.), *Handbook of Clinical Neurology*. Berlin: J. Springer, 1969.

Bannister, D., and Solomon, P. Schizophrenic thought disorder: specific or diffuse. *Brit. J. Med. Psychol.*, 1966, 39: 215–219.

Barbu, Z. *Problems of Historical Psychology*. New York: Grove Press, 1960.

Barker, E. Crusades, Vol. 7, pp. 524–552. In *Encyclopaedia Britannica,* 11th ed. New York: Encyclopaedia Britannica Company, 1910.

Barnett, B. Witchcraft, psychopathology, and hallucinations. *Brit. J. Psychiat.,* 1965, 111: 439–445.

_____. Witchcraft. *Brit. J. Psychiat.,* 1968, 114: 122–123.

Baroja, J. C. Trans. N. Glendinning. *The World of Witches.* London: Weidenfeld and Nicolson, 1961 (1964).

Barr, M. L. The significance of nuclear sexing. In J. G. Howells (ed.), *Modern Perspectives in World Psychiatry.* New York: Brunner/ Mazel, 1971.

Bartlett, F. C. *Thinking: An Experimental and Social Study.* New York: Basic Books, 1958.

Bauers, S. The function of hallucinations: An inquiry into the relationship of hallucinatory experience to creative thought. In W. Keup (ed.), *Origin and Mechanisms of Hallucinations.* New York and London: Pleunum Press, 1970.

Bellak, L. *Schizophrenia.* New York: Logos Press, 1958.

_____. Psychosis, Vol. 13, pp. 126–135. In D. W. Sills (ed.), *International Encyclopedia of the Social Sciences.* New York: Macmillan Co. and Free Press, 1968.

_____. The validity and usefulness of the concept of the schizophrenic syndrome. In R. Cancro (ed.), *The Schizophrenic Reaction.* New York: Brunner/Mazel, 1970.

Bellak, L., and Hurvich, M. A systematic study of ego functions. *J. of Nerv. and Ment. Disease,* 1969, 148: 569–588.

Bellak, L., Hurvich, M., and Gediman, H. K. *Ego Functions in Schizophrenics, Neurotics, and Normals.* New York: John Wiley and Sons, 1973.

Bellak, L., and Loeb, L. *The Schizophrenic Syndrome.* New York: Grune and Stratton, 1969.

Bender, L. Childhood schizophrenia. (Reprinted from *Amer. J. of Orthopsychiat.,* 1947, 17: 40–56.) In S. I. Harrison and J. F. McDermott (eds.), *Childhood psychopathology.* New York: International Universities Press, Inc., 1972.

Benedict, R. K., and Jacks, I. Mental illness in primitive societies. In S. K. Weinber (ed.), *Sociology of Mental Disorders.* Chicago: Aldine, 1967.

Bergin, A. E. The evaluation of therapeutic outcomes. In A. E. Bergin and S. L. Garfield (eds.), *Handbook of Psychotherapy*. New York: John Wiley, 1971.

Bessette, H. J. Learning as related to delusional and hallucinatory behavior. Dissertation, Purdue University, 1955.

Bett, W. R. *The Infirmities of Genius*. London: Christopher Johnson, 1952.

Birenbaum, G., and Zeigarnik, B. A dynamic analysis of thought disturbances. *Soviet Neuropathology, Psychiatry, and Psychohygiene*, 1935, 4, No. 6.

Black, S. The phenomena of hypnosis. In J. G. Howells (ed.), *Modern Perspectives in World Psychiatry*. New York: Brunner/Mazel, 1971.

Blandshard, B. *The Nature of Thought*. London: George Allen and Unwin Ltd., 1939.

Bleuler, E. *Dementia Praecox or The Group of Schizophrenias*. Aschaffenburg's Handbuch, 1911 trans. New York: International Universities Press, 1950.

————. *Textbook of Psychiatry*. Trans. A. A. Brill. New York: Macmillan, 1930.

Bleuler, M. Introduction. In R. Rosenthal and S. S. Kety (eds.), *Transmission of Schizophrenia*. New York: Pergamon Press, 1968.

Boisen, A. T. The form and content of schizophrenic thinking. *Psychiatry*, 1942, 5: 23–33.

de Boismont, A. J. F. Brierre. *A History of Dreams, Visions, Apparitions, Ecstasy, Magnetism, and Somnambulism*. First American trans. from second Paris edition. Philadelphia: Lindsay and Blakiston, 1855.

————. *On Hallucinations: History and Explanation of Apparitions, Visions, Dreams, Ecstasy, Magnetism, and Somnambulism*. Trans. R. T. Hulme. London: Henry Renshaw, 1859.

Bon Le, G. *The Psychology of the Great War*. London: T. Fisher Unwin, 1916.

Bonin, G. von. Architecture of the precentral motor cortex and some adjacent areas. In P. C. Bucy (ed.), *The Precentral Motor Cortex*. Urbana: University of Illinois Press, 1944.

Boring, E. G., Langfeld, H. S., and Weld, H. P. *Foundations of Psychology*. New York: John Wiley and Sons, Chapman Hall, 1948.

Boshes, L. D., and Gibbs, F. A. *Epilepsy Handbook*. Springfield, Ill.: C. C. Thomas, 1972.

Bowman, K. M., and Raymond, A. F. A statistical study of hallucinations in the manic depressive psychoses. *Amer. J. Psychiat.*, 1931, 88: 299–309.

Bradley, P. M. In H. J. Jasper, L. D. Proctor, R. S. Knighton, W. C. Noshay, and R. T. Costello, (eds.), *Reticular Formation of the Brain*. London: Churchill, 1957.

Brain, R. W. Agnosia, apraxia and aphasia, Chapter 83, Vol. 3. In S. A. K. Wilson and A. N. Bruce (eds.), *Neurology*. Baltimore: Williams and Wilkins Co., 1955a.

————. *Diseases of the Nervous System*. London: Oxford Press, 1955b.

Brill, A. A. *Fundamental Conceptions of Psychoanalysis*. New York: Harcourt, Brace and Co., 1921.

Broen, W. E. *Schizophrenia, Research and Theory*. New York and London: Academic Press, 1968.

Brower, D. R., and Bannister, H. M. *A Practical Manual of Insanity*. Philadelphia: W. B. Saunders and Co., 1902.

Brown, N. O. *Life against Death: The Psychoanalytical Meaning of History*. Middletown: Wesleyan University Press, 1959.

Bruner, J. S. The course of cognitive growth. *Amer. Psychologist*, 1964, 19: 1–15.

Bruner, J. S., Goodnow, J. J., and Austin, G. A. *A Study of Thinking*. New York: New York Science Editions, John Wiley and Sons, 1965.

Bryant, M. Charlemagne, Vol. 5, pp. 894–897. In *The Encyclopaedia Britannica*, 11th ed. New York: Encyclopaedia Britannica Co., 1910.

Bryant, W. S. The great psychical importance of ear disease. *J. of Nerv. and Ment. Disease*, September 1906, 33: 553–565.

Bumke, O., and Forester, O. *Handbuch der Neurologie*. Berlin: J. Springer, 1935–37.

Burckhardt, G. Ueber Rindenexcisionen. *Allg. Z. Psychiat.*, 1890–91, 47: 463–548.

Buss, A. H. *Psychopathology*. New York: John Wiley and Sons, 1966.

Buss, A. H., and Lang, P. J. Psychological deficit in schizophrenia: I. affect, reinforcement and concept attainment. *J. Abnorm. Psychol.*, 1965, 70: 2–24.

Bychoswski, G. *Dictators and Disciples*. New York: International University Press, 1969.

Cairns, H. R. Disturbances of consciousness with lesions of the brain stem and diencephalon. *Brain*, 1952, 75: 109–146.

Callaway, E. Schizophrenia and interference, pp. 571–591. In R. Canero (ed.), *The Schizophrenic Syndrome: An Annual Review* New York: Brunner/Mazel, 1971.

Calmeil, L. F. *De la Folia Consideree Sous le Pont de Vue Philosophique, Historique et Judiciare de la folie.* Vol. 2. 1840.

Cameron, N. Reasoning, regression, and communication in schizophrenics. *Psychological Monographs,* 1938, 50: 1; whole No. 221.

————. *Personality Development and Psychopathology: A Dynamic Approach.* Boston: Houghton Mifflin Co., 1963.

Cameron, N., and Margaret, A. *Behavior Pathology.* Boston, Cambridge: Houghton Mifflin Co. and Riverside Press, 1951.

Campbell, J. G. *Witchcraft and Second Sight.* Glasgow: James MacLehose and Sons, 1902.

Cantril, H. Attitudes and opinion, pp. 560–588. In E. G. Boring, H. S. Langeld, and H. P. Weld (eds.), *Foundations of Psychology.* New York: John Wiley and Sons, 1948.

Carpenter, W. T. Current diagnostic concepts in schizophrenia. *Am. J. Psychiat.,* 1976, 133: 172–177.

Carroll, J. B. *Language and Thought.* Englewood Cliffs, N. J.: Prentice-Hall, 1964.

Cartwright, F. F., and Biddiss, M. D. *Disease and History.* New York: Thomas Y. Crowell, 1972.

Carus, P. *History of the Devil and the Idea of Evil.* Chicago: Open Court Publishing Co.; London: Kegal Paul, Trench, Trubner and Co., 1900.

Caston, J. Completion effects and attention in hallucinatory and nonhallucinatory patients and normal subjects. *J. of Nerv. and Ment. Disease,* 1969, 148: 147–157.

Cazzamalli, F. Le allucinazioni creative. *Gioranale de Psichiaturia e di Neuropatologia,* 1937, 3: 336–344.

Cerny, M. Electrophysiological study of verbal hallucinations. *Activitas Nervosa Superior* (Praha), 1964, 6: 94–95.

————. On neurophysiological mechanisms in verbal hallucinations: an electrophysiological study. *Activitas Nervosa Superior* (Praha), 1965, 7: 197–198.

Chapman, J. The early symptoms of schizophrenia. *Brit. J. Psychiat.,* 1966, 112: 225–251.

Chapman, L. J., and Chapman, J. P. *Disordered Thought in Schizophrenia.* Englewood Cliffs, N. J.: Prentice-Hall, 1973.

Chapman, W. P. Depth electrode studies in patients with temporal lobe epilepsy. In E. R. Ramey and D. S. O'Doherty, (eds.), *Electrical Studies on the Unanesthetized Brain*. New York: Paul Hoeber, 1960.

Charcot, J. M. *Lectures on the Diseases of the Nervous System*. Trans. G. Sigerson. London: Sydenham Society, 1877.

Charcot-Schules, P. R. *Etudes cliniques sur la grande hysterie on hysterio-epilepsie*. 2nd ed. Paris, 1885.

Chauchard, P. *The Brain*. New York: Grove Press (London: Evergreen Books), 1962.

Christian, P. *The History and Practice of Magic*. London: Forge Press, 1952.

Chtopicki, W. *Omamy stuchowe jako swoiste zaburzenia czynnosci mowy ze stanowiska nervopatologii i psychopatologii*. Karakow: P. A. V., 1949.

Church, J. *Language and the Discovery of Reality*. New York: Vintage Books, a division of Random House, 1961.

Clark, K. K. *Civilization: A Personal View*. New York: Harper, 1970.

Clark, L. P. A psycho-historical study of the epileptic personality in genius. *Psychoanalytic Review*, 1922, 9: 367–401.

Claude, H. The mechanism of hallucination (syndrome of exterior action). *Psychiat. Quar.*, 1930, 4: 59–73.

Clerambault, G. G. de. Les psychoses hallucinatoieres chroniques analyse. *Bull. Soc. Clin. de Med. Ment.*, 1924, 12:17.

Clissold, A. *The Prophetic Spirit in Its Relation to Wisdom and Madness*. London: Longmans, Green and Co., 1870.

Coffin, T. W. Some conditions of suggestion and suggestibility. *Psychological Monographs*, 1941, 53, No. 4.

Cohen, L. H. Imagery and its relation to schizophrenic symptoms. *J. Ment. Sci.*, 1938, 84: 284–346.

Cohn, N. *The Pursuit of the Millennium*. London: Seckert Warburg, 1957.

———. *The Pursuit of the Millennium*. Revised ed. New York: Oxford University Press, 1970.

Cole, L. E. *Understanding Abnormal Behavior*. Scranton: Chandler Publishing Co., 1970.

Colguhoun, J. C. *A History of Magic, Witchcraft, and Animal Magnetism*. London: Longman, Brown, Green, and Longhmens, 1851.

Connell, P. H. *Amphetamine Psychosis*. London: Chapman and Hall, 1958.

194   Selected References

Conrad, K. Bemerkungen zum psychopathologishe; Problem des Bei-
    ziehingswahns. *Dtsch. Med. Wschr.,* 1950, 84: 1.
_____. *Uber Begriff und Wesen der Apophance in Medhrdimensionale
    Diagnostik und Therapy.* Festschrift zum 70 Geburtstag Ernst
    Kretschmer. Stuttgardt: Thieme, 1958a.
_____. *Die beginnende Schizophrenie versuch einer Gestaltanalyse des
    Wahns.* Stuttgardt: Thieme, 1958b.
Copleston, F. C. *A History of Philosophy.* Westminster, Md.: Newman
    Press, 1950–1966.
Corner, G. W. *Anatomist at Large.* Freeport: Books for Libraries Press,
    1969.
Cossa, P., and Martin, P. Sur les hallucinations temporales. *Ann. Med.
    Psychol.,* 1951, 3: 273–279.
Craig, W. J. Objective measures of thinking integrated with psychiatric
    symptoms. *Psychological Reports,* 1965, 16: 539–554.
Creese, I., Burt, D. R., and Snyder, S. H. Dopamine receptor binding
    predicts clinical and pharmacological potencies of antischizophrenic
    drugs. *Science,* 1976, 192: 481–483.
Critchley, M. The neurology of psychotic speech. *Brit. J. Psychiat.,*
    1964, 110: 353–364.
Cromwell, R. L. Assessment of schizophrenia. In M. R. Rosenzweig and
    L. W. Porter (eds.), *Annual Review of Psychology,* Vol. 26. Palo
    Alto, California: Annual Reviews Inc., 1975.
Darnton, R. *Mesmerism and the End of the Enlightenment in France.*
    Cambridge: Harvard University Press, 1968.
Dashiell, J. F. A physiological description of thinking. *Psychol. Rev.,*
    1925, 32: 54–73.
_____. The role of vision in spatial orientation in the white rat. *J.
    Comp. Physiol. Psychol.,* 1959, 52: 522–526.
Davidman, H. The problem of undiagnosed schizophrenics in prisoners,
    pp. 21–25. In D. V. Siva Sankar (ed.), *Schizophrenia: Current
    Concepts and Research.* Hicksville: PJD Publications, 1969.
Davidson, M. A study of schizophrenic performance on the Stanford-
    Binet scale. *Brit. J. Med. Psychol.,* 1938, 17: 93–97.
_____. Studies in the application of mental tests to psychotic patients.
    Brit. J. Med. Psychol., 1939, 18: 44–52.
De Groot, J. J. M. *The Religious System of China,* Vol. 5. Leiden: E.
    J. Brill, 1907.
Dement, W., Halper, C., Pirik, T., Ferguson, J., Cohen, H., Henrikson,
    S., McGarr, K., Gonda, W., Hoyt, G., Ryan, L., Mitchell, G.,

Barches, J., and Zarcone, V. Hallucinations and dreaming, pp. 335–359. In D. A. Hamburg, K. H. Pribram, and A. J. Stunkard (eds.), *Perception and Its Disorders*. Res. Publ. Ass. Nerv. Ment. Dis., Vol. 48. Baltimore: Williams and Wilkins Co., 1970.

Dempsey, E. W., and Rioch, D. McK. The localization in the brain stem of the oestrous responses of the female guinea pig. *J. Neurophysiol.*, 1939, 2: 9–18.

Dendy, W. C. *The Philosophy of Mystery*. New York: Harper and Brothers, 1847.

Denny-Brown, D. *The Basal Ganglia*. 2nd ed. Oxford: Oxford University Press, 1962.

Dercum, F. X. *A Clinical Manual of Mental Diseases*. Philadephia and London: W. B. Saunders Co., 1914.

Deutsch, H. Foli à deux. *Psychoanalyt. Quar.*, 1938, 7: 307–318.

Devel, W. R. *People under Hitler*. New York: Harcourt, Brace and Co., 1942.

Dewey, J. *How We Think*. Boston: D. C. Heath and Co., 1933.

Dewhurst, K., and Todd, J. The psychosis of association—folie à deux. *J. of Nerv. and Ment. Disease*, 1956, 124: 451–459.

Dewi Rees, W. The hallucinations of widowhood. *Brit. Med. J.*, 1971, 3: 37–41.

Dickinson, R. L. *Human Sex Anatomy: A Topographical Atlas*. 2nd ed. Baltimore: Williams and Wilkins Co., 1949.

Dimmet, E. *The Art of Thinking*. New York: Simon and Schuster, 1928.

Disraeli, I. *The Literary Character. Illustrated by the History of Men of Genius*. London: John Murray, 1818.

Domarus, E. von. Uber die Halluzinationen der Schizophrenen. *Z. Sch. f. d. ges. Nerv. v. Psychiat.*, 1928, 112: 636–638.

Economo, C. F., and Koskinas, G. N. *Die Cytoarchitecktonik der Hirnrinde*. Wien: Springer, 1925.

Edfeldt, A. *Silent Speech and Silent Reading*. Chicago: University of Chicago Press, 1960.

Egdell, H. G., and Kolvin, I. Childhood hallucinations. *J. Child Psychol.*, 1972, 13: 279–287.

Einstein, A. *Why War?* International Institute of Intellectual Cooperation, League of Nations, 1937.

Elkes, J. Mental disorders, biological aspects, Vol. 10, pp. 139–148. In D. L. Sills (ed.), *International Encyclopedia of the Social Sciences*. New York: Macmillan Co. and Free Press, 1968.

Elkind, D. "Good me" or "bad me": The Sullivan approach to personality. *New York Times Magazine*, Sept. 24, 1972, p. 8.

Ellis, H. *A Study of British Genius*. Boston: Houghton, 1926.

English, O. S., and Finch, S. M. *Introduction to Psychiatry*. 3rd ed. New York: W. W. Norton and Co., 1964.

Ennemoser, J. *The History of Magic*. Trans. W. Howitt. London: Henry G. Bohn, 1854.

Erikson, E. H. *Childhood and Society*. Chicago: W. W. Norton Co., 1950.

Erickson, G. D., and Gustafson, G. J. Controlling auditory hallucination. *Hospital and Community Psychiatry*, 1968, 19: 327–329.

Ervin, F., Epstein, A. W., and King, H. E. Behavior of epileptic and nonepileptic patients with temporal spikes. *Arch. Neurol. and Psychiat.*, 1955, 74: 488–497.

Esquirol, J. *Observations on the Illusions of the Insane and on the Medico-legal Question of Their Confinement*. Trans. William Liddell. London: Octavo, Renshaw and Rush, 1833.

————. *Des Maladies mentales*. Vol. 2. Paris, 1838.

————. In C. E. Goshen (ed.), *Documentary History of Psychiatry*. New York: Philosophical Library, 1967.

Evans, P. Henri Ey's concepts of the organization of consciousness and its disorganization: An extension of Jacksonian theory. *Brain*, 1972, 95: 413–440.

Ewalt, J. R., Strecker, E. A., and Ebaugh, F. G. *Practical Clinical Psychiatry*. 8th ed. New York: Blakiston Division, McGraw-Hill Book Co., 1957.

Ey, H. *Hallucination et delire, Les formes hallucinatories de l'automatisme verbal*. Paris: Alcan, 1934.

————. La discussion de 1855 a la Societe Medico-Psychologique sur l'hallucination et l'etut actuel du probleme de l'activito hallucinatoire. *Ann. Med. Psychol.*, 1935, 93: part 1, 584–613.

————. *Manual de Psychiatrie*. Paris: Masson, 1967.

————. *Traite des hallucinations*. 2 tomes. Paris: Masson et Cie, 1973.

Eysenck, H. J. *Crime and Personality*. 2nd ed. London: Granada Publishing Ltd., 1970.

Eysenck, H. J., Granger, G. W., and Brenglemann, J. C. Perceptual processes and mental illness. *Maudsley Monographs* No. 2. London: Institute of Psychiatry, 1951.

Eysenck, S. B. G., and Eysenck, H. J. The personality of female prisoners. *Brit. J. Psychiat.*, 1973, 123: 693–698.

Faaborg-Anderson, K. C. Electromyographic investigation of intrinsic laryngeal muscles in humans. *Acta. Physiol. Scandinva. Suppl.*, 140, 1957, 41: 1–148.

Faaborg-Anderson, K. C., and Edfeldt, A. Q. Electromyography of intrinsic and extrinsic laryngeal muscles during silent speech correlated with reading activity. *Acta. Otolaryng.*, 1958, 49. 478–482.

Faure, H. *Hallucinations et reality perceptive*. Paris: Presses Universitaires de France, 1965.

Ferguson, S. M., Rayport, M., Gardner, R., Kass, W., Weiner, H., and Reser, M. Similarities in mental content of psychotic states, spontaneous seizures, dreams and responses to electrical brain stimulation in patients with temporal lobe epilepsy. *Psychosom. Med.*, 1969, 31: 479–498.

Fey, E. T. The performance of young schizophrenics and young normals on the Wisconsin card sorting test. *J. Consult. Psychol.*, 1951, 15: 311–319.

Finkel, P. Factors Affecting the Level of Aspiration of Delusional and Hallucinatory Patients. Purdue University Thesis, 1956.

Fischer, R. The perception-hallucination continuum. *Diseases of the Nervous System*, 1969, 30: 161–171.

Fish, F., Forrest, A., and MacPherson, E. Hallucinations as a disorder of gestalt function. *J. Ment. Sci.*, 1960, 106: 523–530.

Fish, F. J. A neurophysiological theory of schizophrenia. *J. Ment. Sci.*, 1961, 107: 828–838.

————. *Schizophrenia*. Baltimore: Williams and Wilkins; Briston: J. Wright, 1962.

————. The concept of schizophrenia. *Brit. J. Med. Psychol.*, 1966, 39: 269–274.

Fleming, G. W. T. H. The insane root. *J. Ment Sci.*, 1953, 99: 638–653.

Forester, O. Symptomatologie der Erkrankungen des Grosshirns. Motorische Felder und Bahnen, Vol. 6. In O. Bunke and O. Forester (eds.), *Handbuch der Neurologie*. Berlin: J. Springer, 1935–37.

Forrer, G. R. Benign auditory and visual hallucinations. *Arch. Gen. Psychiat.*, 1960a, 3: 95–98.

————. Effect of oral activity on hallucinations. *Arch. Gen. Psychiat.*, 1960b, 2: 110–113.

————. The psychoanalytic theory of hallucination. *Diseases of the Nervous System*, 1963, 24: 721–727.

Foucault, M. *Madness and Civilization.* Trans. R. Howard. New York and Toronto: New American Library, 1967.

Foulds, G. A., and Dixon, P. The nature of intellectual deficit in schizophrenia. III: A longitudinal study of the sub-groups. *Brit. J. Soc. Clin. Psychol.*, 1962, 1: 199–207.

Frank, J. D. Contributions of behavioral scientists toward a world without war, pp. 205–218. In P. H. Hock and J. Zubin (eds.), *Psychopathology of Schizophrenia.* New York: Grune and Stratton, 1966.

————. *Sanity and Survival.* New York: Random House, 1967.

Frazier, J. G. *The Golden Bough: A Study in Magic and Religion.* London: Macmillan and Co., 1911.

Freeman, T., Cameron, J. L., and McGhie, A. *Studies on Psychosis.* New York: International Universities Press, 1966.

Freeman, W., and Williams, J. M. Human sonar; the amygdaloid nucleus in relation to auditory hallucinations. *J. of Nerv. and Ment. Disease,* 1952, 116: 456–461.

Frete, J. La relation hallucinatorire l'evolution. *Psychiatrique,* 1949, 2: 121–153.

Freud, S. *Collected Papers.* J. Riviere and J. Strachey (eds.). New York and London: International Psycho-Analytical Press, 1924–1950.

————. A metapsychological supplement to the theory of dreams, Vol. 14, pp. 22–235. In J. Riviere and J. Strachey (eds.), *Collected Papers.* New York and London: International Psycho-Analytical Press, 1924–1950.

————. *New Introductory Lectures on Psychoanalysis.* Trans. W. J. Sprott. London: Hogarth Press and the Institute of Psycho-Analysis, 1933.

————. *The Future of an Illusion.* London: Hogarth Press, 1934.

————. Moses and monotheism. In J. Strachey (ed.), *Complete Psychological Works of Sigmund Freud*, Vol. 23 (1937–1938). London: Hogarth Press, 1964.

————. The loss of reality in neurosis and psychosis, Vol. 2. In J. Strachey (ed.), *Collected Papers.* London: Hogarth Press, 1948.

————. *Delusion and Dream.* Philip Rieff (ed.). Boston: Beacon Press, 1956.

Freud, S., and Bullitt, W. G. *Thomas Woodrow Wilson, 28th President, A Psychological Study*. Boston: Houghton Mifflin, 1967.

Furth, H. G. *Thinking without Language*. New York: Free Press, 1966.

Gal'perin, P. Ya. Inner action as the basis of formation of thought and image. (Russian). *Yoprosy Psikhologii*, No. 6, 1957.

————. The development of investigations into the formation of inner action. *Psychological Science in the U.S.S.R.*, Vol. 1. Moscow: RSFSR Academy of Pedagogic Sciences Press, 1959.

Gardiner, S. R. George III, Vol. 11, pp. 740–743. In *Encyclopaedia Britannica*. New York, The Encyclopaedia Britannica, 1910.

Gerard, R. W. Neurophysiology: brain and behavior, Vol. 2. In S. Arieti (ed.), *American Handbook of Psychiatry*. New York: Basic Books, 1959.

Glass, B. A study of concept formation in schizophrenics and non-psychotics. *Dissertation Abstracts*, 1956, 16: 1945.

Glueck, S. S. *Mental Disorder and the Criminal Law*. Boston: Little, Brown and Company, 1925; New York: Kraus Reprint Corporation, 1966.

Godwin, W. *Lives of the Necromancers*. London: Frederick J. Mason, 1834.

Goldstein, K. Methodological approach to the study of schizophrenic thought disorder. In J. S. Kasanin (ed.), *Language and Thought in Schizophrenia*. Berkeley and Los Angeles: University of California Press, 1944.

————. *Language and Language Disturbances*. New York: Grune and Stratton, 1948.

Goldstein, K., and Sheerer, M. Abstract and concrete behavior: An experimental study with special tests. *Psychological Monographs*, 1941, 53: 2 (whole No. 239).

Goodwin, D. W., Alderson, P., and Rosenthal, R. Clinical significance of hallucinations in psychiatric disorders. A study of 116 hallucinatory patients. *Arch. Gen. Psychiat.*, 1971, 24: 76–80.

Gottschalk, L. A., and Gleser, G. C. *The Measurement of Psychological States through the Content Analysis of Verbal Behavior*. Berkeley and Los Angeles: University of California Press, 1969.

Gould, L. N. Verbal hallucinations and activity of vocal musculature: an electromyographic study. *Amer. J. Psychiat.*, 1948, 105: 367–373.

————. Auditory hallucinations and subvocal speech; objective study in a case of schizophrenia. *J. of Nerv. and Ment. Disease,* 1949, 109: 418–427.

————. Verbal hallucinations as automatic speech: The reactivation of dormant speech habit. *Amer. J. Psychiat.,* 1950, 107: 110.

Gowers, W. R. *Epilepsy and Other Chronic Convulsive Disorders.* London: J. A. Churchill, 1901.

Gralnick, A. Folie à deux: The psychosis of association. *Psychiat. Quar.,* 1942, 16: 230.

Grant, V. W. *This Is Mental Illness.* Boston: Beacon Press, 1963.

Greenson, R. D. The psychology of apathy. *Psychoanalyt. Quar.,* 1949, 18: 290.

Griffin, D. R. Acoustic orientation in the oil bird Steatornis. *Proc. Nat. Acad. Sci.,* 1953, 39: 884–893.

————. *Listening in the Dark.* New Haven: Yale University Press, 1958.

————. Echolocation and its relevance to communication behavior. In T. A. Sebeok (ed.), *Animal Communication.* Bloomington: Indiana University Press, 1968.

Grigg, A. E. Hallucinations. *Encyclopedia Americana.* New York: Americana Corporation, 1971.

Grinker, R. R., Sr. An essay on schizophrenia and science. *Arch. Gen. Psychiat.,* 1969, 20: 1–24.

Guiot, G., Hertzog, E., Rondot, P., and Moligna, P. Arrest or acceleration of speech evoked by thalamic stimulation in the course of stereotaxic procedures for Parkinsonism. *Brain,* 1961, 84: 363–380.

Guze, S. B. *Criminality and Psychiatric Disorders.* New York: Oxford University Press, 1976.

Guze, S. B., Goodwin, D. W., and Crane, J. B. Criminality and psychiatric disorder. *Arch. Gen. Psychiat.,* 1969, 20: 583–591.

Haits, G. A contribution to the problem of syndromeshift. *Psychiatria et Neurologia,* 1967, 154: 261–265.

Halleck, S. L. *Psychiatry and the Dilemmas of Crime.* New York and London: Harper and Row, 1967.

Halstead, W. C. *Brain and Intelligence.* Chicago: University of Chicago Press, 1947.

Hamilton, E., and Cairns, H. *The Collected Dialogues of Plato.* New York: Pantheon Books, 1961.

Hamlin, R. M., and Jones, R. E. Vocabulary deficit in improved and unimproved schizophrenic subjects. *J. of Nerv. and Ment. Disease,* 1963, 136: 360.

Hanfmann, E., and Kasanin, J. Conceptual thinking in schizophrenia. *Nervous and Mental Disease Monograph,* No. 67. Washington, D.C.: Nervous and Mental Disease Pub. Co., 1942.

Hansen, C. *Witchcraft at Salem.* New York: George Braziller, 1966.

Harris, A., and Metcalf, M. Inappropriate affect. *J. of Neurology, Neurosurgery, and Psychiatry.* 1956, 19: 308–313.

Harris, J. *The Pseudo-Occult: Notes on Telepathic Vision and Auditory Messages Proceeding from Hypnotism.* London: Philip Wellby, 1908.

Hart, D. S., and Payne, R. W. Language structure and predictability in overinclusive patients. *Brit. J. Psychiat.,* 1973, 123: 643–652.

Hartmann, E. Dreams and other hallucinations: an approach to the underlying mechanisms. In R. K. Siegel and L. J. West (eds.), *Hallucinations: Behavior, Experience and Theory.* New York: John Wiley and Sons, 1975.

Hausman, M. F. A method to objectively demonstrate thinking difficulties. *Amer. J. Psychiat.,* 1933, 13: 613–625.

Haywood, H. D., and Moelis, I. Effect of symptom change on intellectual function in schizophrenia. *J. Abnorm. and Soc. Psychol.,* 1963, 67: 76–78.

Heath, R. G. Pleasure and brain activity in man: Deep and surface electroencephalograms during orgasm. *J. of Nerv. and Ment. Disease,* 1972, 154: 3–18.

————. Brain function and behavior. *J. of Nerv. and Ment. Disease,* 1975, 160: 159–175.

Hecaen, H., and de Ajuriaquerra, J. *Meconnaissances et hallucinations corporelles.* Paris: Masson, 1952.

Hecker, J. F. C. *The Epidemics of the Middle Ages.* Trans. B. G. Babington. London: Trubner and Co., 1859.

Henderson, D., and Batchelor, I. R. C. *Henderson's and Gillespie's Textbook of Psychiatry.* 9th ed. London: Oxford University Press, 1962.

Hernandez-Peon, R. A neurophysiologic model of dreams and hallucinations. *J. of Nerv. and Ment. Disease,* 1965, 141: 3–50.

Herrick, C. J. *The Brain of the Tiger Salamander.* Chicago: University of Chicago Press, 1948.

————. *The Evolution of Human Nature.* Austin: University of Texas Press and Harper and Brothers, 1956.

Herrnstein, R. J. Placebo effect in the rat. *Science,* 1962, 138: 677–678.

Highet, G. *Man's Unconquerable Mind.* New York: Columbia University Press, 1954.

Hilgard, E. R. *The Experience of Hypnosis.* New York: Harcourt, Brace and World, 1965.

Hill, J. M. Hallucinations in psychoses. *J. of Nerv. and Ment. Disease.* 1936, 405–421.

Hirasawa, K., Okano, S., and Kamino, S. Beitrag zur kenntnis uber die corticalen extrapyramidalen Fasern aus der Area temporalis superior (area 22) beim Affen. *Ztsch. F. mikra. anat. Forschg,* 1938, 44: 74–84.

Hirsch, N. D. M. *Genius and Creative Intelligence.* Cambridge: Science Art Publishers, 1931.

Hirsch, S. R., and Leff, J. P. *Abnormalities in Parents of Schizophrenics.* Maudsley Monographs, Number 22. London: Oxford University Press, 1975.

Hodges, A. A developmental study of symbolic behavior. *Child Development,* 1954, 25: 277–280.

Hoenig, J., and Hamilton, C. M. Epilepsy and sexual orgasm. *Acta psychiat. Scand.,* 1960, 35: 355–448.

Hofstadter, R. *The Paranoid Style in American Politics and Other Essays.* New York: Vintage Books, 1967.

Hollingshead, A. B., and Redlich, F. C. *Social Class and Mental Illness.* New York and London: John Wiley and Sons, 1958.

Hollister, L. E. *Chemical Psychoses, L.S.D. and Related Drugs.* Springfield, Ill.: Charles C. Thomas, 1968.

Hume, D. Letter to Dr. John Arbuthnot, 1734. In E. C. Mossner (ed.), *An Enquiry Concerning Human Understanding and Other Essays.* New York: Washington Square Press, 1963.

Humphrey, G. *Thinking.* New York: Wiley, 1951.

Huxley, A. *The Devils of Loudun.* New York: Harper and Brothers, 1952.

Illinois Crime Survey. Illinois Association for Criminal Justice. Montclair, N. J.: Petterson Smith, 1929.

Inglis, J. *The Scientific Study of Abnormal Behavior.* Chicago: Aldine, 1966.

Inhelder, B., and Piaget, J. *The Growth of Logical Thinking.* New York: Basic Books, 1958.

Inouye, T., and Shimizu, A. The electromyographic study of verbal hallucination. *J. of Nerv. and Ment. Disease,* 1970, 151: 415–422.

————. Visual evoked response and reaction time during verbal hallucination. *J. of Nerv. and Ment. Disease,* 1972, 155: 419–426.

Ireland, W. W. *Through the Ivory Gate: Studies in Psychology and History.* Edinburgh: Bell and Bradfute, 1889.

————. *The Blot upon the Brain.* New York: L. P. Putnam's Sons, 1893.

Ivanov-Smolenskii, A. G. (editor). *Works of the Institute of Higher Nervous Activity.* Pathophysiological Series Vols. 1 and 2. Moscow: The Academy of Sciences of the USSR, 1955, 1956, Washington, D. C.: Office of Technical Services, U. S. Department of Commerce, 1960.

Ives, G. *A History of Penal Methods.* London: Stanley Paul and Co., 1914.

Jackson, D. D. *The Etiology of Schizophrenia.* New York: Basic Books, 1960.

Jackson, J. H. *Med. Times.* London, 1874, 1: 123.

Jacobson, A. C. An analysis of genius. *Critic and Guide,* 1909, 12: 206–209.

————. *Genius: Some Revelations.* New York: Greenberg, 1926.

Jacobson, E. Electrophysiology of mental activities. *Amer. J. Psychol.,* 1932, 44: 677–694.

Jaffe, S. L. Hallucinations in children at a state hospital. *Psychiat. Quar.,* 1966, 40: 88–95.

James, W. *The Principles of Psychology.* New York: Dover Publications, 1890.

Janet, P. *Major Symptoms of Hysteria.* New York: Macmillan Co., 1906 (1929).

————. *Psychological Healing.* Trans. E. C. Paul. New York: Macmillan Co.; London: George Allen and Unwin, 1925.

————. Le langage interieur dans l'hallucination psychique. *Ann. Medicopsychol.,* 1936, 2: 377–386.

————. Caracteres de l'hallucination du persecute. *Miscellanea psychologica,* Albert Michotte. Paris: Librairie Philosophique, 1947.

Jasper, K. *General Psychopathology.* Chicago: University of Chicago Press, 1963.

Jefferson, G. The reticular formation and clinical neurology, pp. 729–744. In H. H. Jasper and L. D. Proctor (eds.), *Reticular Formation of the Brain.* Boston and Toronto: Little, Brown and Co., 1958.

Johnson, A. War. In E. R. A. Seligman and A. Johnson (eds.), *Ency-clopedia of the Social Sciences*. New York: Macmillan Co., 1935.

Johnson. F. H. An anatomicophysiological study of the mesencephalic reticular formation. *Cornell University Thesis Summaries*. Ithaca, N. Y.: Cornell University Press, 1951.

————. Experimental study of spino-reticular connections in the cat. *Anatomical Record*, 1954, 118: 316.

————. Auditory hallucinations as interpreted by means of recorders. *Anatomical Record*, 1958, 130: 321.

————. A study on the cause of brain waves. *Federation Proceedings*, 1960, 19: 290.

————. The nucleus cuneiformis and decerebrate rigidity. *Anatomical Record*, 1962, 142: 244.

————. Neurophysiological disuse of inner speech as used in thinking in schizophrenia. *Anatomical Record*, 1967, 157: 366.

————. Observations from medical history concerning hallucinatory suggestibility. *Anatomical Record*, 1972, 172: 456–457.

Johnson, F. H., and Russell, G. V. The locus coeruleus as a pneumo-taxic center. *Anatomical Record*, 1952, 112: 464.

Johnson, F. H., Sherry, C. J., and Millichap, J. G. A study of experi-mental epilepsy in the cat. *Anatomical Record*, 1969, 163: 205.

Johnson, R. L., and Miller, M. D. Auditory hallucinations and intellec-tual deficit. *J. Psychiat. Res.*, 1965, 3: 37–41.

Jones, H. B. Learning and abnormal behavior, pp. 488–528. In D. D. Jackson (ed.), *The Etiology of Schizophrenia*. New York: Basic Books, 1960.

Jouvet, M. Telencephalic and rhombencephalic sleep in the cat, pp. 188–208. In Ge. E. W. Wolstenholme and M. O'Connor (eds.), *The Nature of Sleep*. Boston: Little, Brown and Co., 1960.

————. Mechanism of the states of sleep, pp. 86–126. In S. S. Kety , E. V. Evarts, and H. L. Williams (eds.), *Sleep and Altered States of Consciousness*. Res. Publ. Ass. Nerv. Ment. Dis., Vol. 45. Balti-more: Williams and Wilkins Co., 1967.

Jowett, B. Translation of Plato. In C. W. Eliot (ed.), *The Harvard Classics*. New York: P. F. Collier and Sons Corp., 1909.

Jung, C. G. *The Psychogenesis of Mental Disease*. Bollingen Series XX. New York: Pantheon, 1960a.

————. *Psychology of Dementia Praecox*. 1907 Bollingen Series XX. New York: Pantheon, 1960b.

Kandinsky, V. Zur lehre von den Hallucination. *Arch. F. Psychiat.,* 1881, 11: 453.

Karagrlla, I., and Robertson, E. E. Psychical phenomena in temporal lobe epilepsy and the psychoses. *Brit. Med. J.,* 1955, 26: 748–752.

Karpman, B. *Case Studies in the Psychopathology of Crime.* Vol. 2. Washington, D. C.: Medical Science Press, 1944.

Kasanin, J. S. (ed.). *Language and Thought in Schizophrenia.* Berkeley and Los Angeles: University of California Press, 1944 (1951).

Katan, M. Dream and psychosis: their relationship to hallucinatory processes. *Int. J. Psychoanal.,* 1960, 41: 341–351.

Kelley, A. H., Beaton, L. E., and Magoun, H. W. A midbrain mechanism for facio-vocal activity. *J. Neurophysiol.,* 1946, 9: 181–189.

Kellogg, W. N. *Porpoises and Sonar.* Chicago: Phoenix Science Series, University of Chicago Press, 1961.

Keup, W. (ed.). *Origin and Mechanisms of Hallucination.* New York and London: Pleunum Press, 1970.

Kinsbourne, M., and Warrington, E. K. Jargon aphasia. *Neuropsychol.,* 1963, 1: 27.

Kinsey, A. C., Pomeroy, W. B., Martin, C. E., and Gebhard, R. H. *Sexual Behavior in the Human Female.* Philadelphia: W. B. Saunders Co., 1953.

Kirton, F. *A Collection Out of the Best Approved Authors. Histories of Visions, Apparitions.* London: John Gaule, 1660.

Klass, W. Inter-relationship of hallucinations and dreams in spontaneously hallucinating patients. *Psychiat. Quar.,* 1970, 44: 488–499.

Klein, G. S. Ego psychology, Vol. 11. In D. L. Sills, *International Encyclopedia of the Social Sciences.* New York: Macmillan Co. and Free Press, 1968.

Klein, K., and Mayer-Gross, W. *The Clinical Examination of Patients with Organic Cerebral Disease.* Springfield, Ill.: Charles C. Thomas, 1957.

Kleist, K. Aphasia und Giesteskrankhest. *Munch Med. Wschr.,* 1914, 61: 8.

Klimes, K. "Audible thoughts" as a preliminary stage of acoustic hallucination. *Arch. F. Psychiat.,* 1941, 114: 358–365.

Kluver, H. *Mescal and Mechanisms of Hallucinations.* Chicago: Phoenix Science Series, University of Chicago Press, 1966.

Kohn, M. L. The interaction of social class and the factors in the etiology of schizophrenia. *Amer. J. Psychiat.,* 1976, 133: 177–184.

Kolb, L. C. *Noyes' Modern Clinical Psychiatry*. 7th ed. Philadelphia, London, and Toronto: W. B. Saunders Co., 1968.

Konorski, J. *Integrative Activity of the Brain*. Chicago and London: University of Chicago Press, 1967, Second Impression, 1970.

Kraepelin, E. *Dementia Praecox and Paraphrenia*. Edinburgh: E. and S. Livingston, 1919.

_____. *Manic-depressive Insanity and Paranoia*. Edinburgh: E. and S. Livingston, 1921.

Krech, D., and Crutschfield, R. *Elements of Psychology*. New York: Knopf, 1969.

Kreisman, D. E., and Joy, U. D. Family response to the mental illness of a relative: A review of the literature. *Schizophrenia Bulletin*: NIMH No. 10. Washington, D. C.: Government Printing Office, 1974.

Kretschmer, E. *The Psychology of Men of Genius*. Trans. R. B. Cattell. London: Kegan Paul, Trench, Trubner and Co.; New York: Harcourt, Brace and Co., 1931.

Krieg, W. J. S. *Functional Neuroanatomy*. 3rd ed. Evanston: Brain Books, 1966.

Kris, E. *The New York Times*. December 8, 1940.

Kubie, L. S. *Neurotic Distortion of the Creative Process*. New York: Noonday Press, Division Farrar, Straus and Giroux, 1968.

Lagache, D. *Les Hallucinations verbal et le parole*. Paris: Librairie Felix Alcan, 1934.

_____. Les hallucinations. *Psychol. Abstr.*, 1935, 9: 529.

Landis, C. *Varieties of Psychopathological Experience*. F. A. Mettler (ed.). New York: Holt, Rinehart and Winston, 1964.

Lange, J. The other side of hallucinations. *Amer. J. Psychiat.*, 1938, 94: 1089–1097.

_____. The other side of hallucinations. *Amer. J. Psychiat.*, 1939a, 96: 423–430.

_____. The other side of the affective aspect of schizophrenia. *Psychiatry*, 1939b, 2: 195–202.

_____. The other side of the ideological aspect of schizophrenia. *Psychiatry*, 1940, 3: 389–399.

Lange, P. J. The effect of aversive stimuli on reaction time in schizophrenia. *J. Abnorm. and Soc. Psychol.*, 1959, 59: 263–268.

Lange, P. J., and Buss, A. H. Psychological deficit in schizophrenia: II. Interference and activation. *J. Abnorm. Psychol.*, 1965, 70: 77–106.

Lange-Eichbaum, W. *The Problem of Genius.* Trans. E. Paul and C. Paul. New York: Macmillan Co., 1932.

————. *Genie, Irrsinn and Ruhum.* (von Wolfram Kurth). Munchen and Basel: Ernst Beinhardt Verlag, 1956.

Lashley, K. S. The problem of cerebral organization in vision. *Biol. Symposia,* 1942, 7: 301–322.

Lawn, A. M. The localization in the nucleus ambiguus of the rabbit, of the cells of origin of motor nerve fibers in the glossopharyngeal nerve and various branches of the vagus nerve by means of retrograde degeneration. *J. Comp. Neurol.,* 1966, 127: 293–305.

Leaf, A., and Launois, J. A scientist visits some of the world's oldest people. *National Geographic Magazine,* 1973, 143: 93–119.

Leff, J. Perceptual phenomena and personality in sensory deprivation. *Brit. J. Psychiat.,* 1968, 114: 1499–1508.

Lehmann, H. E. Schizophrenia IV: Clinical features, pp. 621–648. In A. M. Freedman, and H. I. Kaplan (eds.), *Comprehensive Textbook of Psychiatry.* Baltimore: Williams and Wilkins Co., 1967.

Lelut, M. Demon de Socratei specimen d'une application de la Science Physiologique a cell de l'Histoire. Membre de l'Institute Nouvell Ed., 1836.

————. del'Amulette de Pascal, pour servir c' l'histoire des hallucinations, analy. par. M. E. Carriere Gazette Medicale. Paris, 1847.

Lenneberg, E. H. *Biological Foundations of Language.* New York, London and Sydney: John Wiley and Sons, 1967.

Lennox, W. G., with Lennox, M. A. *Epilepsy and Related Disorders.* 2 vols. Boston and Toronto: Little, Brown and Co., 1960.

Lerner, J. Disability evaluation of hallucination in psychiatric illness. *Amer. J. Psychiat.,* 1964, 121: 586–588.

Lester, J. R. Production of associative sequences in schizophrenia and chronic brain syndrome. *J. Abnorm. and Soc. Psychol.,* 1960, 60: 225–233.

L'Etang, H. *The Pathology of Leadership.* New York: Hawthorn Books, 1970.

Levin, M. The basic symptoms of schizophrenia. *Amer. J. Psychiat.,* 1931, 11: 215–236.

————. Auditory hallucinations in "non-psychotic" children. *Amer. J. Psychiat.,* 1932, 11: 1119–1152.

————. On the causation of mental symptoms. *J. Ment. Sci.,* 1936, 82: 1–27.

Levinson, H. Auditory hallucinations in a case of hysteria. *Brit. J. Psychiat.*, 1966, 112: 19–26.

Lewinsohn, P. M. Characteristics of patients with hallucinations. *J. Clin. Psychol.*, 1968, 24: 423 (suppl.).

Lhermitte, F., and Gautier, J. C. Aphasia, Vol. 4, chapter 5, pp. 84–104. In P. J. Vinken and G. W. Bruyn (eds.), *Handbook of Clinical Neurology*. Amsterdam: North-Holland Publishing Co.; New York: Wiley Interscience Division, John Wiley and Sons, 1969.

Lhermitte, J. Comment comprendre les hallucinations. *Gazette Modicale de France, Paris*, 1949, 56: 345–351.

————. *Les hallucination, clinique et physiopathologie*. Paris: G. Doin, 1951.

Liddell, H. S. The nervous system as a whole: The conditioned reflex. In J. F. Fulton (ed.), *Physiology of the Nervous System*. London and New York: Oxford University Press, 1943.

————. In H. W. Brosin (ed.), *Lectures on Experimental Psychiatry*. Pittsburgh: University of Pittsburgh Press, 1961.

Lidz, T. Schizophrenia. In D. L. Sills (ed.), *International Encyclopedia of the Social Sciences*. New York: Macmillan Co. and Free Press, 1968.

————. Family settings that produce schizophrenic offspring, pp. 196–210. In P. Doucet and C. Lauvin (eds.), *Problems of Psychosis*. Amsterdam: Excerpta Medica, 1971.

————. *The Origin and Treatment of Schizophrenic Disorders*. New York: Basic Books, 1973.

Lilly, J. D. Mental effects of reduction of ordinary levels of physical stimuli in intact healthy persons. *Psychiat. Res. Rep.*, 1956, No. 5.

Lindsley, O. R. Operant conditioning methods applied to research in chronic schizophrenia. *Psychiat. Res. Rep.*, 1956, 5: 118–139.

————. Characteristics of the behavior of chronic psychotics as revealed by free-operant conditioning methods. *Diseases of the Nervous System Monograph Supplement*, 1960, 21: 66–78.

————. Direct measurement and functional definition of vocal hallucinatory symptoms in chronic psychosis. *Proceedings of the Third Congress of Psychiatry*. Montreal: McGill University Press, 1961.

————. Operant conditioning methods in diagnosis. In J. H. Nodine and J. H. Moyer (eds.), *Psychosomatic Medicine: The First Hahnemann Symposium*. Philadelphia: Lea and Febiger, 1962.

_____. Free-operant conditioning and psychotherapy, Vol. 3. In J. H. Masserman (ed.), *Current Psychiatric Therapies.* New York: Grune and Stratton, 1963*a*.

_____. Direct measurement and functional definition of vocal hallucinatory symptoms. *J. of Nerv. and Ment. Disease*, 1963*b*, 136: 293–297.

_____. Characteristics of the behavior of chronic psychotics as revealed by free-operant conditioning methods, pp. 250–271. In W. H. Gantt, L. Pickenhain, and C. H. Zwingman (eds.), *Pavlovian Approach to Psychopathology.* New York: Pergamon Press, 1970.

Linn, L. Clinical manifestations of psychiatric disorders, pp. 546–577. In A. M. Freedman and H. I. Kaplan (eds.), *Comprehensive Textbook of Psychiatry.* Baltimore: Williams and Wilkins Co., 1967.

Logan, W. J. Neurological aspects of hallucinogenic drugs. In W. J. Friedlander (ed.), *Advances in Neurology.* Vol. 13. New York: Raven Press, 1975.

Lombroso, C. *The Man of Genius.* London: Walter Scott, 1891.

Loosten, G. de. *Jesus Christus von Standpunkte des Psychiaters.* Bamberg: 1905.

Lorant, S. Lincoln's darker side. *The New York Times,* August 6, 1972, Section 4, p. 12.

Lothrop, W. W. A critical review of research on the conceptual thinking of schizophrenics. *J. of Nerv. and Ment. Disease*, 1961, 132: 118–126.

Lowe, G. R. The phenomenology of hallucinations as an aid to differential diagnosis. *Brit. J. Psychiat.*, 1973, 123: 621–633.

Lowell, P. *Occult Japan or The Way of the Gods.* Boston and New York: Houghton, Mifflin and Co., 1895.

Lucas, C., Sansbury, P., and Collins, J. A social and clinical study of delusions in schizophrenia. *J. Ment. Sci.*, 1962, 108: 747–758.

Ludecke, K. G. W. *I Knew Hitler.* New York: C. Scribner's Sons, 1938.

Lunn, V. On body hallucinations. *Acta Psychiat. Scand.*, 1965, 41: 387–399.

Luria, A. R. Verbal regulation of behavior, pp. 359–424. In M. A. B. Brazier (ed.), *The Central Nervous System and Behavior.* Trans. of 3rd Conference, J. Macy, Jr. Foundation. Madison, N. J.: Madison Printing Co., 1960.

_____. *The Role of Speech in the Regulation of Normal and Abnormal Behavior.* New York: Liveright, 1961.

————. *Restoration of Function after Brain Injury*. Trans. B. Haigh and O. L. Zanguill. New York: Macmillan Co., 1963.

————. *Human Brain and Psychological Processes*. New York and London: Harper and Row, 1966*a*.

————. *Higher Cortical Functions in Man*. New York: Basic Books, Consultants Bureau, 1966*b*.

————. *The Working Brain: An Introduction to Neuropsychology*. Trans. B. Haigh. New York: Basic Books, 1973.

Luria, A. R., and Yudovich, F. I. *Speech and the Development of Mental Processes in the Child*. London: Stapes, 1959.

Macalpine, I., and Hunter, R. *George III and the Mad-Business*. New York: Pantheon Books, A Division of Random House, 1969.

McGhie, A. *Pathology of Attention*. Baltimore: Penguin Books, 1969.

McGuigan, F. J. *Thinking: Studies of Covert Language Processes*. New York: Appleton-Century Crofts, Division of Meredith Publishing Co., 1966*a*.

————. Covert oral behavior and auditory hallucinations. *Psychophysiology*, 1966*b*, 3: 73–80.

McGuigan, F. J., Keller, B., and Stanton, E. Covert language responses during silent reading. *J. Educ. Psychol.*, 1964, 55: 339–343.

Machen, A. *The Angels of Mons*. London: Simpkin, Marshall, Hamilton, Kent and Co., 1915.

MacKay, C. *Memoirs of Extraordinary Popular Delusions*. London: Richard Bentley, 1841.

McKeller, P. *Imagination and Thinking*. New York: Basic Books, 1957.

McReynolds, P. Chapter 9. In L. Bellack, and L. Loeg (eds.), *The Schizophrenic Syndrome*. New York: Grune and Stratton, 1969.

Mac Robert, R. G. Hallucinations of the sane; The psychiatric significance of the "vertical" or truth-telling variety. *J. Insurance Med.*, 1949–1950, No. 3: 5–15.

Madden, R. R. *Phantasmata or Illusions and Fanaticism*. London: T. C. Newby, 1857.

Magnus, O., and Loventz De Haas, A. M. (eds.). The epilepsies, Vol. 15. In P. J. Vinken and C. W. Bruyn (eds.), *Handbook of Clinical Neurology*. Berlin: J. Springer, 1974.

Magoun, H. W. Discussion, p. 381. In M. A. B. Brazier (ed.), *The Central Nervous System and Behavior*. Trans. of 3rd Conference, J. Macy, Jr. Foundation. Madison, N. J.: Madison Printing Co., 1960.

Maher, B. A. *Principles of Psychopathology*. New York: McGraw-Hill, 1966.

Mahesh, M. D. Intelligence and verbal knowledge in relation to Epstein's overinclusion test. *J. Clin. Psychol.*, 1960, 16: 417–419.

Malzberg, B. Mortality among patients with mental disease in the New York Civil State Hospitals. *J. Insurance Med.*, 1949–1950, 5: 5–13.

Marcus, E. L. *Hypnosis: Fact and Fiction*. Baltimore: Penguin Books, 1959.

Marie, P., and Foix, C. Rev. Neurol. See P. Bailey, Aphasia and Apriaxia. *Arch. Neurol. and Psychiat.*, 1924, 11: 501–529.

Maritain, J. *Creative Intuition in Art and Poetry*. London: Pantheon Books, 1953.

Marrazzi, A. S. The effects of drugs on neurons and synapses. In W. S. Fields (ed.), *Brain Mechanisms and Drug Action*. Springfield, Ill.: Charles C. Thomas, 1957.

————. The action of psychotogens and a neurophysiological theory of hallucination. *Amer. J. Psychiat.*, 1960, 116: 911–914.

Maslow, A. H., and Mittleman, B. *Principles of Abnormal Psychology*. New York and London: Harper and Brother, 1941.

Masserman, J. H. The biodynamic approaches, Vol. 2, pp. 1,680–1,696. In S. Arieti (ed.), *American Handbook of Psychiatry*. New York: Basic Books, 1959.

Mathers, L. H. The synaptic organization of the cortical projection to the pulvinar of the squirrel monkey. *J. Comp. Neurol.*, 1972, 146: 43–60.

Matle-Blanco, I. A study of schizophrenic thinking. *Int. J. Psychiat.*, 1965, 1: 91.

Maudsley, H. *Natural Causes and Supernatural Seemings*. London: Kegan Paul, Trench and Co., 1886.

————. *Responsibility in Mental Disease*. New York: Appleton and Co., 1888.

————. *The Pathology of Mind*. London: Macmillan and Co., 1895.

Max, L. W. An experimental study of the motor theory of consciousness. IV. Action of current responses in the deaf during awakening, kinaesthetic imagery, and abstract thinking. *J. Comp. Psychol.*, 1937, 24: 301.

Mayer-Gross, W., Slater, E., and Roth, M. *Clinical Psychiatry*. Baltimore: Williams and Wilkins Co., 1960.

Mazlish, B. *Psychoanalysis and History*. New York: G & D Publishers, 1963.

Meadow, A., Greenblatt, M., and Solomon, H. C. Looseness of association and impairment in abstraction in schizophrenia. *J. of Nerv. and Ment. Disease*, 1953, 118: 27–35.

Medlicott, R. W. An inquiry into the significance of hallucinations with special reference to their occurrence in the sane. *Int. Rec. Med.*, 1958, 171: 664–677.

Meinecke, F. *The German Catastrophe*. Cambridge: Harvard University Press, 1950.

Mellor, C. S. First rank symptoms of schizophrenia. *Brit. J. Psychiat.*, 1970, 117: 15–23.

Mendel, E. *Textbook of Psychiatry*. Trans. W. C. Krauss. Philadelphia: F. A. Davis Co., 1907.

Menninger, K. *A Manual for Psychiatric Case Study*. New York: Grune and Stratton, 1962.

————. Syndrome, yes; disease entity, no. In R. Cancro (ed.), *The Schizophrenic Reactions*, pp. 71–78. New York: Brunner/Mazel, 1970.

Menninger, K., with Mayman, M., and Pruyser, P. *The Vital Balance*. New York: Viking Press, 1963.

Mettler, F. A. Corticifugal fiber connections of the cortex of Macaca mulatta. The parietal region. *J. Comp. Neurol.*, 1935, 62: 263–291.

————. In J. D. Page (ed.), *Approaches to Psychopathology*. New York and London: Temple University Publication, Distributed by Columbia University Press, 1966.

Meyer, A. The problems of mental reaction types, mental causes and disease. *Psychol. Bull.*, 1908, 5: 243–261.

Michaud, J. F. *The History of the Crusades*. Trans. W. Robson. London: A. C. Armstrong and Son, 1852.

Middleton, J. *Magic, Witchcraft and Curing*. Garden City, N. Y.: Natural History Press, 1967.

Milgram, N. A. Cognitive and empathic factors in role-taking by schizophrenic and brain damaged patients. *J. Abnorm. and Soc. Psychol.*, 1960, 60: No. 2.

Miller, M. D., Johnson, R. L., and Richmond, L. H. Auditory hallucinations and descriptive language skills. *J. Psychiat. Res.*, 1965, 3: 43–56.

Modell, A. H. The theoretical implications of hallucinatory experiences in schizophrenia. *J. Amer. Psychoanalyt. Assoc.*, 1958, 6: 442–480.

————. An approach to the nature of auditory hallucinations in schizophrenia. *Arch. Gen. Psychiat.*, 1960, 3: 259–266.

————. Hallucination in schizophrenic patients and their relation to psychic structure. In L. West (ed.), *Hallucinations*. New York: Grune and Stratton, 1962.

Monchaux, C. de. The psycho-analytic study of thinking. Thinking and negative hallucination. *Int. J. Psychoanal.*, 1962, 43: 311–314.

Mora, G. One hundred years from Lombroso's first essay, "Genius and Insanity." *Amer. J. Psychiat.*, 1964, 121: 562–571.

Morel, F. L'echo de la lecture et l'echo de la pensee. Contribution a l'etude des hallucinations audives verbales. *Encephale.*, 1934, 29: 18–31.

————. Examen audiome trique de malades presentant des hallucination auditives verbales. *Ann. Med. Psychol.*, 1936, 94: 520–533.

Morgan, C. T. *Physiological Psychology*. New York: McGraw-Hill, 1965.

Mosovich, A., and Tallaferro, A. Studies of EEG and sex function orgasm. *Diseases of the Nervous System*, 1954, 15: 218–220.

Moss, G. C. The mentality and personality of the Julio-Clardian emperors. *Med. Hist.*, 1963, 7: 165–175.

————. Mental disorder in antiquity, pp. 709–722. In D. Brothwell and A. T. Sandison (eds.), *Diseases in Antiquity*. Springfield, Ill.: Charles C. Thomas, 1967.

Mott, R. H., Small, I. F., and Anderson, J. M. Comparative study of hallucinations. *Arch. Gen. Psychiat.*, 1965, 12: 595–601.

Mourgue, R. *Neurobiologie de l'Hallucination*. Bruxelles: Lameitin, 1932.

Mousier de. Le mechanisme des hallucination. *Ann. Med. Psychol.*, 1930, 88: 365–389.

Mowrer, U. H. *Learning theory and the symbolic processes*. New York: Wiley, 1960.

Munn, N. L. *Psychology*. Boston: Houghton Mifflin Co., 1961.

————. *The Evolution and Growth of Human Behavior*. Boston: Houghton Mifflin Co., 1965.

Nathan, P. E., and Harris, S. L. *Psychopathology and Society*. New York: McGraw-Hill, 1975.

Naudi, G. *The History of Magic*. London: John Streater, 1657.

Neisser, U. *Cognitive Psychology*. New York: Appleton-Century-Crofts, 1967.

Nevius, J. L. *Demon Possession and Allied Themes*. Chicago, New York, and Toronto: Fleming H. Revell Co., 1894.

Newman, C. *The Evolution of Medical Education in the Nineteenth Century*. London: Oxford University Press, 1957.

Nielsen, J. M. *Agnosia, Apraxia, Aphasia. Their Value in Cerebral Localization*. 2nd ed. New York and London: P. B. Hoeber, 1946.

————. *A Textbook of Clinical Neurology*. New York: P. B. Hoeber, 1951.

Nisbet, J. F. *The Insanity of Genius*. London: Grant Richard, 1891.

Nitsche, P., and Wilmanns, K. *The History of the Prison Psychoses*. New York: The Journal of Nervous and Mental Disease Publishing Co., 1912.

Noland, M. J. Hallucinations and sanity. *J. Ment. Sci.*, 1928, 74: 49–59.

Noland, R. L. Presidential disability and the proposed constitutional amendment. *Amer. Psychologist,* 1966, 21: 230–235.

Noyes, A. P. *Modern Clinical Psychiatry*. Philadelphia and London: W. B. Saunders Co., 1953.

Oesterreich, T. K. *Possession, Demoniacal and Other*. London: Kegal Paul, Trench, Trubner and Co., 1930.

Ojemann, G. A., Fedio, P., and van Buren, J. M. Anomia from pulvinar and subcortical parietal stimulation. *Brain,* 1968, 91: 99–116.

Osgood, C. E. *Method and Theory in Experimental Psychology*. New York: Oxford University Press, 1953.

Othmer, E., Hayden, M. P., and Segelbaum, R. Encephalic cycles during sleep and wakefulness in humans: A 24 hour pattern. *Science,* 1969, 164: 447–449.

Papez, J. W. A proposed mechanism of emotion. *Arch. Neurol. and Psychiat.*, 1937, 38: 725–743.

————. Connections of the pulvinar. *Arch. Neurol. and Psychiat.*, 1939, 41: 277–289.

————. *Human Growth and Development*. Ithaca: Cornell Co-operative Society, 1948.

————. *Fragments of Verse*. Los Angeles: New Age Publishing Co., 1957.

Parish, E. *Hallucinations and Illusions*. London: Walter Scott, 1897.

Patterson, R. M., and Kaelbling, R. The clinical diagnosis of schizophrenia, pp. 11–27. In A. R. Kaplan (ed.), *Genetic Factors in Schizophrenia*. Springfield, Ill.: C. C. Thomas, 1972.

Paulus, J. Le probleme de l'hallucination et evolution de la psychologie d'Esquirol a Pierre Janet. *Faculte de Philosophie et Lettres*, Liege Fascicule No. 91, 1941.

Pavlov, I. P. *Lectures on Conditioned Reflexes*. Vol. 2. *Conditioned Reflexes and Psychiatry*. Trans. W. H. Gantt. New York: International Publication, 1941.

Payne, R. W. Cognitive abnormalities, pp. 193–261. In H. J. Eysenck (ed.), *Handbook of Abnormal Psychology*. New York: Basic Books, 1961.

————. The measurement and significance of overinclusive thinking and retardation in schizophrenic patients, pp. 77–97. In P. H. Hoch and J. Zubin (eds.), *Psychopathology of Schizophrenia*. New York: Grune and Stratton, 1966.

Payne, R. W., Ancevich, S., and Laverty, S. G. Overinclusive thinking in symptom-free schizophrenics. *Can. Psychiat. Assoc. J.*, 1963, 8: 225–234.

Payne, R. W., Caird, W. K., and Laverty, S. G. Overinclusive thinking and delusions in schizophrenic patients. *J. Abnorm. and Soc. Psychol.*, 1964, 68: 562–566.

Payne, R. W., and Hewlett, J. H. G. Thought disorder in psychotic patients, vol. 2. In H. J. Eysenck (ed.), *Experiments in Personality*. London: Routledge and Kegan Paul, 1960.

Payne, R. W., and Hirst, H. L. Overinclusive thinking in a depressive and a control group. *J. Consult. Psychol.*, 1957, 21: 186–188.

Peak, H. Observations on the characteristics and distribution of German Nazis. *Psychological Monographs*, 1945, 59: No. 276.

Penfield, W. Memory and perception. In D. A. Hamburg, K. H. Pribram, and A. J. Stunkard (eds.), *Perception and Its Disorders*, Vol. 48. Baltimore: Williams and Wilkins Co., 1970.

————. The neurophysiological basis of thought. In J. G. Howells(ed.), *Modern Perspectives in World Psychiatry*. New York: Brunner/Mazel, 1971.

Penfield, W., and Perot, P. The brain's record of auditory and visual experience. *Brain*, 1963, 86: 595–696.

Penfield, W., and Rasmussen, T. *The Cerebral Cortex of Man*. New York: Macmillan Co., 1950.

Penfield, W., and Roberts, L. *Speech and Brain Mechanisms*. Princeton: Princeton University Press, 1959.

Penrose, L. S. Critical survey of schizophrenia genetics. In J. G. Howells (ed.), *Modern Perspective in World Psychiatry*. New York: Brunner/Mazel, 1971.

Perceval, J. *A Narrative of the Treatment Experienced by a Gentleman, During a State of Mental Derangement*. London: Effingham Wilson, 1840.

Perria, L. Auadri allucinosici in parkinsonian. *Congresso di Psichiatria Italiana*, 1943, 10: 18–20.

————. Hallucinations accompanying lesion of cerebral peduncle during parkinsonism, 6 cases. *L. Perria Riv. Neurol.*, 1947, 17: 81–100.

Piaget, J. *The Child's Conception of the World*. New York: Harcourt Brace, 1929.

Pinel, P. *Traite medico-philosophique sur l'alienation mentale, ou la mani*. Paris: Richard, Caille et Ravier, an IX, 1801.

Pintner, R. Inner speech during silent reading. *Psychol. Rev.*, 1913, 20: 129–153.

Pond, D. A. Personality disorders, vol. 15, pp. 576–592. In P. J. Vinken and C. W. Bruyn (eds.), *Handbook of Clinical Neurology*. Berlin: J. Springer, 1974.

Powell, B. J. Role of verbal intelligence in the field approach to selective groups of psychotics. *J. Abnorm. Psychol.*, 1970, 76: 47–49.

Prichard, J. C. *A Treatise of Insanity and Other Disorders Affecting the Mind*. London, 1835.

Quercy, P. *L'hallucination*. Paris: F. Alcan, 1930.

Quinton, A. Knowledge and belief. In P. Edwards (ed.), *The Encyclopedia of Philosophy*. New York: Macmillan Co. and Free Press, 1967.

Rabinovitch, R. D. Dyslexia: Psychiatric considerations. In J. Money (ed.), *Reading Disability*. Baltimore: Johns Hopkins Press, 1962.

Rabkin, R. Ego functions and hallucinations. *Amer. J. Psychiat.*, 1966, 123: 481–484.

Rainer, J. D., Abdullch, S., and Alshuler, K. Z. Phenomenology of hallucinations in the deaf, pp. 449–456. In W. Keup (ed.), *Origin and Mechanism of Hallucination*. New York: Plenum Press, 1970.

Ramey, E. R., and O'Doherty, D. S. *Electrical Studies on the Unanesthetized Brain*. New York: Paul Hoeber, 1960.

Rapaport, D. *Organization and Pathology of Thought.* New York: Columbia University Press, 1951.

Rappaport, S. R., and Webb, W. An attempt to study intellectual deterioration by premorbid and psychotic testing. *J. Consult. Psychol.*, 1950, 14: 95–98.

Rashkins, H. A. Three types of thinking disorders. *J. of Nerv. and Ment. Disease*, 1947, 106: 650–670.

Raskin, A. Effect of background conversation and darkness on reaction time in anxious, hallucinating and severely ill schizophrenics. *Perceptual and Motor Skills*, 1967, 25: 353–358.

Rauschning, H. *The Voice of Destruction.* New York: G. P. Putnam's Sons, 1940.

Rechtschaffen, A., and Kales, A. *A Manual of Standardized Terminology, Techniques and Scoring System for Sleep Stages of Human Subjects.* Bethesda, Maryland: U. S. Government Printing Office, 1968.

Rechtschaffen, A., Shelsinger, F., and Mednick, S. Schizophrenia and physiological indices of dreaming. *Arch. Gen. Psychiat.*, 1964, 10: 89–93.

Redlich, F. C., and Freedman, D. X. *The Theory and Practice of Psychiatry.* New York and London: Basic Books, 1966.

Reed, H. B. The existence and function of inner speech in thought process. *J. Exp. Psychol.*, 1916, 1: 365–392.

Reed, J. L. Schizophrenic thought disorder: a review and hypothesis. *Comprehensive Psychiatry*, 1970, 11: 403–432.

Reeves, J. W. *Thinking about Thinking.* New York: Dell Publishing Co., 1965.

Reicse, W. *A History of Neurology.* New York: MD Publications, 1959.

Reik, T. *Listening with the Third Ear.* New York: Pyramid Books, 1948.

Reis, D. J. The relationship between brain norepinephrine and aggressive behavior. In I. J. Kopin (ed.), *Neurotransmitters*, Vol. 50. Baltimore: Williams and Wilkins, 1972.

Reitan, R. M. Investigation of the validity of Halstead's measures of biological intelligence. *Arch. Neurol. and Psychiat.*, 1955, 73: 109–119.

Reitman, W. R. *Cognition and Thought.* New York: John Wiley and Sons, 1965.

Rennie, T. A. C., and Fowler, J. B. Prognosis in manic-depressive psychoses. *Amer. J. Psych.*, 1942, 98: 801–814.

Retterstol, N. *Paranoid and Paranoiac Psychoses.* Springfield, Ill.: Charles C. Thomas; Oslo: Universitetsferlaget, 1966.

————. *Prognosis in Paranoid Psychoses.* Springfield, Ill.: Charles C. Thomas, 1970.

Riesen, A. H. (ed.), *The Developmental Neuropsychology of Behavior. Deprivation.* New York: Academic Press, 1975.

Riklan, M., and Levita, E. *Subcortical Correlates of Human Behavior.* Baltimore: Williams and Wilkins Co., 1969.

Riley, D. A., and Rosenzweig, M. R. Echolocation in rats. *J. Comp. Physiol. Psychol.*, 1957, 50: 323–328.

Riss, E. Are hallucinations illusions? An experimental study of non-veridical perception. *J. Psychol.*, 1959, 48: 367–373.

Ritchie, J. M. The Xanthines. In L. S. Goodman and A. Gilman (eds.), *The Pharmacologic Basis of Therapeutics.* Toronto: The Macmillan Co., 1970.

Roberts, B. H., Greenblatt, M., and Solomon, H. C. Movements of the vocal apparatus during auditory hallucination. *Amer. J. Psychiat.*, 1952, 108: 912–914.

Robinson, C. History and pathology. *American Historical Association; Annual Report for the Year 1916 (1919)*, pp. 343–369.

Robinson, J. H. Civilization and culture. In *Encyclopaedia Britannica.* Chicago: William Benton, 1968.

Robsjohn-Gibbings, T. H. *Mona Lisa's Mustache: A Dissection of Modern Art.* New York: Alfred A. Knopf, 1947.

Rochford, G. The breakdown of language associated with organic brain damage. Thesis offered for D. Phil. *Oxon*, 1969.

Roe, A. Personal problems and science. In C. W. Taylor and F. Barron (eds.), *Scientific Creativity.* New York: John Wiley and Sons, 1963.

Rogers, A. A study of hallucinations and the sense modality used in learning. *Dissertation Abstracts*, 1959, 19: 3371–3372.

Rogow, A. A. Psychiatry, history and political science. In J. Marmor (ed.), *Modern Psychoanalysis: New Directions and Perspectives.* New York: Basic Books, 1968.

Roman, R., and Landis, C. Hallucinations and mental imagery. *J. of Nerv. and Ment. Disease*, 1945, 102: 327–331.

Russell, G. V. The centrencephalic system. In E. R. Ramey and D. S. O'Doherty (eds.), *Electrical Studies on the Unanesthetized Brain.* New York: Paul Hoeber, 1960.

Rutner, I. T., and Bugle, C. An experimental procedure for the modification of psychotic behavior. *J. Consult. Clin. Psychol.,* 1969, 33: 651–653.

Ryle, G. *The Concept of Mind.* New York: Barnes and Noble, 1967, c1949.

————. A puzzling element in the notion of thinking. *Proceedings of the British Academy.* Oxford University Press, 1958, 44: 129–144.

Sandison, A. T. The madness of the Emperor Caligula. *Med. Hist.,* 1958, 2: 202–209.

Sarbin, T. R. The concept of hallucinations. *J. Personality,* 1967, 35: 359–380.

Sartre, J. *The Psychology of Imagination.* New York: Philosophical Library, 1948.

Satten, J. Crime and mental disorders. In A. Deutsch and H. Fishman (eds.), *The Encyclopedia of Mental Health.* New York: Franklin Watts, 1963.

Schaltenbrand, G. The effects of stereotactic electrical stimulation in the depth of the brain. *Brain,* 1965, 88: 835–840.

Schilling, R. Significance of "internal speaking" for normal and abnormal development of speech. *Medizin Klinik.,* 1934, 30: 289–290.

Schneider, C. Beringer Beitrag zur Analyse schizophrener Denkstruungen. *Z. Neur.,* 1924, 93.

————. *Die Schizophrenen Symptom Verbande.* Berlin: Springer, 1942.

Schneider, K. Wesen und Erfassung des Schizophrenen. *Zeitschrift. ges. Neurol. Psychiat.,* 1924, 99: 542.

————. Primare und sekundare Symptome bei Schizophrenie. *Fortsch. Neurol. Psychiat.,* 1957, 25: 487.

Schulman, C. A. Hallucinations and disturbances of affect, cognition, and physical state as a function of sensory deprivation. *Percept. Motor Skill,* 1967, 25: 1001–1024.

Schulz, C. G., and Kilgalen, R. K. *Case Studies in Schizophrenia.* New York and London: Basic Books, 1968.

Schwartz, S. Cognitive deficit among remitted schizophrenics: The role of a life-history variable. *J. Abnorm. Psychol.,* 1967, 72: 54–58.

Schwartzman, A. E., Douglas, V. I., and Muir, W. R. Intellectual loss in schizophrenia. Part II. *Canad. Psychol.*, 1962, 16: 161–168.

Schwarz, R. Auditory hallucinations in prison psychosis. *Psychiat. Quar.*, 1936, 10: 149–157.

Schweitzer, A. *The Psychiatric Study of Jesus, Exposition and Criticism.* Trans. C. R. Joy. *Also* Introduction by Overholser on paranoia. Boston: Beacon Press, 1948.

Scoppa, A., and Fasullo, S. Rilieri Pathogenetici sulle allucinazioni E. Sulle pseudoallucinazioni. *Osped. Psichiat.*, 1970, 38: 74–107.

Searles, H. The effort to drive the other person crazy: An element in the aetiology and psychotherapy of schizophrenia. *Brit. J. Med. Psychol.*, 1959, 32: 1–18.

Sedman, G. "Inner Voices" phenomenological and clinical aspects. *Brit. J. Psychiat.*, 1966, 112: 485–490.

Seitz, P. F. D., and Molholm, H. B. Relation of mental imagery to hallucinations. *Arch, Neurol. and Psychiat.*, 1947, 57: 469–480.

Sem-Jacobsen, C. W. *Depth-Electrographic Stimulation of the Human Brain and Behavior.* Springfield, Ill.: Charles C. Thomas, 1968.

Seredina, M. I. The influence of caffeine on the interactivity of the first and second signalling systems in cases of chronic alcoholic hallucinations. In A. G. Ivanov-Smolenskii (ed.), *Works of the Institute of Higher Nervous Activity.* Pathophysiological Series Vol. 2. Moscow: The Academy of Sciences of the USSR, 1955; Washington, D. C.: Office of Technical Services, U. S. Department of Commerce, 1960.

Shakow, D. *The Nature of Deterioration in Schizophrenic Conditions.* New York: Durnham, 1946.

————. Psychological deficit in schizophrenia. *Behavioral Science*, 1963, 8: 275–305.

Shapiro, W. K. Placebo effects in medicine, psychotherapy, psychoanalysis. In A. E. Gergin and S. L. Garfield (eds.), *Handbook of Psychotherapy and Behavior Change.* New York: John Wiley and Sons, 1971.

Sheppard, S. The comparative study of millenarian. In S. L. Thrupp (ed.), *Millennial Dreams in Action.* New York: Schocken Books, 1970.

Sherman, N., and Beverly, G. I. Hallucinations in children. *J. Abnorm. and Soc. Psychol.*, 1924, 19: 165.

Siegel, R. K., and West, L. J. *Hallucinations: Behavior, Experience and Theory.* New York: John Wiley and Sons, 1975.

Sigerist, H. E. *Civilization and Disease.* Ithaca: Cornell University Press, 1943.

Sim, M. *Guide to Psychiatry.* Philadelphia: Williams and Wilkins Co., 1968.

Simmel, E. Anti-semitism and mass psychopathology. In E. Simmel (ed.), *Anti-Semitism, a Social Disease.* New York: International Universities Press, 1946.

Singer, C. *Vesalius: On the Human Brain.* New York: Oxford University Press, 1952.

Skinner, B. R. *Verbal Behavior.* New York: Appleton-Century-Crofts, 1957.

Small, I. T., Small, J. G., and Anderson, J. M. Clinical characteristics of hallucinations of schizophrenia. *Diseases of the Nervous System,* 1966, 27: 349–353.

Smart, F. *Neurosis and Crime.* New York: Barnes and Noble, 1970.

Smirnov, A. A. Intelligence. Chapter 8. In A. A. Smirnov, A. N. Leonter, S. L. Ruginshtein, and B. M. Teplov (eds.), *Psychology.* Moscow: Uchpedgiz, 1956.

Smythies, J. R. A logical and cultural analysis of hallucinatory sense-experience. *J. Ment. Sci.,* 1956, 102: 336–342.

Snezhnevsky, A. V. The symptomatology, clinical forms and nosology of schizophrenia, pp. 425–447. In J. G. Howells (ed.), *Modern Perspectives in World Psychiatry.* New York: Brunner/Mazel, 1971.

Solomon, P. *Sensory Deprivation.* Cambridge: Harvard University Press, 1961.

Solomon, P., and Rossi, M. Sensory deprivation. In J. G. Howells (ed.), *Modern Perspectives in World Psychiatry.* New York: Brunner/Mazel, 1971.

Spence, J. T., and Lair, C. V. Associative interference in the paired-associated learning of remitted and non-remitted schizophrenics. *J. Abnorm. Psychol.,* 1965, 70: 119–122.

Sperling, G. The information available in brief visual presentations. *Psychological Monographs,* 1960, 74 (11): 1–29.

Springer, J., and Kramer, H. *Malleus Maleficarum.* Trans. and introduction by M. Summers. London: Pushkin Press, 1951.

Stein, M. I., and Heinze, S. J. *Creativity and the Individual.* Glencoe, Ill.: Free Press of Glencoe, 1960.

Stoddart, W. H. B. *Mind and Its Disorders.* Philadelphia: P. Blakiston's Son & Co., 1919.

Storch, A. Erlebnisanalyse und Sprachwissenschaft. *Z. Psychol.*, 1924, 94: 146–152.

Storr, A. *The Dynamics of Creation.* New York: Atheneum, 1972.

Strauss, H. Epileptic disorders, Vol. 2, pp. 1,109–1,143. In S. Arieti (ed.), *American Handbook of Psychiatry.* New York: Basic Books, 1959.

Strecker, E. A. *Basic Psychiatry.* New York: Random House, 1952.

Stukat, K. G. *Suggestibility: A Factorial and Experimental Analysis.* Stockholm: Almquist and Wiksell, 1958.

Sullivan, H. S. Mental disorders. In E. R. A. Seligman, and A. Johnson (eds.), *Encyclopedia of the Social Sciences,* Vol. 10, p. 313. New York: Macmillan, 1933.

————. The language of schizophrenia. In J. S. Kasanin (ed.), *Language and Thought in Schizophrenia.* Berkeley and Los Angeles: University of California Press, 1944 (1951).

————. *The Psychiatric Interview.* New York: W. W. Norton and Co., 1954.

Sully, J. *Illusions: A Psychological Study.* New York: D. Appleton and Co., 1886.

Swanson, D. W., Bohnert, P. J., and Smith, J. A. *The Paranoid.* Boston: Little, Brown and Co., 1970.

Szentagothai, J. Die Lokalisation der Kehlkopfmus kulatur in den Vauskernen. *Z. Anat. Entwickl. Gesch.*, 1943, 112: 704–710.

Taylor, J. N. A comparison of delusional and hallucinatory individuals using field dependency as a measure. Dissertation at Purdue University, 1956.

Temkin, O. *The Falling Sickness.* 2nd ed. Baltimore and London: Johns Hopkins Press, 1971.

Thomas, N. W. Witchcraft. In *Encyclopaedia Britannica.* 11th Edition. New York: The Encyclopaedia Britannica Co., 1911.

Thompson, C. J. S. *The Mystery and Lore of Apparitions.* London: Harold Shaylor, 1930.

Thomson, R. *The Psychology of Thinking.* Baltimore: Penguin Books, 1959.

Thorndike, L. *A History of Magic and Experimental Science.* Vols. 1 to 8. New York: Macmillan Co., 1923–58.

Thrupp, S. L. *Millennial Dreams in Action.* New York: Schocken Books, 1970.

Titchnener, E. B. *Lectures on the Experimental Psychology Thought Process.* New York: Macmillan Co., 1909.

Toynbee, A. J. *A Study of History.* Vol. 5. London: Oxford University Press, 1939.

————. *A Study of History.* Abridgement by D. C. Somervell. London and New York: Oxford University Press, 1947.

————. *A Study of History.* Vol. 12, *Reconsiderations.* London and New York: Oxford University Press, 1961.

————. The desert hermits. *Horizon,* 1970, 12: 22–39.

————. The year 2000: Crises, trends. *Chicago Tribune,* October 21, 1972, Section 1, p. 14.

Tredennick, H. *Plato: The Last Days of Socrates.* Baltimore: Penguin Books, 1969.

Trevor-Roper, H. R. Essay on the mind of Adolph Hitler. In N. Cameron and R. H. Stevens (trans.), *Hitler's Secret Conversation.* New York: Farrar Straus and Young, 1953.

————. *Religion, the Reformation and Social Change.* London: Macmillan Co., 1967.

Tringo, J. L. Work reviewed in *Human Behavior.* 1972, 1: 27.

Turner, B. Pathology of paralysis agitans. In P. J. Vinken and G. W. Bruyn (eds.), *Handbook of Clinical Neurology.* Amsterdam: North-Holland Publishing Co.; New York: Wiley Interscience Division, John Wiley and Sons, 1968.

Unna, K. R., and Martin, W. R. The action of chlorpromazine on the electrical activity of the brain. In S. Garattini and V. Ghetti (eds.), *Psychotropic Drugs.* New York: Elsevier, 1957.

Ushakov, G. K. O paranoicheskikh gallyutsinctisiyokh vcobrazheniya pri paranoiyal'nykh sustoyaniyakh. *Zhurnal Neuropathologii i Psikhiartii,* 1971, 71: 106–112.

Van Buren, J. M. Confusion and disturbance of speech from stimulation in vicinity of the head of the caudate nucleus. *J. Neurosurg.,* 1963, 20: 148–157.

Vermeylen, G. Hallucinations et niveau mental. *Ann. Med. Psychol.,* 1934, 92: Part 2, 429–440.

Vesalius, A. *De humani corpus fabrica.* 1543, II, 42, p. 303.

Vetter, H. J. *Language Behavior and Psychopathology.* Chicago: Rand McNally and Co., 1969.

Vinacke, W. A. *The Psychology of Thinking.* New York: McGraw-Hill, 1952.

von Neumann, J. *The Computer and the Brain.* New Haven: Yale University Press, 1969.

Vygotsky, L. S. Thought in schizophrenia. *Arch. Neurol. and Psychiat.*, 1934, 31: 1063–1077.

————. Selected psychological investigations. *Isd. Akad. Ped. Nauk. RSFSR.* Moscow, 1956.

————. *Thought and Language.* Cambridge: M. I. T. Press, 1962.

Waelder, R. Lettre sur L'Etiologies de L'Evolution des Psychoiss Collectives. L'Esprit, L'Ethique Et La Guerre. *Institut International De Co-operation Intellectuelle Societe des Nations,* 1934, 85–151.

Walker, A. E. *The Primate Thalamus.* Chicago: University of Chicago Press, 1938.

Walker, N. *Crime and Insanity in England.* Edinburgh: University Press, 1968.

Wallace, A. F. C. Cultural determinants of response to hallucinatory experience. *Arch. Gen. Psychiat.,* 1959, 1: 58–69.

Walsh, E. G. *Physiology of the Nervous System.* London: Longman, 1964.

Wanley, N. *The Wonders of the Little World or a General History of Man.* London: T. Davies, 1774.

Watson, J. B. *Behaviorism.* Chicago: University of Chicago Press, 1924.

Weber, M. Science as a vocation. In H. H. Gerth and C. W. Mills (eds.), *Essays in Sociology.* New York and London: Oxford University Press, 1946.

Weiner, M. F. Hallucinations in children. *Arch. Gen. Psychiat.,* 1961, 5: 544–553.

Weingaertner, A. H. Self-administered aversive stimulation with hallucinating hospitalized schizophrenia. *J. Consult. Clin. Psychol.,* 1971, 36: 422–429.

Welch, L. A behavioristic explanation of the mechanism of suggestion and hypnosis. *J. Abnorm. and Soc. Psychol.,* 1947, 42: 359–364.

Werner, H. *Comparative Psychology of Mental Development.* Trans. E. B. Garside. New York: Harper Brothers, 1940.

Werner, H., and Kaplan, B. *Symbol Formation.* New York: Wiley, 1967.

West, L. J. *Hallucinations.* New York: Grune and Stratton, 1962.

————. Hallucinations. In J. G. Howells (ed.), *Modern Perspectives in World Psychiatry.* New York: Brunner/Mazel, 1971.

————. A clinical and theoretical overview of hallucinatory phenomena. In R. K. Siegel and L. J. West (eds.), *Hallucinations: Behavior, Experience and Theory*. New York: John Wiley and Sons, 1975.

West, R. H. *The Invisible World*. Athens: University of Georgia Press, 1939.

Westermarck, E. *Pagan Survivals in Mohammedan Civilization*. London: Macmillan and Co., 1933.

White, W. A. The language of schizophrenia. *Arch. Neurol. and Psychiat.*, 1926, 16: 395–413.

Whitehorn, J. G., and Zipf, C. K. Schizophrenic language. *Arch. Neurol. and Psychiat.*, 1943, 49: 831–851.

Whitlock, D. G., and Nauta, W. J. H. Subcortical projections from the temporal neocortex in Macaca mulatta. *J. Comp. Neurol.*, 1956, 106: 183–212.

Whorf, B. L. *Language, Thought and Reality*. J. R. Carrol (ed.), New York: Wiley, 1956.

Williams, J. G. L. A resonance theory of microvibrations. *Psychol. Rev.*, 1963, 70: 547–555.

Williams, M. *Brain Damage and the Mind*. Middlesex, England: Penguin Books, 1970.

Wing, J. K., Cooper, J. E., and Soutorius, N. *The Description and Classification of Psychiatric Symptomatology*. New York: Cambridge University Press, 1974.

Winslow, F. B. *Obscure Diseases of the Brain and Disorders of the Brain*. 2nd ed. Philadelphia: H. C. Lea, 1866.

Witkin, H. A. Psychological differentiation and forms of pathology. *J. Abnorm. Psychol.*, 1965, 70: 311–336.

Wolman, B. B. *The Psychoanalytic Interpretation of History*. New York. Basic Books, 1971.

Woodworth, R. S. *Experimental Psychology*. New York: Henry Holt and Co., 1st ed. 1938, 2nd ed. 1960.

Words and Phrases. Vol. 19 (legal dictionary). St. Paul, Minn.: West Publishing Company, 1940–52.

Wright, Q. *The Causes of War and the Conditions of Peace*. London, New York, and Toronto: Longmans, Green and Co., 1935.

————. *The Study of War*. Vols. 1 and 2. Chicago: University of Chicago Press, 1942.

————. The study of war. In D. L. Sills (ed.), *International Encyclopedia of the Social Sciences*. New York: Macmillan Co. and Free Press, 1968.

Wyatt, R. J. Introduction: current concepts of schizophrenia. *Amer. J. Psychiat.*, 1976, 133: 171–172.

Wynee, L. C., and Singer, T. Thought disorders and family relations in schizophrenia. II. A classification of forms of thinking. *Arch. Gen. Psychiat.*, 1963, 9: 199–206.

Yap, P. M. The culture-bound reactive syndromes. In W. Caudill and T. Lin (eds.), *Mental Health Research in Asia and the Pacific*. Honolulu: East-West Center Press, 1969.

Zeigarnick, B. *The Pathology of Thinking*. New York: Consultant Bureau, International Behavior Science Series, 1965.

Zentay, P. J. Motor disorders of the central nervous system and their significance for speech. Part I. Cerebral and cerebellar dysarthrias. *Laryngoscope*, 1937, 47: 147–156.

Zucker, K. Funklionsanalyse in der schizophrenia. *Arch. Psychiat.*, 1939, (D), 110: 465.

Zucker, K., and de B. Hubert, W. H. A study of changes in function found in schizophrenic thought disorder. *J. Ment. Sci.*, 1935, 81: 1–45.

Zuckerman, M. Stress and hallucinatory effects of perceptual isolation. *Psychological Monographs*, 1962, 76: 549.

Author Index

227

Subject Index

Fred H. Johnson, Ph.D., has worked as a research associate in the Department of Neuropsychiatry, Institute of Research, Walter Reed Army Hospital (1951-1952); the Department of Psychiatry, Neuro-psychiatric Institute, University of Illinois (1957-1959); the Research Laboratory in Neuropsychiatry of the VA, Pittsburgh, Pa. (1962-1963); the Division of Neurology, Children's Memorial Hospital, Chicago (1967-1969); and held the rank of associate professor at the University of Oregon Medical School and New York University at Buffalo.

Dr. Johnson received his A.B., A.M. and Ph.D. from Cornell University. In addition to numerous articles in professional journals of anatomy, physiology, and neurology, he has written the monograph *Brain Tracts* (1958).